T0144506

A Brief History of Cyberspace

A Brief History of Cyberspace

Huansheng Ning

CRC Press
Taylor & Francis Group

AN AUERBACH BOOK

First edition published 2022
by CRC Press
6000 Broken Sound Parkway NW, Suite 300, Boca Raton, FL 33487-2742

and by CRC Press
4 Park Square, Milton Park, Abingdon, Oxon, OX14 4RN

CRC Press is an imprint of Taylor & Francis Group, LLC

© 2022 selection and editorial matter, Huansheng Ning

ISBN: 978-1-032-07832-8 (hbk)
ISBN: 978-1-032-19020-4 (pbk)
ISBN: 978-1-003-25738-7 (ebk)

DOI: 10.1201/9781003257387

Typeset in Garamond
by codeMantra

Contents

Preface

With the widespread growth of the Internet, a new space, cyberspace, has appeared and has rapidly integrated into our daily life and industrial manufacture, becoming the fourth basic living space for human beings. In recent years, cyberspace has become a hot topic of widespread concern. However, it is still confusing for most people to understand cyberspace well, because of its definitions, content, and differences from other similar concepts.

This book attempts to establish a complete knowledge system of the evolution history of cyberspace and cyber-enabled spaces (i.e., cyber-enabled physical space, cyber-enabled social space, and cyber-enabled thinking space) to better understand cyberspace. By providing an overall and comprehensive overview, this book aims to help readers understand the history of cyberspace and lay a solid foundation for researchers and learners who are interested in cyberspace.

The book accomplishes three main objectives as follows:

- It provides a comprehensive understanding of the development of cyberspace, ranging from its origin, evolutions, and research status to open issues and future challenges, as well as related hot topics in industry and academia.
- It discusses cyber life, syndrome, and health in addition to cyber-enabled spaces guiding for better living.
- It describes cyberspace governance from the perspectives of individual, society, national, and international levels, and promotes it toward a more profound and reasonable direction.

The book, consisting of 16 chapters, is divided into three parts. Chapter 1 introduces the origin and basic concepts of cyberspace, cyber philosophy, and cyberlogic, helping readers get an overall understanding of cyberspace. Chapters 2–7 discuss a wide variety of topics related to the human behaviors, psychology, and health of cyberspace to help people better adapt to cyberspace. Chapters 8–16 present the history of cyberspace governance and connotation from different aspects. Additionally, at the end of each chapter, some discussions of future development are put forward to help explore cyberspace.

Author

Huansheng Ning received a PhD degree from Beihang University in 2001. From 2002 to 2003, he worked in Aisino Co. From 2004 to 2013, he worked as a post-PhD and then as an associate professor in the School of Electronics and Information Engineering, Beihang University. From 2013, he worked as a professor and vice dean in the School of Computer and Communication Engineering, University of Science and Technology Beijing. From December 2021, he worked as a professor and vice president of Jinzhong University, Shanxi Province. He is an IEEE senior member, founder, and director of Cybermatics and Cyberspace International Science and Technology Cooperation Base; co-founder and director of DMU – USTBSmart Healthcare Co–Laboratory; and co-founder and co-chair of IEEE SMC Society Technical Committee on Cybermatics. He was elected as IET fellow in 2018 and appointed as a visiting chair professor of Cyber Science in Ulster University, United Kingdom (2020–2023).

He has presided over many research projects and published more than 200 journal/conference papers at Science China Information Science, Computer, IEEE TPDS/TIFS/TSG/TMC/TITS/TLT/TII/IOTJ, etc. He has launched and organized many successful and influential international conferences such as the IEEE Conference of Internet of Things (http://www.china-iot.net/iThings2013.htm), the 2015 Smart World Congress, the International Conference on Cyberspace Data and Intelligence (CyberDI), and the International Conference on Cyber-Living, Cyber-Syndrome, and Cyber-Health (CyberLife) in 2019. He has authored/edited/co-edited seven books on the Internet of Things or cyberspace.

He serves as an associate editor of *IEEE Systems Journal* (2013–2020), *IEEE Internet of Things Journal* (Associate editor: 2014–2018; area editor: 2020–2022; Steering Committee Member: 2017–2021), *Digital Communications and Networks* (2017–2020), etc.; and guest editor for *Science China Information Science, IEEE Sensors Journal, IEEE Transactions on Multimedia*, etc. His research interests include IoT (Internet of Things), CyberDIS (Cyberspace data, intelligence, and security), and CyberLife (Cyber-Living, Cyber-Syndrome, and Cyber-Health).

Acknowledgments

I thank my graduate students, Wenxi Wang, Zhimin Zhang, Shan Cui, Rongyang Li, Yang Xu, Zhenyu Wang, Sahraoui Dhelim, Xiao Zhang, Feifei Shi, Zhangfeng Pi, Yidi Zuo, Haochen Huang, Hang Wang, Zhijie Guo, Dazhi Gao, and Xiaorui Ren, for their help in collecting and preparing chapters.

I am also grateful to authors and institutions which have provided valuable messages and ideas listed in the chapters and references. Finally, I am very grateful to the editor, John Wyzalek, for his guidance and suggestions, and other staff for their help with the production of this book.

Chapter 1

Cyberspace, Cyber Philosophy, and Cyberlogic

1.1 Introduction

This chapter introduces cyberspace and the most basic concepts related to it, including the three traditional spaces, cyber science, cyber philosophy, and cyberlogic, and lays the foundation for the following chapters.

1.2 The Definition of Cyberspace

The term "cyberspace" comes from the word "cybernetics", which is originally derived from the Ancient Greek "kybernētēs" and means steersman, governor, pilot, or rudder. Specifically, the term initially appeared in the artwork *Atelier Cyberspace*, co-created by Danish artist Susanne Ussing and architect Carsten Hoff in the late 1960s. In this work, cyberspace referred to a series of installations and images called "sensory spaces", representing the open physical space that could sense and adapt to various behaviors or changes of human beings and other materials in space.[1] In the 1980s, American author William Gibson published a series of cyberpunk science fiction, including *Burning Chrome* (1982) and *Neuromancer* (1984). The term "cyberspace" was first defined as a concept concerning the digital world created by computers. Specifically, it was described as "a consensual hallucination experienced daily by billions of legitimate operators" and "a graphic representation of data abstracted from the banks of every com-

---

[1] https://en.wikipedia.org/wiki/Cyberspace

DOI: 10.1201/9781003257387-1

1

puter in the human system" [1,2]. The term "cyberspace" was then widely used in various novels, arts, films, and television works. It became popular as a synonym of computer networks and the Internet during the 1990s.

Different definitions of cyberspace can be found in diverse artistic works, scientific literatures, and official governmental sources. There is still no generally accepted definition due to people's different understandings and use purposes. In artistic works, cyberspace is usually used as a metaphor to represent a notional or virtual world created by computers and related infrastructure. It is a disembodied space, but people can do anything they do in the real world in cyberspace without the limitation of time and space, such as communicating, interacting, playing, shopping, learning, and working. For example, in the movie *The Matrix*, cyberspace was described as an imaginary world that looked like a normal real world but controlled by a computer and artificial intelligence (AI) system. Human beings could exist in cyberspace by connecting using hardware equipment. They played different roles in both the real world and cyberspace and met their various needs by switching between the two spaces. Inversely, scientific literatures and official governmental sources emphasized more the constitution and functionality of cyberspace. The term "cyberspace" is generally utilized as a generic terminology on computer and communication technologies, which is conceptualized as a digital world with which people can interact. For example, in *DoD Dictionary of Military and Associated Terms* of the U.S. (2017), cyberspace was defined as "a global domain within the information environment consisting of the interdependent network of information technology infrastructures and resident data, including the Internet, telecommunication networks, computer systems, and embedded processors and controllers".[2]

1.3 The History of Cyberspace

Technically, the development of cyberspace could track back to the birth of the world's first computer in 1946. As the commercialization and mass production of computers in the 1950s, cyberspace gradually walked into people's daily life and production. In this case, connecting distributed computers and realizing mutual communication became the major concern to share the information and resources. Thus, the first experimental network, Advanced Research Projects Agency Network (ARPANET), was built by the Advanced Research Projects Agency (ARPA) in 1969. It realized the information exchange between distributed computers, which was regarded as the original prototype of the Internet.

In 1975, ARPANET was transformed from an experimental network into a commercial network. The computer network with the ideas of resource sharing, decentralized control, packet switching, and network communication was formed as the increasing scale of ARPANET. However, communication could only occur between

---

[2] https://www.jcs.mil/Portals/36/Documents/Doctrine/pubs/dictionary.pdf

computers within the same network in that period. To achieve intercommunication between different computer networks, ARPA started a new project called "inter-network" (*Internet* in short) to support the research on network interconnection in academia and industry. The term "Internet" has been used to denote the interconnected computer network until today. The project promoted the emergence of TCP/IP protocol, which made the Internet an open system and contributed to the fast development of it. In the early 1980s, some organizations began to build the national Wide Area Network (WAN). Hereinto, the National Science Foundation Network (NSFNET) gradually replaced ARPANET to become the backbone of the Internet. In 1989, ARPANET disbanded, and NSFNET was connected to Military Network (MILNET) that was separated from ARPANET for military applications. By 1990, ARPANET withdrew from the stage of history after completing its historical mission. The Internet also shifted from military to civilian use.

Commercial organizations began to have access to the Internet. In 1992, IBM, MCI, and MERIT in the U.S. jointly set up Advanced Network Services (ANS) cooperation and built the ANSNET, which became another backbone of the Internet. The intervention of enterprises also resulted in a new process of commercialization of the Internet. In 1995, NSFNET was terminated and entirely replaced by the commercialized Internet. So far, the Internet has become an international network covering different countries and various fields. Cyberspace, in a conventional sense, was formed with the development of the Internet. It metaphorically refers to everything that exists within the communication network itself, including objects, identities, activities, etc. The term "cyberspace" was even used as a synonym for the Internet or a symbolic and figurative space that exists within the scope of the Internet for a long time.

According to the recent draft definitions, conventional cyberspace consists of the following aspects: (a) the basic physical infrastructures, such as computers, mobile devices, servers, and routers, which allow the connection between technology and communication system networks; (b) computer systems and various supporting software for guaranteeing its functionality and connectivity; (c) networks between distributed computers and the networks of networks; (d) resident data and information as well as related activities such as storage, transmission, exchange, processing, and sharing.[3] In addition, cyberspace has features of virtualization, interactivity, and time-space ambiguity. Despite the infrastructure and elements involved in traditional physical, social, and thinking (PST) spaces, cyberspace in this stage was still relatively independent of the three traditional spaces. It is largely limited to the Internet that only deals with the interconnections between entities existing in the digital/information space.

Considering the separation of physical and telecommunication infrastructures among different fields, the Cyber-Physical System (CPS) was proposed to deal with the integration of computation, communication, and physical system. CPS enabled

---

[3] https://en.wikipedia.org/wiki/Cyberspace

the connections of physical devices, machines, and objects to cyberspace and further realized the networking of physical space by the combination and coordination of computing and physical resources. As people's increasing demands of Information and Communication Technology (ICT), the idea of ubiquitous interconnection attracted wide attention, thereby contributing to the emergence of the Internet of Things (IoT). IoT extended the clients of cyberspace to things in physical space, including traditional and limited devices (e.g., computers, servers, printers, and cameras), ordinary objects in our daily life (e.g., various electric appliances, commodities, and vehicles), animals, and human beings. Based on new generation ICTs such as sensor and infrared technology, Radio Frequency Identification (RFID), Global Positioning System (GPS), and embedded technology, IoT has realized the interconnections between things and things as well as things and humans to achieve more intelligent, efficient, and safe management and services.

The ubiquitous connection of IoT significantly promoted the interconnection among humans in cyberspace. Accordingly, the attributes and complex social issues of humans were also mapped and connected to cyberspace, such as personal information, social relationships (e.g., affiliation, family, friend, and employment relationships), social rights, obligation, and duty. The increasing concerns of human-oriented applications generated the emergence of the Internet of People (IoP),[4] which allowed people to communicate and interact with each other without the restrictions of time and space. Besides, the Social Internet of Things (SIoT) developed as the integration of IoT with social aspects such as social community, organization, activity, phenomenon, and rule [3,4]. The generation of Cyber-Physical-Social (CPS) space has given rise to several novel human-oriented technologies, such as social computing, social network, and collective intelligence, supporting more people-centric services and applications.

Additionally, human thinking and its related aspects (e.g., instinct, awareness, and consciousness) embodied in cyberspace attracted numerous studies along with the interconnection of humans. In recent years, a series of thinking-oriented discipline branches and technologies have emerged, such as brain information, AI, and affective computing, which lead to the emergence and development of the Internet of Thinking (IoTk). In 2012, the question "Is it possible to have Internet of Thinking" was selected as one of the top ten questions in intelligent informatics/computing.[5] On the one hand, it allowed people to share ideas collaboratively in more extensive space-time. On the other hand, human thinking and natural wisdom were learned and applied in diverse scenarios to realize a more intelligent and harmonious ecosystem.

The ubiquitous connection and deep convergence of cyberspace and traditional spaces made cyberspace no longer limited to the scope of the Internet. It became a hyperspace encompassing every aspect of conventional cyberspace as well as PST

---

[4] http://www.cybermatics.org/SmartWorldCongress2015/SWC2015/IoP/IoP2015.htm

[5] Huansheng Ning, "Internet of Thinking," *The World Intelligence Congress*, Macau, Dec.4-7. 2012. (http://wi-consortium.org/blog/top10qi/)

space. Furthermore, it significantly impacted traditional spaces, even traditional philosophy, science, and technology. The two phenomena were named Cyberization and Cyber-enabled, respectively. The cyber-physical-social-thinking (CPST) hyperspace was called General Cyberspace [5–9]. Moreover, a novel concept, cybermatics, was put forward to address science and technology issues in the heterogeneous CPST hyperspace [10].

1.4 Cyber Philosophy

The advancement of cyber science, which is discussed in the following chapters, brings significant effects to mankind. All these phenomena were summarized into a new world outlook and methodology and eventually formed the concept of cyber philosophy [11]. Then, the concept of cyberlogic was developed as a bridge from cyber philosophy to cyber science [12].

If the establishment of ARPANET in the 1950s was taken as the beginning of cyberspace's influence on the real world, it was not until 1996 that the academic world expounded the concept of cyber philosophy for the first time. In the past half-century, the rapid development of cyberspace has impacted all aspects of human life, and the concept of cyber philosophy has gradually sprouted in this process.

The period from 1996 to 2003 was the foundation period of cyber philosophy. The clear explanation of cyber philosophy can be traced back at least to 1996 when Frank published *Cyber Philosophy: Medientheoretische Auslotungen* [13]. In the following years, groundbreaking works in the field of cyber philosophy were done. From 2002 to 2003, Moor and Bynum successively published *Introduction to Cyberphilosophy* [1] and *Cyberphilosophy: The Intersection of Philosophy and Computing* [14]. The work defined cyber philosophy that was widely used in academia: "cyber philosophy is an intersection of philosophy and computer science and is associated with new topics, models, methods, and issues revolving around five themes: minds; agency; reality; communication; and ethics". So far, the discussion on the basic concepts of cyber philosophy has reached a certain degree of unity. Then, some scholars put forward new descriptions from other perspectives of cyber philosophy and continued to improve the concept of cyber philosophy [12].

After 2003, the basic concept of cyber philosophy was relatively clear. However, with the continuous development of cyber medical, legal, social, public opinion, and other fields, the content of cyber philosophy has also been greatly enriched. Thus, the concept of cyber philosophy has also become more familiar to scholars in various fields, and cyber philosophy has entered a period of development. In 2009, Rahman et al. studied cyber-enabled jurisprudential philosophy [15], and Beycioglu studied the cyber philosophy issue in education [16]. In 2010, Bynum presented philosophical contributions of cybernetics and philosophy of information [17]. In 2012, Crosston studied cyber philosophy from a political perspective [18]. In 2017, Ning et al. studied the relationship between cyber philosophy and cyber science [12]. In 2018, Papadimitriou studied the influence of culture on cyber philosophy [19]. On the one hand, scholars paid more attention to the relationship among cyber philosophy and other fields and other spaces. On the other hand, various subdivisions of cyber philosophy were also developed rapidly, especially theories, such as cyberpunk and cybernetic capitalism, which effectively led the development direction of today's society.

1.5 Cyberlogic

With the development of cyberspace, unique logic has emerged in cyberspace. However, for an extended period of time and in the field of computer science, people were more concerned with circuit logic [20] and computer logic [21,22].

As a bridge between cyber philosophy and cyber science, it was not until 2017 that the concept of cyberlogic was first systematically proposed to represent the logic in cyberspace [12]. Cyberlogic covers the informal logic of natural language arguments and the formal logic of inference with purely formal content of cyber and cyber-enabled entities in CPST hyperspace. Cyberlogic mainly includes (a) the essences and rules of cyber entities and cyber-enabled PST entities that exist in cyber-enabled PST spaces, and (b) the rules of single CPST hyperspace, the interactions among cyber-enabled physical, cyber-enabled social, and cyber-enabled thinking spaces, and the essences of CPST convergence space [12]. Since it was proposed, cyberlogic has become an essential part of general cyberspace [1,9] and has been quickly applied to smart homes [23], IoT [24], and other fields. Furthermore, in 2021, the concept of cyber-driven logic was proposed to describe the new logic in traditional spaces generated by the influence of cyberspace [25].

References

1. W. Gibson, *Burning Chrome*, Hachette, UK, 2017.
2. W. Gibson, Neuromancer, Aleph, New Delhi, 2003.
3. H. Ning, Z. Wang, Future internet of things architecture: Like mankind neural system or social organization framework? *IEEE Communications Letters*, Vol. 15; No. 4, pp. 461–463, 2011.
4. A. Luigi, I. Antonio, and M. Giacomo, SIot: Giving a social structure to the internet of things, *IEEE Communications Letters*, Vol. 15; No. 11, pp. 1193–1195, 2011.
5. H. Ning, H. Liu, Cyber-physical-social-thinking space based science and technology framework for the internet of things, *Science China (Information Sciences)*, Vol. 58; No. 3, pp. 17–35, 2015.
6. H. Ning, X. Ye, M. A. Bouras, D. Wei, and M. Daneshmand, General cyberspace: Cyberspace and cyber-enabled spaces, *IEEE Internet of Things Journal*, Vol. 5; No. 3, pp. 1843–1856, 2018.
7. H. Ning, *General Cyberspace*, Publishing House of Electronics Industry, China, 2017. [in Chinese]

8. H. Ning, H. Liu, J. Ma, L. T. Yang, Y. Wan, X. Ye, and R. Huang, From Internet to smart world, *IEEE Access*, Vol. 3; pp. 1994–1999, 2015.

9. S. Dhelim, H. Ning, S. Cui, J. Ma, R. Huang, and K.I. Wang, Cyberentity and its consistency in the cyber-physical-social-thinking hyperspace, *Computers & Electrical Engineering*, Vol. 81; pp. 106506, 2020.

10. H. Ning, H. Liu, J. Ma, L.T. Yang, and R. Huang, Cybermatics: Cyber–physical–social–thinking hyperspace based science and technology, *Future Generation Computer Systems*, Vol. 56; pp. 504–522, 2016.

11. J.H. Moor, T.W. Bynum, Introduction to cyberphilosophy, *Metaphilosophy*, Vol. 33; No. 1/2, pp. 4–10, 2002.

12. H. Ning, Q. Li, D. Wei, H. Liu, and T. Zhu, Cyberlogic paves the way from cyber philosophy to cyber science, *IEEE Internet of Things Journal*, Vol. 4; No. 3, pp. 783–790, 2017.

13. F. Hartmann, *Cyber. Philosophy: MedientheoretischeAuslotungen*, Passagen-Verlag, Austria, 1996.

14. J.H. Moor, T. W. Bynum, *Cyberphilosophy: The Intersection of Philosophy and Computing*, Wiley-Blackwell, United States, 2002.

15. M. M. Rahman, M. A. Khan, N. Mohammad, and M. O. Rahman, Cyberspace claiming new dynamism in the jurisprudential philosophy, *International Journal of Law and Management*, Vol. 51; No. 5, pp. 274–290, 2009.

16. K. Beycioglu, A cyberphilosophical issue in education: Unethical computer using behavior–The case of prospective teachers, *Computers & Education*, Vol. 53; No. 2, pp. 201–208, 2009.

17. T. W. Bynum, Philosophy in the information age, *Metaphilosophy*, Vol. 41; No. 3, pp. 420–442, 2010.

18. M. Crosston, Virtual patriots and a new American cyber strategy: Changing the zero-sum game, *Strategic Studies Quarterly*, Vol. 6; No. 4, pp. 100–118, 2012.

19. F. Papadimitriou, Philosophy of cyberspace, society, culture and transparency in ICTs, in *Proceedings of the XXIII World Congress of Philosophy*, pp. 41–46, 2018.

20. K. W. Martin, *Digital Integrated Circuit Design*, Oxford University Press, New York, 2000.

21. I. Flores, *Computer Logic: The Functional Design of Digital Computers*, Prentice-Hall, United States, 1960.

22. E. F. Morris and T. E. Wohr, Automatic implementation of computer logic, *Communications of the ACM*, Vol. 1; No. 5, pp. 14–20, 1958.

23. S. Dhelim, H. Ning, M. A. Bouras, and J. Ma, *Cyber-Enabled Human-Centric smart home architecture*, 2018 IEEE SmartWorld, Ubiquitous Intelligence & Computing, Advanced & Trusted Computing, Scalable Computing & Communications, Cloud & Big Data Computing, Internet of People and Smart City Innovations, pp. 1880–1886, 2018.

24. K. M. Abbasi, T. A. Khan, and I. U. Haq, Hierarchical modeling of complex internet of things systems using conceptual modeling approaches, *IEEE Access*, Vol. 7; pp. 102772–102791, 2019.

25. Y. Xu, H. Ning, Y. Wan, and F. Zhou, Cyberlogic and cyber-driven logic, *Chinese Journal of Engineering*, Vol. 43; No. 5, pp. 702–709, 2021.

Chapter 2

Cyberspace Behavior: Development and Research History

2.1 Introduction

Cyberspace is one of the basic spaces representing human existence. The development of the Internet has promoted the interaction between humans and cyberspace and has changed our behavior patterns. This chapter describes the development and research history of cyberspace behavior.

2.2 Human Behavior in Cyberspace

The earliest research on cyberspace behavior can be traced back to the book *Second Self: Computers and the Human Spirit*[1] published by Sherry Turkle in 1984, which marked the birth of cyberspace behavior. Cyberspace behavior refers to all activities that an individual does in cyberspace. There are many types of human behaviors in cyberspace. This chapter discusses the following six types of cyberspace behaviors, as shown in Table 2.1[2,3] [1].

---

[1] https://monoskop.org/images/5/55/Turkle_Sherry_The_Second_Self_Computers_and_the_Human_Spirit_20th_ed.pdf
[2] https://en.wikipedia.org/wiki/Cybercrime
[3] https://en.wikipedia.org/wiki/Online_shopping

DOI: 10.1201/9781003257387-2

Table 2.1 Types of Human Behavior in Cyberspace

Behavior Types	Examples
Online Information Seeking and Sharing Behavior	Seek health information, share daily life, etc.
Online Social Behavior	Make a new friend, chat with someone, etc.
Online Shopping Behavior	Buy something, browse products, etc.
Online Game Behavior	Play an online game
Online Activism Behavior	Participate in a protest
Cybercrime Behavior	Illegal intrusion, electronic theft, etc.

2.2.1 Online Information Seeking and Sharing Behavior

Online information is the information transmitted through the Internet. Its spread has the characteristics of high retention, wide range, and multiple channels. There are many behaviors related to online information. In this chapter, two representative types are introduced: online information seeking behavior and online information sharing behavior.

Early online information was transmitted in one direction, that was, from the website to the user. Online information sharing behavior was the exclusive behavior of the administrator of the bulletin board or website, and administrators were responsible for publishing information on the Internet for users to view. Users could only get the information that has been published on the Internet. Therefore, earlier researches mainly focused on online information seeking behavior.

Researches on online information seeking behavior mainly focused on its features and theoretical research. Some scholars have studied the features of online information seeking behavior. For example, in 1994, Pitkow and Recker found that as the preference for using web browsers for Internet exploration increased, users seemed to prefer text-based search. On the contrary, as the preference for using web browsers for Internet exploration decreased, users preferred to search by using keywords [2]. Other researchers have studied the theoretical research of this behavior. For example, Dervin proposed an information seeking behavior model called the Sense-Making Model in 1998 [3], and Wilson proposed the Information Behavior Model in 1999 [4].

In the 21st century, the Internet has developed by leaps and bounds. Information technology applications, such as search engines and social networking sites, have emerged one after another, and their functions have become more and more powerful. This changed the online information seeking and sharing behavior. At this time, online information involved two-way transmission, and users became the obtainer, creator, and communicator of online information. Besides, they could freely post information on the Internet. Naturally, online information sharing behavior has also aroused the attention of researchers. For example, in 2000, Rioux put forward the theory of information seeking and sharing on the Internet. He believed that online information sharing behavior is the behavior of Internet users discovering useful and attractive information, and sharing the information with others [5,6]. Besides, different from the previous stage, online information seeking and sharing behaviors have shown diversified characteristics. Researchers have conducted in-depth studies to explore the underlying factors of the occurrence of different characteristics. For example, in 2007, Zimmer et al. found that the quality and accessibility of information sources were closely related to the seeking of online information [7]. In the same year, Lu and Hsiao found that self-efficacy and personal outcome expectation directly affect online information sharing behavior [8]. In 2013, Stefanone et al. found that global uncertainty had a positive relationship with the information of actively seeking new friends, and the communication of fear had a positive relationship with the information of finding existing friends [9]. In 2020, Lin and Wang found that women pay more attention to privacy risks, social ties, and commitment than men in their attitudes towards online information sharing behavior [10]. See Tables 2.2 and 2.3 for details.

2.2.2 Online Social Behavior

Online social behavior is an important part of human cyberspace behavior. With the development of the Internet, as people's online social behavior is constantly changing, its research keeps progressing.

In the 1970s and 1980s, the forms of social behavior in cyberspace were simple. Sending e-mails was the main form of social behavior. With the development of the Internet, the form of online social behaviors continuously varied in the late 1990s. Some social networking platforms were developed at this time, such as Geocities and TheGlobe.com, in which people gathered together through chat rooms and shared personal information and ideas with publishing tools.

In the 21st century, richly functional social networking platforms appeared, such as Friendster, MySpace, Facebook, and Twitter. Accordingly, people had a higher degree of freedom, which provides great convenience for posting information, making friends, etc. In this period, researchers carried out various extended studies related to online social behaviors, such as their purpose and influencing factors. First, there are abundant researches on the purpose of online social behaviors. In 2007, Golder et al. found that the purpose of online social behaviors is to maintain and establish long-distance social connections [21]. In the following year, Raacke and Bonds-Raacke stated that the common purposes of users' online social behaviors are: "keep in touch with old friends", "keep in touch with current friends", "upload/view photos", "make new friends", and "find old friends" [22]. In 2010, to distinguish the relevance of online social behavior's many purposes, Raacke and Bonds-Raacke further divided them into three dimensions [23]. In 2015, Basak and Calisir found that users' online social behaviors had significant connections with entertainment and status seeking [24]. Second, the influencing factors of online social behaviors were also one of the important research topics. In

**Table 2.2 Researches on Influencing Factors of
Online Information Seeking Behavior**

Literature Source	Research Content	Influencing Factors
Rieh [11]	The relationship between people's online search behaviors and domestic settings were studied.	Home environment
Heinström [12]	The relationship between the personality traits of 305 master students and their online information seeking behaviors were investigated and analyzed.	Personality traits
Zimmer et al. [7]	The selection of information sources (relational sources and nonrelational sources) for 204 working professionals was surveyed.	Source accessibility and quality
Zhao [13]	The online health information seeking behaviors of parents and teenagers under different educational backgrounds was analyzed.	Education backgrounds
Niuand Hemminger [14]	The online information seeking behavior of 2063 academic scientists was analyzed.	Demographic, psychological, role-related, and environmental factors
Stefanone et al. [9]	The relationship between the online information seeking behavior of 337 Facebook users and their personality traits and social context were analyzed.	Personality traits and social context
Dengand Liu [15]	Combining the risk perception attitude framework and social support, the online health information seeking behaviors of 486 patients was investigated.	Risk perception and social support
Parija et al. [16]	The relationship between online health information seeking behaviors and various socio-demographic variables of 321 adult Indian residents was investigated and analyzed.	Various socio-demographic variables

Table 2.3   Researches on Influencing Factors of Online Information Sharing Behavior

Literature Source	Research Content	Influencing Factors
Hennig-Thuraud et al. [17]	The structure and relevant information of 2,000 consumers' online information sharing behavior motivation was analyzed.	The desire for social interaction, attention to other consumers, and enhancement of user's own value
Lu and Hsiao [8]	The relationship between online information-sharing behavior and four factors of 155 blog users was studied.	Knowledge self-efficacy, personal outcome expectation, subjective norms, and feedback
Oh [18]	257 health information sharers' behaviors were investigated, and ten related factors were proposed and tested.	Altruism, enjoyment, sense of accomplishment and status, etc.
Stieglitz and Dang-Xuan [19]	Based on more than 165,000 Twitter users' data, the relationship between users' information-sharing behavior and emotions was analyzed.	Emotions contained in social media content
Liu et al. [20]	The online behavior of 1,177 users of social commerce sites was analyzed, and a theoretical model of user information-sharing behavior was put forward and empirically tested.	Reputation, enjoyment, out-degrees' post, in-degrees' feedback, customer expertise, and reciprocity
Lin and Wang [10]	The gender differences in the decision-making of information-sharing behavior of 405 social networking sites' users were analyzed by using rationed action theory and social role theory.	Gender

2008, Joinson found that women paid more attention to their privacy than men in social networking [25]. In 2013, Toubia Olivier et al. pointed out that user-created content behavior was affected by intrinsic utility and impression. The increase in user fans would both stimulate users to create content and reduce the enthusiasm of users to create content, depending on different motivations [26]. Certainly, there are also many other studies related to influencing factors, as shown in Table 2.4.

Table 2.4 Researches on Influencing Factors of Online Social Behavior

Literature Source	Research Content	Influencing Factors
Thayer and Ray [27]	The relationship between gender, age, Internet usage time, and online social behavior of 174 users was explored.	Age, gender, and duration
Hargittai [28]	The relationship between user characteristics and the use of social networking sites was studied.	Gender, race, and education
Joinson [25]	The online social behavior data of 241 Facebook users was analyzed.	Gender and satisfaction
Ryan and Xenos [29]	The survey studied how personality traits affected the online social behavior of 1,158 Facebook users and 166 non-Facebook users.	Personality traits
McAndrew and Jeong [30]	1,026 Facebook users' using behaviors was studied.	Age and gender
Moore and McElroy [31]	The general behavioral patterns of 219 college students on the Facebook platform were analyzed.	Personality traits and experience
Toubia and Stephen [26]	The relationship between the changes in the number of followers and fans of 2,493 Facebook users and the user behavior of creating content was analyzed.	Intrinsic utility, impression, and fans
Varol et al. [32]	The changes of users' tweets in 25 days during the Gezi Park campaign were studied.	Society state
Shakya and Christakis [33]	The relationship between the online social activities and real-life social activities of 5,208 subjects was studied by using some subjective measures of well-being.	Physical health, mental health, life satisfaction, and body mass index
Shchebetenko [34]	The data of 830 users of a social networking site were analyzed, and the relationship between online social behavior and personality traits was examined.	Personality traits

Additionally, due to the increase of cyber-enabled psychological disease, some researchers have studied the relationship between online social behavior and psychological health. In 2007, Ellison et al. found that people who seldom socialized online had lower life satisfaction and self-esteem than those who regularly associated online [35]. Pantic et al. and Banjanin et al. believed that the increase in adolescents' online social time is related to the increase in depression and anxiety [36,37]. However, Best et al. and Huang said the relationship between the two was minimal [38,39]. In 2020, a recent 8-year study by Coyne et al. found no evidence that the increase in online social behavior time has an impact on psychological health [40].

2.2.3 Online Shopping Behavior

Online shopping behavior overcomes the disadvantages of traditional shopping, such as time-consuming and laborious, so that people can buy any goods they want without leaving home.

Back in the 1960s, online shopping behavior occurred. IBM's online transaction processing (OLTP) allowed processing financial transaction processing in real-time,[4] such as the computer ticket booking system. In 1972, Mohamed M. Atalla realized a secure transaction system over telecommunication networks, which used encryption technology to ensure telephone links' security. In 1984, Gateshead SIS/Tesco, the early B2C online shopping system was published. Mrs. Snowball became the first online home shopper. However, few people were shopping online at that stage because of the limitations of computer technology and the Internet.

In the 1990s, online shopping behaviors began to attract people's attention gradually. In 1989, Sequoia Data Corporation launched Compumarket, in which sellers could post items for sale, and buyers could search the database and make purchases with credit cards. In 1994, "Amazon.com" was established, which was positioned as the world's largest bookstore at first, and then it tried to be the largest retailer in the world. In the next year, eBay was established by Pierre Omidyar as an auction site. This was an earlier online auction site for person-to-person transactions. In 1999, Alibaba was launched as a large shopping platform in China. Although the online shopping platforms began to be booming, the products that people could buy at that time were relatively minimal, and the online shopping process was still cumbersome.

In the 21st century, with the increase in the functions and product categories of online shopping platforms, more and more people chose to shop online. Online shopping behavior presents a state of diversified development. To have a deeper understanding of online shopping behavior, people have begun to study its influencing factors. In 2008, based on the trust and Technology Acceptance Model (including perceived usefulness and ease-of-use), Kim et al. found that reputation, privacy, security, consumer's trust tendencies, and platform's information quality had a significant impact on online shopping behavior [41]. In 2010, Tsao and

---

[4] https://en.wikipedia.org/wiki/Online_shopping#History

Chang found that neuroticism, extraversion, and openness to experience positively impacted consumers' online shopping behavior [42]. More relevant studies on the influencing factors of online shopping behavior are described in Table 2.5.

In the 2010s, with the advance in virtual reality and augmented reality, there were some novel functions and behaviors for online shopping, for example, trying on clothes online. The development of Artificial Intelligence (AI) made the product recommendation of shopping websites more in line with consumers' shopping habits and psychological expectations. These have brought great convenience to our online shopping and promoted the development of online shopping behavior. For example, the IKEA Place app could automatically measure the space of the living room and recommend furniture suitable for that space to the user by taking a photo of the living room. Users could observe, mix, and match the furniture according to their ideas in the 3D living room generated by the App.

2.2.4 Online Game Behavior

Online game behaviors eliminate the boundaries between physical space and cyberspace, which provide people a new entertainment way. There are many kinds of online games, such as shooting puzzles, leisure, and the behaviors of online games have great variety, including battle, coordination, and communication, etc.

Multi-User Dungeon (MUD) was an early example of online games connected to ARPANET in 1980. In the 1990s, since the Internet has not yet been widely popularized, the development of online games was in its initial stage. Consequently, the types of online games were relatively few, basically including two types of games. One was the first-person shooter (FPS), such as Counter-Strike and Unreal Tournament. The other was real-time strategy (RTS), such as Age of Empires and StarCraft. Therefore, the players' online game behavior was simple. Common online game behavior includes the following: players control the avatar to simulate a gunfight with others, and players cultivate their forces in the virtual world to fight against the forces of other players.

In the 2000s, with the development of game technology and the Internet, online games developed rapidly and became popular. Besides, the types of online games became rich and diverse. Massive Multiplayer Online Role-Playing Game (MMORPG), as a popular video game, received much attention. In MMORPG, players can create their characters, fight various monsters, communicate with others, and try novel things (e.g., travel through space-time).

In the 2010s, the development of online games gradually became mature, and the types of online game behaviors become more and more diversified. To understand online game behavior deeply, researchers began to study its influencing factors and its impacts on our health. There are various influencing factors, such as gender, age, and personality traits, as shown in Table 2.6. Besides, some researchers found that online game behavior is bad for our health. In 2012, Kuss and Griffiths pointed out personality was related to online game addiction [51]. In 2018, Jung et al. found

Table 2.5 Researches on Influencing Factors of Online Shopping Behavior

Literature Source	Research Content	Influencing Factors
Gefen and Straub [43]	The authors investigated whether the primary task of using information technology of 217 MBA students directly affects the use intention of information technology.	Perceived ease of use
Reichheld and Schefter [44]	The authors described the meaning of loyalty in online shopping behavior.	Trust
Lee et al. [45]	The impact of perceived ease of use, perceived usefulness, and perceived risk on the online shopping behavior of 176 consumers were investigated.	Perceived usefulness, perceived ease of use, and trust
Salam et al. [46]	Theoretical analysis of the impact of economic incentives on online shopping behavior was studied.	Economic incentives and perceived risk
Hsu et al. [47]	The reasons why 201 online consumers continue to shop online were researched.	Disconfirmation and satisfaction with prior use
Tsao and Chang [42]	The influence of personality traits of 429 e-shoppers on their online shopping behaviors was studied.	Personality traits
Wei and Lu [48]	The impact of customer reviews and celebrity endorsements on 176 women's online shopping behavior was studied.	Customer reviews and celebrity endorsements
Zhou et al. [49]	Nearly 30,000 consumer reviews on Amazon were analyzed to compare the online shopping behavior between the U.S. and China.	Online market maturity
González et al. [50]	Five experiments were conducted to explore the influence of gender and product usage context on online shopping behavior.	Gender and product usage context

that escaping from reality, attack motivations, and achievement motivations were related to online game addiction [52]. Although online games have brought much convenience to people's lives, they should abide by reasonable and healthy principles to create a better online game environment.

Table 2.6 Researches on Influencing Factors of Online Game Behavior

Literature Source	Research Content	Influencing Factor(s)
Griffiths et al. [53]	The relationship between basic demographic information, game frequency, and game history of 540 young and adult players was investigated and analyzed.	Basic demographic information
Lee et al. [54]	A theoretical model was proposed to explain and predict the online game behavior of players. Four hundred and fifty eight players were analyzed using the model.	Game experience, interaction, gender, and age
Yee et al. [55]	The authors researched how the online game behavior preferences of 2,037 players of the "World of Warcraft" map to their demographic data.	Basic demographic information
Worth and Book [56]	The relationship between the personality traits of 205 players of "World of Warcraft" and online game behavior was investigated and studied.	Personality traits
Alzahrani et al. [57]	The influencing factors of 1,584 college students' online game behavior were analyzed.	Game experience, subject norms, and attitude
Lemercier-Dugarin et al. [58]	The relationship between an anti-social behavior in the online game of 816 players and several potential factors was investigated and studied.	Personality traits, emotion reactivity, and motivations

2.2.5 Online Activism Behavior

The development of the Internet has changed people's lives, and it has provided people with a faster and more effective way to express their ideas.

In the 1990s, people used e-mail and static web pages for online activism behavior. For example, in 1990, a product contained the names, addresses, and purchase behaviors of 120 million Americans in the form of CD-ROMs, named Lotus Marketplace: Households. This product quickly sparked a heated discussion, and about 30,000 people organized and protested via e-mail and message boards. In 1998, Joan Blades and Wes Boyd published a petition online to Washington called Moveon.org. The petition was initially sent to only about 100 family members and friends, but it received 100,000 signatures in a week. Eventually, 5 million signatures were obtained. At this stage, the speed of information transmission was low, but it is not difficult to see that the spread and effects of online activism behavior were remarkable.

In the 21st century, with the development of online social information technology tools, people's online activism behavior shifted to social media (e.g., MySpace, Facebook, and Twitter). For example, during the California immigration protests in 2006, high school students in the Los Angeles area contacted other teenagers in the Central Valley of California on MySpace, which inspired 1,000 Fresno students to join the strike. In the same year, "#MeToo" was initiated by Tarana Burke on MySpace to help victims of sexual assault in impoverished areas. In July 2013, the social hashtag "#BlackLivesMatter" appeared on social media and was usually used to advocate against police violence against blacks and various other policy changes related to black liberation. Until today, this is also a significant activity. From July 2013 to May 1, 2018, the hashtag "BlackLivesMatter" has been released more than 30 million times, with an average of 17,002 times per day. A survey[5] conducted by the Pew Research Center in June 2020 found that 67% of adult Americans supported it. Table 2.7 lists some other examples of online activism behavior.

At this stage, online activism behavior was closely related to traditional social activities. A rally was usually completed by a combination of online and offline, which attracted the attention of researchers and prompted them to carry out researches on the impact between the two.

First, some researchers expressed negative views on online activism behavior, for example, online activism behavior has low effect with lazy activism and insubstantial support [59,60]. Drumbl believed that click activism has a short attention span and a limited shelf life [61]. Schumann and Klein found that engaged in online actions would inhibit offline participation, which is consistent with the lazy activism hypothesis [62].

Second, other researchers expressed affirmative views. Harlow and Harp found that respondents believed that online activism behavior could be transformed into traditional activism behavior. Moreover, compared with online activism behavior, offline movement develops better [63]. Kende et al. believed that when Internet actions are used to express group identity and establish politicized identity, online activism behavior can promote future participation [64]. Dookhoo found that people who engage in online activism mainly use online activism behavior to meet their intrinsic needs for interaction and belonging, and millennials' online activism behavior is higher than offline activism behavior [65]. Greijdanus et al. found that online and offline activisms are positively related and intertwined [66].

Third, some researchers expressed a neutral view. For example, Wilkins et al. stated that whether it is positive or not depends on the previous level of activism and belief in the effectiveness of individual contributions to collective activities [67].

---

[5] https://www.pewresearch.org/social-trends/2020/06/12/amid-protests-majorities-across-racial-and-ethnic-groups-express-support-for-the-black-lives-matter-movement/

Table 2.7 Examples of Online Activism Behavior

Online Activism Behavior	Date	Online Social Media
California Immigration Protests	March 2006	Myspace
#MeToo	2006 to present	Myspace
Colombian Las Farc Protests	February 2008	Facebook
Iran Election Protests	June 2009	Twitter and YouTube
Greek Protests	May 2010	Facebook
Arab Spring	December 2010 to May 2014	Blogs, Facebook, and Twitter
Spain 15-M Protests	May 2011	Facebook
Saudi Woman Driving	June 2011	Facebook and Twitter
London Riots	August 2011	Twitter
Protests against SOPA and PIPA	January 2012	Websites
Human Rights Campaign	March 2013	Facebook
#Black Lives Matter	July 2013 to present	Twitter
He For She	September 2014 to present	Twitter and YouTube
#Stop Funding Hate	August 2016	Facebook
#Womens March	January 2017	Facebook, Twitter, and YouTube
#March for Our Lives	March 2018	Facebook, Instagram, Twitter, and Snapchat
Youth Climate Change Strike	March 2019	Slack and WhatsApp
Justice for George Floyd	May 2020	Change.org, Facebook, and Twitter

2.2.6 *Cybercrime Behavior*

Cybercrime refers to the general term for people using computer technology to attack and destroy systems, networks, and information centers or using networks to commit other crimes. Cybercrime behavior has its typical characteristics. First, cybercrime behavior has the characteristics of low cost, fast transmission speed, and wide range. For example, Melissa virus in 1999, which was the first large-scale e-mail virus, attacked more than one million e-mail accounts around the world, causing losses of about $80 million. Second, due to the anonymity of the Internet, cybercrime has the characteristics of high interactivity, high secrecy, and difficulty in obtaining evidence. Third, cybercrime endangers the safety and order of the Internet and its information all the time. Common cybercrime behaviors include spreading network rumors and computer viruses, excessive cyberbullying, attacking computer systems, selling contraband, and online sexual transactions. The research on cybercrime involves detection, prevention and governance, and legislation. It is further explored in Chapter 14.

2.3 Human Behavior Analysis Development

In the 1990s, online behavior analysis based on packet and traffic levels appeared. It involved technologies, such as network traffic identification, message classification, and packet reassembly, to isolate information related to user cyberspace behavior. Afterward, the information was analyzed in-depth to explain human cyberspace behavior. The technology was often used to detect abnormal traffic and hacker attacks. In the 21st century, with the advancement of computers and intelligent technology, user-level behavior analysis became more and more popular. Technology needs to process user behavior's picture, audio, and text information. Image processing technology, audio conversion technology, and natural language processing technology, respectively, are used to convert data of image content, audio content, and text content into structured data, respectively. User's payment, purchase, and access can be directly represented by structured tables. Finally, knowledge graphs, users' profile, and data mining techniques are used to analyze user behavior.

2.4 Prospect and Discussion

The development of the Internet has provided a new way of life for mankind, involving information seeking and sharing, social interaction, shopping, gaming, and expressing personal thoughts, etc. It has also brought new challenges to mankind, such as cybercrime. With the development of various human behaviors in cyberspace, the connection between individuals in real life and cyberspace is getting closer. This motivates researchers to study their behaviors more deeply. In the late 2000s and during the 2010s, there were already some immature intelligent individuals in cyberspace, such as Siri, Google Assistant, and Alexa, etc. They could perform some behaviors in cyberspace the same as humans do, such as simple office work. In the future, intelligent individuals will gradually become mature, and they will have the same wisdom and thinking ability as humans. There are three issues worthy of consideration as follows:

- How do humans get along with intelligent individuals?
- Is the intelligent individual behavior in cyberspace related to its individual characteristics?
- Does the behavior of the intelligent individual need moral and legal constraints and norms?

References

1. X. Zha, J. Zhang, Y. Yan, and J. Li, Review on the research status and development trend of network users' information behavior, *Journal of Library Science in China*, Vol. 40; No. 4, pp. 100–115, 2014.
2. J. Pitkow and M. Recker, Results from the first world-wide web user survey, *Computer Networks and ISDN Systems*, Vol. 27; No. 2, pp. 243–254, 1994.
3. B. Dervin, Sense-making theory and practice: An overview of user interests in knowledge seeking and use, *Journal of Knowledge Management*, Vol. 2; No. 2, pp. 36–46, 1998.
4. T. D. Wilson, Models in information behaviour research, *Journal of Documentation*, Vol. 55; No. 3, pp. 249–270, 1999.
5. K. Rioux, Sharing information found for others on the World Wide Web: A preliminary examination, *Proceedings of the ASIS Annual Meeting*, Vol. 37; pp. 68–77, 2000.
6. C. Zhang and X. Wang, Review on the study of network information sharing behavior, *Journal of Chongqing Technology and Business University (Social Science Edition)*, Vol. 35; No. 5, pp. 94–102, 2018.
7. J. C. Zimmer, R. M. Henry, and B. S. Butler, Determinants of the use of relational and nonrelational information sources, *Journal of Management Information Systems*, Vol. 24; No. 3, pp. 297–331, 2007.
8. H. Lu and K. L. Hsiao, Understanding intention to continuously share information on weblogs, *Internet Research*, Vol. 17; No. 4, pp. 345–361, 2007.
9. M. A. Stefanone, C. M. Hurley, and Z. Yang, Antecedents of online information seeking, *Information, Communication & Society*, Vol. 16; No. 1, pp. 61–81, 2013.
10. X. Linand and X. Wang. Examining gender differences in people's information-sharing decisions on social networking sites, *International Journal of Information Management*, Vol. 50; pp. 45–56, 2020.
11. S. Y. Rieh, Investigating Web searching behavior in home environments, *Proceedings of the American Society for Information Science and Technology*, Vol. 40; No. 1, pp. 255–264, 2003.
12. J. Heinström, Fast surfing, broad scanning and deep diving: The influence of personality and study approach on students' information-seeking behavior, *Journal of Documentation*, Vol. 61; No. 2, pp. 228–247, 2005.
13. S. Zhao, Parental education and children's online health information seeking: Beyond the digital divide debate, *Social Science & Medicine*, Vol. 69; No. 10, pp 1501–1505, 2009.

14. X. Niu and B. M. Hemminger, A study of factors that affect the information-seeking behavior of academic scientists, *Journal of the American Society for Information Science and Technology*, Vol. 63; No. 2, pp. 336–353, 2012.
15. Z. Deng and S. Liu, Understanding consumer health information-seeking behavior from the perspective of the risk perception attitude framework and social support in mobile social media websites, *International Journal of Medical Informatics*, Vol. 105; pp. 98–109, 2017.
16. P. P. Parija, P. Tiwari, P. Sharma, and S. K. Saha, Determinants of online health information-seeking behavior: A cross-sectional survey among residents of an urban settlement in Delhi, *Journal of Education and Health Promotion*, Vol. 9; No. 1, pp. 344, 2020.
17. T. Hennig-Thurau, K. P. Gwinner, G. Walsh, and D. Gremler, Electronic word-of-mouth via consumer-opinion platforms: What motivates consumers to articulate themselves on the Internet? *Journal of Interactive Marketing*, Vol. 18; No. 1, pp. 38–52, 2004.
18. O. Sanghee, The characteristics and motivations of health answerers for sharing information, knowledge, and experiences in online environments, *Journal of the American Society for Information Science and Technology*, Vol. 63; No. 3, pp. 543–557, 2012.
19. S. Stieglitz and L. Dang-Xuan, Emotions and information diffusion in social media—sentiment of microblogs and sharing behavior, *Journal of Management Information Systems*, Vol. 29; No. 4, pp. 217–248, 2013.
20. L. Liu, C. M. K. Cheung, and M. K. O. Lee, An empirical investigation of information sharing behavior on social commerce sites, *International Journal of Information Management*, Vol. 36; No. 5, pp. 686–699, 2016.
21. S. A. Golder, D. M. Wilkinson, and B. A. Huberman, Rhythms of social interaction: Messaging within a massive online network, In: C. Steinfield, B. T. Pentland, M. Ackerman, and N. Contractor (eds), *Communities and Technologies*, Springer, London, pp. 41–66, 2007.
22. J. Raacke and J. Bonds-Raacke, MySpace and Facebook: Applying the uses and gratifications theory to exploring friend-networking sites, *Cyberpsychology & Behavior*, Vol. 11; No. 2, pp. 169–174, 2008.
23. J. Bonds-Raacke and J. Raacke, MySpace and Facebook: Identifying dimensions of uses and gratifications for friend networking sites, *Individual Differences Research*, Vol. 8; No. 1, 2010.
24. E. Basakand and F. Calisir, An empirical study on factors affecting continuance intention of using Facebook, *Computers in Human Behavior*, Vol. 48; pp. 181–189, 2015.
25. A. N. Joinson, Looking at, looking up or keeping up with people? Motives and use of Facebook, *Proceedings of the SIGCHI Conference on Human Factors in Computing Systems*, pp. 1027–1036, 2008.
26. O. Toubiaand and A. T. Stephen, Intrinsic vs. image-related utility in social media: Why do people contribute content to twitter? *Marketing Science*, Vol. 32; No. 3, pp. 368–392, 2013.
27. S. E. Thayer and S. Ray, Online communication preferences across age, gender, and duration of Internet use, *CyberPsychology& Behavior*, Vol. 9; No. 4, pp. 432–440, 2006.
28. E. Hargittai, Whose space? Differences among users and non-users of social network sites, *Journal of Computer-Mediated Communication*, Vol. 13; No. 1, pp. 276–297, 2007.

29. T. Ryan and S. Xenos, Who uses Facebook? An investigation into the relationship between the big five, shyness, narcissism, loneliness, and Facebook usage, *Computers in Human Behavior*, Vol. 27; No. 5, pp. 1658–1664, 2011.
30. F. T. McAndrew and H. S. Jeong, Who does what on Facebook? Age, sex, and relationship status as predictors of Facebook use, *Computers in Human Behavior*, Vol. 28; No. 6, pp. 2359–2365, 2012.
31. K. Moore and J. C. McElroy, The influence of personality on Facebook usage, wall postings, and regret, *Computers in Human Behavior*, Vol. 28; No. 1, pp. 267–274, 2012.
32. O. Varol, E. Ferrara, C. L. Ogan, F. Menczer, and A. Flammini, Evolution of online user behavior during a social upheaval, *Proceedings of the 2014 ACM conference on Web science*, pp. 81–90, 2014.
33. H. B. Shakya and N. A. Christakis, Association of Facebook use with compromised well-being: A longitudinal study, *American Journal of Epidemiology*, Vol. 185; No. 3, pp. 203–211, 2017.
34. S. Shchebetenko, Do personality characteristics explain the associations between self-esteem and online social networking behavior? *Computers in Human Behavior*, Vol. 91; pp. 17–23, 2019.
35. N. B. Ellison, C. Steinfield, and C. Lampe, The benefits of Facebook "friends:" Social capital and college students' use of online social network sites, *Journal of Computer-Mediated Communication*, Vol. 12; No. 4, pp. 1143–1168, 2007.
36. I. Pantic, A. Damjanovic, J. Todorovic, D. Topalovic, D. Bojovic-Jovic, S. Ristic, and S. Pantic, Association between online social networking and depression in high school students: Behavioral physiology viewpoint, *Psychiatria Danubina*, Vol. 24; No. 1, pp. 90–93, 2012.
37. N. Banjanin, N. Banjanin, I. Dimitrijevic, and I. Pantic, Relationship between internet use and depression: Focus on physiological mood oscillations, social networking and online addictive behavior, *Computers in Human Behavior*, Vol. 43; pp. 308–312, 2015.
38. P. Best, R. Manktelow, and B. Taylor, Online communication, social media and adolescent wellbeing: A systematic narrative review, *Children and Youth Services Review*, Vol. 41; pp. 27–36, 2014.
39. C. Huang, Time spent on social network sites and psychological well-being: A meta-analysis, *Cyberpsychology, Behavior, and Social Networking*, Vol. 20; No. 6, pp. 346–354, 2017.
40. S. M. Coyne, A. A. Rogers, J. D. Zurcher, L. Stockdale, and M. Booth, Does time spent using social media impact mental health?: An eight year longitudinal study, *Computers in Human Behavior*, Vol. 104; pp. 106160, 2020.
41. D. J. Kim, D. L. Ferrin, and H. R. Rao, A trust-based consumer decision-making model in electronic commerce: The role of trust, perceived risk, and their antecedents, *Decision Support Systems*, Vol. 44; No. 2, pp. 544–564, 2008.
42. W. C. Tsao and H. R. Chang, Exploring the impact of personality traits on online shopping behavior, *African Journal of Business Management*, Vol. 4; No. 9, pp. 1800–1812, 2010.
43. D. Gefen and D. W. Straub, The relative importance of perceived ease of use in IS adoption: A study of e-commerce adoption, *Journal of the association for Information Systems*, Vol. 1; No. 1, pp. 8, 2000.
44. F. F. Reichhelland and P. Schefter, E-loyalty: Your secret weapon on the web, *Harvard Business Review*, Vol. 78; No. 4, pp. 105–113, 2000.

45. D. Lee, J. Park, and J. H. Ahn, On the explanation of factors affecting e-commerce adoption, *ICIS 2001 Proceedings*, 2001.
46. A. F. Salam, H. R. Rao, and C. C. Pegels, Consumer-perceived risk in e-commerce transactions, *Communications of the ACM*, Vol. 46; No. 12, pp. 325–331, 2003.
47. M. H. Hsu, C. H. Yen, C. M. Chiu, and C. M. Chang, A longitudinal investigation of continued online shopping behavior: An extension of the theory of planned behavior, *International Journal of Human-Computer Studies*, Vol. 64; No. 9, pp. 889–904, 2006.
48. P. Wei and H. P. Lu. An examination of the celebrity endorsements and online customer reviews influence female consumers' shopping behavior, *Computers in Human Behavior*, Vol. 29; No. 1, pp. 193–201, 2013.
49. Q. Zhou, R. Xia, and C. Zhang, Online shopping behavior study based on multi-granularity opinion mining: China versus America, *Cognitive Computation*, Vol. 8; No. 4, pp. 587–602, 2016.
50. E. M. González, J. H. Meyer, and M. P. Toldos, What women want? How contextual product displays influence women's online shopping behavior, *Journal of Business Research*, Vol. 123; pp. 625–641, 2021.
51. D. J. Kuss and M. D. Griffiths, Internet gaming addiction: A systematic review of empirical research, *International Journal of Mental Health and Addiction*, Vol. 10; No. 2, pp. 278–296, 2012.
52. H. Wei, M. Chen, P. Huang, and Y. Bai, The association between online gaming, social phobia, and depression: An internet survey, *BMC Psychiatry*, Vol. 12; No. 1, pp. 1–7, 2012.
53. M. N. O. Griffithsand and D. C. Davies, Online computer gaming: A comparison of adolescent and adult gamers, *Journal of Adolescence*, Vol. 27; No. 1, pp. 87–96, 2004.
54. M.C. Lee, Understanding the behavioral intention to play online games: An extension of the theory of planned behavior, *Online Information Review*, Vol. 33; No. 5, pp. 849–872, 2009.
55. N. Yee, N. Ducheneaut, H. T. Shiao, L. Nelson, Through the azerothian looking glass: Mapping in-game preferences to real world demographics, *Proceedings of the SIGCHI Conference on Human Factors in Computing Systems*, pp. 2811–2814, 2012.
56. N. C. Worth and A. S. Book, Personality and behavior in a massively multiplayer online role-playing game, *Computers in Human Behavior*, Vol. 38; pp. 322–330, 2014.
57. A. I. Alzahrani, I. Mahmud, T. Ramayah, O. Alfarraj, and N. Alalwan, Extending the theory of planned behavior (TPB) to explain online game playing among Malaysian undergraduate students, *Telematics and Informatics*, Vol. 34; No. 4, pp. 239–251, 2017.
58. M. Lemercier-Dugarin, L. Romo, C. Tijus, and O. Zerhouni, "Who are the CykaBlyat?" How empathy, impulsivity, and motivations to play predict aggressive behaviors in multiplayer online games, *Cyberpsychology, Behavior, and Social Networking*, Vol. 24; No. 1, pp. 63–69, 2021.
59. M. Gladwell, Small change, *The New Yorker*, Vol. 4; pp. 42–49, 2010.
60. H. S. Christensen, Political activities on the internet: Slacktivism or political participation by other means? *First Monday*, Vol. 16; No. 2, 2011.
61. M. A. Drumbl, Child soldiers and clicktivism: Justice, myths, and prevention, *Journal of Human Rights Practice*, Vol. 4; No. 3, pp. 481–485, 2012.
62. S. Schumann and O. Klein, Substitute or stepping stone? Assessing the impact of low-threshold online collective actions on offline participation, *European Journal of Social Psychology*, Vol. 45; No. 3, pp. 308–322, 2015.

63. S. Harlow and D. Harp, Collective action on the web: A cross-cultural study of social networking sites and online and offline activism in the United States and Latin America, *Information, Communication & Society*, Vol. 15; No. 2, pp. 196–216, 2012.

64. A. Kende, M. Zomeren, A. Ujhelyi, and N. A. Lantos, The social affirmation use of social media as a motivator of collective action, *Journal of Applied Social Psychology*, Vol. 46; No. 8, pp. 453–469, 2016.

65. S. Dookhoo, How millennials engage in social media activism: A uses and gratifications approach (Master's Thesis), University of Central Florida, United States, 2015.

66. H. Greijdanus, C. A. M. Fernandes, F. Turner-Zwinkels, A. Honari, C. Roos, H. Rosenbusch, and T. Postmes, The psychology of online activism and social movements: Relations between online and offline collective action, *Current Opinion in Psychology*, Vol. 35; pp. 49–54, 2020.

67. D. J. Wilkins, A. G. Livingstone, and M. Levine, All click, no action? Online action, efficacy perceptions, and prior experience combine to affect future collective action, *Computers in Human Behavior*, Vol. 91; pp. 97–105, 2019.

Chapter 3

History of Online Social Network

3.1 Introduction

Social networks have been widely concerned by scholars. The emergence of a social network makes people's communication more and more convenient, and the way of life and thinking has been greatly affected. This chapter mainly introduces the history of online social networks and the history of social networks analysis.

3.2 The History of Online Social Networks

With the advance of computing and communication technologies, and the interconnection of multiple machines, the concept of social machines appeared. The emergence of social machines has been widely empowered by the recently developed technologies such as the Internet, mobile smartphones, social networks, and the World Wide Web, by connecting users in new ways. The concept of social machines was proposed as early as the sixteenth century. The invention of the telegraph in 1792 made it the fastest method of communication over a long distance, and it was revolutionary at the time. After that, the telephone and the radio were invented during the 1800s, making everything change since they provided fast and instant communication. Figure 3.1 shows the milestones of Internet history.

With the invention of the first computer, the development of computing and communication technologies underwent unprecedented changes. For example, e-mails first appeared in 1966, followed by the Usenet network in 1979. In 1960,

DOI: 10.1201/9781003257387-3

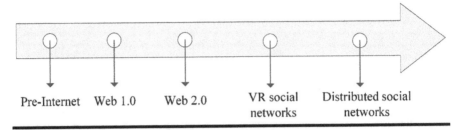

| Pre-Internet | Web 1.0 | Web 2.0 | VR social networks | Distributed social networks |

Figure 3.1 Brief history of social networks.

the Programmed Logic for Automated Teaching Operations (PLATO) was developed by the University of Illinois. It provided the first shape of social media functions with 1973-era innovations that included PLATO's message-forum function known as TERM-talk and its instant-messaging function, Talkomatic, which was the earliest online chat room, News Report, a blog, and online newspaper crowdsourcing system, in addition to Access Lists function that enabled the note owner to access other functions used by similar users, such as colleagues and classmates. The first social system in the pre-internet era was Bulletin Board System (BBS), also known as Community Memory. It was an online meeting venue that allowed people to communicate through a centralized system in which they could download games and files. The users accessed BBS using telephone lines through modems, which was the main social network throughout the 1980s and 1990s until the creation of the Internet.

After the creation of the Internet and Web 1.0, the development of social networking websites began with simple sites. In 1994, GeoCities was launched, and it was considered one of the earliest social networking websites. Classmates.com and SixDegrees.com were launched in 1995 and 1997, respectively. The latter was considered the first professional social network, as users were required to use their real identity. It also included the information of school affiliations during the registration process. However, these sites did not stand a long time, and due to their static nature, which was mainly oriented for content display and download, the early social networks gradually vanished over time. Table 3.1 shows the major social networks and their launch time.

Web 2.0 was introduced in the early 2000s, and the world has witnessed a social network explosion – Facebook and Twitter were the most prominent examples of this era. The widespread of mobile smartphones revolutionized social networking and the way people used them. The era of smartphone-based social networks marked the birth of many photos and video-sharing applications, such as Snapchat and Instagram. With the emergence of virtual reality technology, many social networks tried to integrate this technology within their systems, such as Facebook's Oculus VR. The centralized nature of dominant social networks and the criticism related to free speech on these networks inspired the creation of many distributed networks and blockchain-based social networks.

Table 3.1   Major Social Networks Launch Time

Year	Social Network	Type
1960	PLATO	Forum social network
1973	Bulletin Board System	File sharing social network
1994	GeoCities	Locations social network
1995	Classmates	Colleagues social network
1996	ICQ	Instant messenger
1997	AIM	Instant messenger
1997	SixDegrees	Professional social network
1998	OpenDiary	Diary social network
1998	LiveJournal	Diary social network
2003	LinkedIn	Professional social network
2003	Myspace	Friend social network
2004	Facebook	Friend social network
2004	YouTube	Video social network
2006	Twitter	Text social network
2010	Instagram	Photo social network

3.3 The History of Social Networks Analysis

With the popularity of social networks and the increasing size of user-generated data, social network analysis has emerged as a new study field that takes advantage of rich social network data. Generally speaking, social networks analysis is the procedure of studying social structures using network analysis and graph theory techniques. One of the common tasks in social networks analysis is to classify and study the network structures based on the type of nodes and the links that connect them. Social networks analysis is applied to many types of networks in the field of social media networks, such as friendship networks, rumors spreading networks, and collaboration graphs. These networks are usually analyzed and visualized using the sociograms network model in which nodes are denoted as points and links are represented as lines connecting these points. Network visualization offers a way of qualitative analysis of the studied networks. Figure 3.2 shows a visual representation of the relationships between Internet IP addresses in 1995.

Social scientists have studied the field of "social networks" since the late 19th century to model complex sets of relationships between entities of social systems at

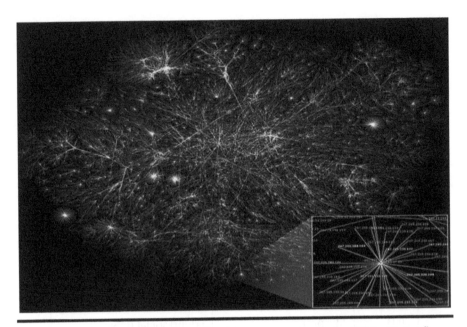

Figure 3.2 Representational graph of Internet network in 2005. Note: figure from Creative Commons Zero.

all levels, varying from interpersonal to international. The theoretical foundation of social network analysis goes back to the early works of Émile Durkheim and Ferdinand Tönnies in the 1980s. On the one hand, Tönnies proposed that social groups can exist as personal and direct social links that either connect individuals who have common shared beliefs and values or formal, impersonal, and instrumental social ties [1]. On the other hand, Émile Durkheim proposed a nonindividualistic description of social facts, claiming that social phenomena happen when interacting individuals form a reality that can no longer be represented in terms of the properties of individual level [2]. In the early 1900s, Georg Simmel discussed the importance of studying patterns of relationships that linked social entities and showed the nature of networks and the relationship between network size and entity interaction. He also studied the likelihood of network interactions in loose networks instead of groups. The 1930s witnessed many major developments led by various independently working scholars of mathematics, psychology, and anthropology. In psychology, Jacob L. Moreno started to systematically record, study, and analyze social interaction in small social groups, notably classrooms and workgroups. In anthropology, the theoretical and ethnographic works of Claude Lévi-Strauss, Alfred Radcliffe-Brown, and Bronislaw Malinowski were the foundation for social network theory. Besides, the British anthropologist Siegfried Frederick Nadel proposed a theory of social structure that was influential in later social network analysis [3]. In sociology, the works of Talcott Parsons enabled the scholars to study social structures using relational network analysis [4]. Following that, based

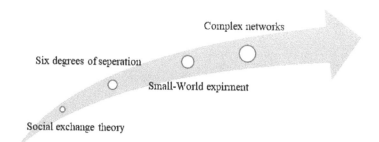

Figure 3.3   Milestones in social network analysis.

on Parsons' social structure theory, Peter Blau proposed a solid impetus for analyzing the relational links of social entities with his work on social exchange theory [5]. In the 1970s, the field of social networks analysis witnessed a growing number of scholars who worked to combine different theories. Notably, Harrison White and Charles Tilly concentrated on networks of political and community sociology and social movements. In the 1990s, the theories of social network analysis were applied in many new application domains, and scholars applied new models and methods to study the structure of data available from online social networks, as well as "digital footprints" about face-to-face interaction networks. Figure 3.3 shows the milestone phases of social network analysis theory.

References

1. F. Tonnies and C. P. Loomis, *Community and Society*, Courier Corporation, United States, 2002.
2. E. Durkheim, *The Division of Labor in Society*, Simon and Schuster, United States, 2014.
3. S. F. Nadel, *The Theory of Social Structure*, Routledge, UK, 2013.
4. L. Wirth, The Structure of Social Action: A Study in Social Theory with Special Reference to a Group of Recent European Writers, *American Sociological Review*, Vol. 4; No. 3, pp. 399–404, 1939.
5. P. M. Blau, A theory of social integration, *American Journal of Sociology*, Vol. 65; No. 6, pp. 545–556, 1960.

Chapter 4

Research History on Cyber-Enabled Disease (Cyber Syndrome)

4.1 Introduction

The development of Internet technology promotes the interaction between cyberspace and us, bringing great convenience for our living. However, if we interact with cyberspace excessively, our physical and psychological health will be compromised. Generally, the physical or psychological disease caused by cyberspace is commonly referred to as Cyber-enabled Disease (Cyber Syndrome, or Cyber-Syndrome). This chapter introduces Cyber-enabled Disease and its classification, rehabilitation, and treatment. Besides, Internet addiction and its treatment are also discussed. Finally, future development discussion is drawn for the research on Cyber-enabled Disease.

4.2 Cyber-Enabled Disease

With the emergence of Internet technology, people interact with cyberspace more and more frequently. Statistics[1] suggest that the number of Internet users worldwide is large and increased rapidly, from 1.1 billion in 2005 to 3.969 billion in 2019. The average access time for Internet users is as high as 4 hours per day and some users can even go online for several days without interruption.[2] Furthermore,

---

[1] https://www.statista.com/statistics/273018/number-of-internet-users-worldwide
[2] https://ourworldindata.org/internet

https://doi.org/10.1201/9781003257387-4

DOI: 10.1201/9781003257387-4

Table 4.1 The Classification of Cyber-Enabled Disease

Cyber-Enabled Disease (Cyber Syndrome)	Types	Examples
	Cyber-enabled Physical Disease	Spinal disease, cervical spondylosis, eye disease, dizziness, insomnia, dermatitis, obesity, etc.
	Cyber-enabled Psychological Disease	Social phobia, gaming addiction, shopping addiction, pathological gambling, depression, etc.

evidence shows that the interaction between people and cyberspace is in a very frequent or even excessive state, which leads to the birth of Cyber-enabled Disease, also named Cyber Syndrome or Cyber-Syndrome.

We put forward "Cyber Syndrome" in [1] and defined Cyber Syndrome as the physical, social, and mental health that affects the human being due to the excessive interaction with cyberspace. We also divided Cyber Syndrome into three categories: physical disorder, social disorder, and mental disorder. Additionally, Cyber Syndrome's formation stages, recovery, and prevention methods were presented in [1].

Here, based on our previous work, we further improve the definition and classification of Cyber Syndrome as follows: Cyber Syndrome, also called Cyber-enabled Disease, is a disease that endangers the physical and psychological health of Internet users due to excessive interaction between users and can be divided into two major categories: Cyber-enabled Physical Disease and Cyber-enabled Psychological Disease. Cyber-enabled Disease and its classification are presented in Table 4.1.

4.2.1 Cyber-Enabled Physical Disease

Cyber-enabled Physical Disease will bring the human body a series of diseases, such as dizziness, insomnia, spinal disease, eye disease, etc. In 1995, Haughie et al. conducted an experiment in which some people were asked to continue using computer terminals for more than 4 hours, and all those people reported having pain in the cervical or neck after the experiment ended [2]. Their result showed that long-time use of computers could cause muscle and bone strain. In 1996, World Health Organization (WHO) launched a project to investigate the effects of radiation on human health. The result suggested that radiation emitted by electronic devices will adversely affect human organs, making organs unable to work normally and deteriorate and causing eye strain, hair loss, cardiovascular disease, weakened immune system, etc. Thus, radiation is designated as the fourth largest pollution by WHO.[3]

Entering the 21st century, Internet technologies have come to an unprecedented fast-paced stage and its penetration rate has increased dramatically. Consequently, more Cyber-enabled Physical Disease followed naturally.

---

[3] https://zhidao.baidu.com/question/316703607.html

In the first 5 years of the 21st century, researchers collected people's self-assessment data on their physical conditions by follow-up visits. For example, Siivola et al. conducted experiments to explore the causes of neck and shoulder pain in young adults. They discovered that one of the most important reasons is the long-term use of computers in 2004 [3].

In the late 2000s and early 2010s, professional standard questionnaires and scientific sampling methods have been applied to the investigation of Cyber-enabled Physical Disease. In 2006, Suhail et al. used the Internet Effect Scale (IES) to investigate the effects of excessive Internet use on undergraduate students, and the result showed that excessive use of the Internet caused certain physical discomfort [4]. In 2007, Ma et al. recruited 300 college students and asked them to complete questionnaires using a nonprobabilistic quota sampling method [5]. The result illustrated that the Internet causes physical health problems, causing arm or wrist pain, backache, and vision disturbances. In 2012, Kelley applied Internet Use Questionnaire and SF-36v2Health Survey to explore the relationship between the using duration of the Internet and physical health and found that excessive Internet use is associated with poor physical health [6].

In the mid- to late 2010s, the questionnaire survey method is still used. Additionally, statistical data analysis methods are used in questionnaire data analysis to obtain more objective and convincing evidence to verify that the Internet is harmful to people's physical health. In 2014, Moon et al. investigated the relationship between eye diseases and the use of video display terminals by questionnaires and found that there is a clear correlation between the two [7]. In 2016, we collected data through a questionnaire in [8], analyzed Pearson correlation coefficients, and concluded that overuse of the Internet was highly correlated with the occurrence of Cyber-enabled Disease, including decreased vision and cervical pain. Through statistical analysis of data on Scopus, Web of Science, and Google Scholar, Aghasi et al. concluded that there is a positive correlation between time spent on the Internet and the probability of obesity based on the results of the meta-analysis in 2019 [9].

Briefly, Cyber-enabled Physical Disease research sprouted in the 1990s and gradually became a research hotspot in the 21st century. In the future, there will be more and more people paying attention to Cyber-enabled Physical Disease.

4.2.2 Cyber-Enabled Psychological Disease

Research on the impact of the Internet on people's psychological health began early. Back in 1995, Goldberg et al. proposed the concept of Internet Addictive Disorder (IAD). They described it as, due to over access to cyberspace, people have the following symptoms: unwilling to participate in social activities, dreaming the Internet-related things frequently [10]. Next, Kandell et al. defined Internet disorder in 1998 as "a kind of psychological dependence on the Internet that appears once you log on to the Internet" [11]. In 2005, Beard presented that Internet Addictive occurs when an individual's psychological states, including social interactions and emotional states, are impaired by the overuse of the Internet [12]. Considering these above researches, some of them hold that psychological diseases directly caused by the Internet belong to Internet disorder, while others regarded psychological complications caused by the Internet as Internet disorder. For clarity, this book collectively refers to all situations in which cyberspace harms people's psychological state as Cyber-enabled Psychological Disease.

In this chapter, Cyber-enabled Psychological Disease is divided into two categories: Cyber-enabled Social Disease and Cyber-enabled Mental Disease.

Cyber-enabled Social Disease causes people to be addicted to the virtual social environment (e.g., Facebook, Wechat, Instagram, etc.) in cyberspace, which seriously affects their ability to communicate with others face-to-face in real life.

Cyber-enabled Mental Disease leads to patients' mental disorders, and its common symptoms are irritability, personality disorder, irritability, inattention, and sleep disturbance caused by a strong desire to use the Internet.

Yet, Cyber-enabled Social Disease and Cyber-enabled Mental Disease are very closely related, and there is no boundary to separate them. Therefore, in this chapter, they were regarded as Cyber-enabled Psychological Disease, and the development history of Cyber-enabled Psychological Disease was discussed in detail below.

As early as the 1990s, although the well-defined correlation between psychological health and Internet overuse needed to be verified, some researchers have proved that psychological health and Internet use are related to a certain degree. For example, in 1993, Zhu et al. designed a questionnaire (Internet-related social-psychological health, ISHS-CS) and used it to investigate the impact of the Internet on the psychological health of college students [13]. The survey concluded that there is no obvious correlation between the frequency of Internet using and psychological health, while there is indeed a certain connection. In 1997, Young et al. researched the qualitative analysis of the relationship between pathological Internet use and psychological health and found that excessive use of the Internet does harm to psychological health [14].

In the late 20th century and early 21st century, researchers used statistics to conduct definitive research on the relationship between Internet use and psychological health. In 1998, Young et al. collected people's depression self-assessment data by using Beck Depression Inventory. The authors found a clear correlation between depression and excessive Internet use by analyzing variance and mean of self-assessment data [15]. In 2001, Moody et al. recruited volunteers and asked them to complete the Social and Emotional Loneliness Scale (SELS) [16]. The results showed that those people who use the Internet frequently tend to feel lonely more.

From the late 2000s to the 2010s, researchers began to study the role of other factors (e.g., age, gender, education background, etc.) in the relationship between the Internet and psychological health. In 2007, Jenaro et al. investigated the relationship between the Internet using and psychological health using questionnaires (Internet Overuse Scale, Cell-Phone Over-Use Scale, Beck Depression Inventory, General Health Questionnaire) and logistic regression analyses [17]. They found that, compared with men, excessive use of the Internet seems to be more likely to cause psychological diseases such as anxiety and insomnia among female users. In 2018, Ioannidis et al. explored the moderating role of age and gender in associations between Internet use and psychological health using lasso regression and found that social phobia and attention deficit hyperactivity disorder are more common in young users, while anxiety and obsessive-compulsive disorder are more common in older users [18].

Cyber-enabled Psychological Disease is caused by long-term addiction to the Internet. At first, people found that there may be a certain relationship between Internet overuse and psychological health. After that, definitive research was conducted on the relationship between them using statistics. Come into the 21st century, more studies have focused on the role of other factors in the relationship between Internet use and psychological health.

4.3 Rehabilitation and Treatment

Throughout the related research, the development of cyberspace provides the breeding ground for Cyber-enabled Disease. Further, Cyber-enabled Disease brings people many physical and psychological health problems. Faced with these problems, people actively seek and study corresponding methods and solutions. Next, the rehabilitation and treatment methods for Cyber-enabled Disease are described in detail.

With continuous convergence among physical space, social space, thinking space, and cyberspace, Cyber-enabled Disease not only adversely affects people's living in cyberspace but also affects people's normal activities in other spaces. Correspondingly, rehabilitation and treatment methods are discussed from physical, social, psychological, and cyber perspectives, respectively.

Physical space is the basic living space for people [19], which suggests that physical methods are of positive significance for rehabilitation and treatment of Cyber-enabled Disease. Several physical methods for rehabilitation and treatment of Cyber-enabled Disease are listed as follows:

- Protect your body properly, such as buying antielectromagnetic radiation clothing or glasses, and eat more vegetables and fruits.
- Strengthen physical exercise and actively participate in physical activities to divert your attention away from the Internet.
- Shorten the time on the Internet. Make a plan to limit and reduce your online time and reduce online time and frequency.

From a social perspective, research shows that participating in meaningful social activities reasonably is beneficial to our health [20]. Similarly, participation in social activities also has a place in the rehabilitation and treatment of Cyber-enabled Disease. Some social methods are discussed as follows:

- Actively participate in group activities, communicate with others, and make more friends.
- Cultivate hobbies, such as outdoor sports, reading books, listening to music, and so on.
- Participate in interested and meaningful organizations and participate in active social activities.

Cyber-enabled Disease also affects people's thinking space adversely. To face this situation, it is necessary to guide patients correctly to form a positive psychological state. There are some psychological methods for reference as follows:

- Communicate with patients equally to understand their real and inner thinking, and give them psychological care and comfort.
- Take measures to divert attention and steer the curiosity on the positive, help patients establish positive living values, set ambitious goals, cultivate their noble sentiments, and strengthen their self-control.
- Family members and friends should pay more attention to patients and create a warm living environment for patients.

With the development of the Internet, cyberspace and information technologies play an essential role in the rehabilitation and treatment of Cyber-enabled Disease. Some cyber methods for rehabilitation and treatment of Cyber-enabled Disease are listed below:

- Advanced technologies, such as Machine Learning, Natural Language Processing, and Knowledge Graphs, can help people diagnose diseases. Many companies have developed corresponding inquiry products (e.g., Baidu Muzhi Doctor,[4] Sonde Health Vocometer,[5] etc.).
- Monitor people's physical state using sensors. While using the Internet, once the physical state is abnormal, devices alarm users to rest and adjust their states. For instance, Nie et al. [21] researched real-time fatigue monitoring of mobile phone users by analyzing people's electromyogram of the neck. Besides, many companies have launched health monitoring products, such as Apple Watch,[6] Huawei Watch,[7] Redmi Watch,[8] etc.
- Monitor human online behavior. Common network traffic monitoring technologies include protocol analysis technology based on traffic image, monitoring technology based on SNMP, and monitoring technology based on NetFlow [22]. They can realize the real-time monitoring of people's online behavior, such as the time spent on the Internet and the content and information browsed on Internet, to protect people from harmful effects in cyberspace.

---

[4] https://baike.baidu.com/item/%E6%8B%87%E6%8C%87%E5%8C%BB%E7%94%9F/17561608?fr=aladdin

[5] https://apps.apple.com/cn/app/id1147192738

[6] https://www.apple.com/

[7] https://consumer.huawei.com/en/

[8] https://www.mi.com/global/

4.4 Internet Addiction

Generally speaking, Cyber-enabled Disease is caused by Internet Addiction which has a bad influence on human physics and psychology or brings other physical and psychological complications. Internet Addiction is a pathological state of Internet use that is different from normal Internet use.

To distinguish Internet Addiction from normal Internet use, many countries have launched Internet Addiction diagnostic criteria. The most commonly used are *Clinical Diagnostic Criteria for Internet Addiction* issued by China in 2008,[9] which considered 6 hours a day for three consecutive months as Internet Addiction, and *American Psychological Association (APA)*, which has also issued criteria to diagnose Internet addiction and stipulated that those who meet five or more of the conditions shown in Table 4.2 are regarded as Internet addiction.

There are many treatment methods for Internet Addiction. Some are universally acknowledged methods, and others are some controversial methods. On the one hand, common methods are mainly divided into psychological therapy and pharmacological therapy. Psychological therapy[10] refers to changing patients' attitudes toward the Internet by psychological interventions to get rid of Internet Addiction. Common psychological therapies include cognition behavior therapy methods, family therapy, and so on, as shown in Table 4.3. Pharmacological therapy[11] refers to implementing intervention and treatment using drugs, but the therapeutic effect of pharmacological therapy on Internet Addiction remains to be verified. On the other hand, there are some controversial treatment methods, such as corporal punishment, electro-convulsive therapy, etc., which cause greater harm to patients' physics and psychology and have very limited effect on Internet Addiction treatment.

To treat Internet Addiction systematically, many institutions have been established. For example, in 2009, the first Internet Addiction rehabilitation center, named Heavensfield Retreat Center,[12] was set up in the U.S. The Restart project initiated by this center controls the deterioration of patients' conditions by changing their living habits and has proved that it is effective. Besides, United Kingdom National Health Service[13] also opened a treatment center, called Centre for Internet and Gaming Disorder, specifically for young patients aged 13–25. Also, in China, many treatment centers are established by individuals or officials, among which TAORAN Internet Addiction Treatment Center[14] is the most recognizable. In South Korea, more than 140 psychological counseling institutions were established to help patients get rid of Internet addiction through military training and

---

[9] https://baike.baidu.com/item/%E7%BD%91%E7%98%BE%E6%A0%87%E5%87%86/6103254?fr=aladdin

[10] https://en.wikipedia.org/wiki/Psychotherapy

[11] https://en.wikipedia.org/wiki/Pharmacotherapy

[12] https://www.gamersky.com/news/200908/148100.shtml?tag=wap

[13] https://www.nhs.uk/

[14] http://www.chinayoung.net/news.php?class=276

Table 4.2 APA's Criteria for Diagnosing Internet Addiction[16]

Numbers	Contents
1	The online time exceeds 144 hours per month, that is, more than 4 hours a day.
2	Things related to the Internet always come to mind.
3	The urge to surf the Internet cannot be suppressed.
4	The purposes of going online are to escape reality and get rid of anxiety.
5	Do not dare to tell your families the time to go online.
6	Problems of schoolwork and interpersonal relationship caused by the Internet.
7	The online time is often longer than expected.
8	A lot of money is spent on updating network equipment or going online.
9	More time is spent surfing the Internet to satisfy you.

[16] https://www.apa.org/

Table 4.3 Part of Psychological Therapies for Internet Addiction

Methods	Description
Cognitive behavioral therapy [23], the 1960s	By communicating with patients, reconstruct patients' cognition of the Internet and correct their behavior of Internet overuse.
Family therapy [24], 1984	Family members, especially parents, should give patients more care and create a comfortable and warm environment for patients to get rid of Internet Addiction.
Systemic desensitization therapy [25], 1976	Induce patients to expose the situation at the onset of Internet Addiction and fight with this situation using psychological relaxation.
Attention shift therapy[17]	Cultivate other positive hobbies of patients and find happiness in other activities, such as traveling, reading, dancing, listening to music, etc.
Reinforcement methods [26], 1982	Give patients rewards or punishment depending on the performance of the day to reduce the desire to surf the Internet.

[17] http://www.hnlfjy.com/wtzl/wyzt/2217.html

psychological rehabilitation training. Among these methods, horse riding therapy is a representative and effective method in South Korea.[15] However, despite the continuous improvement of Internet Addiction treatment institutions, there are still illegal institutions that cause physical and psychological harm to patients through some extreme treatment methods. Relevant departments should formulate relevant laws and regulations to strengthen the standardization of institutions.

4.5 Future Development Discussion

Nowadays, the frequency of interaction between people and cyberspace is extremely high and shows a rapid growth trend, which increases the incidence of Cyber-enabled Disease (Cyber Syndrome) and poses a great challenge to our health. People have discovered Cyber-enabled Disease, conducted extensive research on its diagnosis and treatment, and opened corresponding treatment institutions. However, these existing treatment methods and institutions still have certain irrationality, which causes harm to patients' physical and psychological health. To address this issue, individuals should be strict with themselves, society should create correct public opinion and moral orientation, and governments should establish relevant laws and regulations to restrict inappropriate behaviors.

In the future, Cyber-enabled Disease and its treatment will continue to be a hot topic of research. There are two issues worthy of consideration as follows:

■ **Privacy protection**
    During treatment, to grasp the patient's physical condition and the use of the Internet, we need to take some methods to monitor the patient's physical condition. In this process, how to ensure that the patient's privacy is not violated is a problem worth thinking about.
■ **Laws and regulations**
    Some patients will be taken extreme treatment methods which may cause inevitable physical and psychological damage by some institutions. The corresponding laws and regulations are needed to restrict unreasonable therapeutic behaviors and institutions.

References

1. H. Ning, S. Dhelim, M. A. Bouras, A. Khelloufi, and A. Ullah, Cyber-syndrome and its formation, classification, recovery and prevention, *IEEE Access*, Vol. 6; pp. 35501–35511, 2018.
2. L. J. Haughie, I. M. Fiebert, and K. E. Roach, Relationship of forward head posture and cervical backward bending to neck pain, *Journal of Manual & Manipulative Therapy*, Vol. 3; No. 3, pp. 91–97, 1995.

---

[15] https://zh.wikipedia.org/wiki/

3. S. M. Siivola, S. Levoska, K. Latvala, E. Hoskio, H. Vanharanta, and S. Keinänen-Kiukaanniemi, Predictive factors for neck and shoulder pain: A longitudinal study in young adults, *Spine*, Vol. 29; No. 15, pp. 1662–1669, 2004.

4. K. Suhail and Z. Bargees, Effects of excessive internet use on undergraduate students in Pakistan, *Cyberpsychology & Behavior*, Vol. 9; No. 3, pp. 297–307, 2006.

5. M. A. Coniglio, V. Muni, G. Giammanco, and S. Pignato, Excessive internet use and internet addiction: Emerging public health issues, *Igiene e SanitaPubblica*. Vol. 63; No. 2, pp. 127–136, 2007.

6. K. J. Kelley and E. M. Gruber, Problematic internet use and physical health, *Journal of Behavioral Addictions*, Vol. 2; No. 2, pp. 108–112, 2013.

7. J. H. Moon, M. Y. Lee, and N. J. Moon, Association between video display terminal use and dry eye disease in school children, *Journal of Pediatric Ophthalmology and Strabismus*, Vol. 51; No. 2, pp. 87–92, 2014.

8. Y. Zheng, D. Wei, J. Li, T. Zhu, and H. Ning, Internet use and its impact on individual physical health, *IEEE Access*, Vol. 4; pp. 5135–5142, 2016.

9. M. Aghasi, A. Matinfar, M. Golzarand, A. Salari-Moghaddam, Internet use in relation to overweight and obesity: A systematic review and meta-analysis of cross-sectional studies, *Advances in Nutrition*, Vol. 11; No. 2, pp. 349–356, 2020.

10. I. Goldberg, Internet addictive disorder (IAD) diagnostic criteria, http://www.psycom.net/iadcriteria.html, 1995.

11. J. J. Kandell, Internet addiction on campus: The vulnerability of college students, *Cyberpsychology & Behavior*, Vol. 1; No. 1, pp. 11–17, 1998.

12. K. W. Beard, Internet addiction: A review of current assessment techniques and potential assessment questions, *Cyberpsychology & Behavior*, Vol. 8; No. 1, pp. 7–14, 2005.

13. H. Zhu, F. Zhang, M. Shen, and M. Xu, Development of concept of internet-related social-psychological health for undergraduates, *Chinese Journal of Clinical Psychology*, Vol. 1; pp. 4–8, 2005.

14. K. S. Young, What makes the internet addictive: Potential explanations for pathological internet use, *105th Annual Conference of the American Psychological Association*, Chicago, Vol. 15; pp. 12–30, 1997.

15. K. S. Young and R. C. Rogers, The relationship between depression and Internet addiction, *Cyberpsychology & Behavior*, Vol. 1; No. 1, pp. 25–28, 1998.

16. E. J. Moody, Internet use and its relationship to loneliness, *Cyberpsychology & Behavior*, Vol. 4; No. 3, pp. 393–401, 2001.

17. C. Jenaro, N. Flores, M. Gómez-Vela, F. Gonzalez-Gil, and C. Caballo, Problematic internet and cell-phone use: Psychological, behavioral, and health correlates, *Addiction Research & Theory*, Vol. 15; No. 3, pp. 309–320, 2007.

18. K. Ioannidis, M. S. Treder, S. R. Chamberlain, F. Kiraly, S. Redden, D. Stein, C. Lochner, and J. E. Grant, Problematic internet use as an age-related multifaceted problem: Evidence from a two-site survey, *Addictive Behaviors*, vol. 81; pp. 157–166, 2018.

19. H. Ning and T. Zhu. *Generalized Cyberspace*, Publishing House of Electronics Industry, Beijing, 2017.

20. Y. Li, L. Xu, I. Chi, and P. G. Ma, Participation in productive activities and health outcomes among older adults in urban China, *The Gerontologist*, Vol. 54; No. 5, pp. 784–796, 2014.

21. L. Nie, X. Ye, S. Yang, and H. Ning, sEMG-based fatigue detection for mobile phone users, In: H. Ning (eds), *Cyberspace Data and Intelligence, and Cyber-Living, Syndrome, and Health, Communications in Computer and Information Science*, Springer, Singapore, Vol. 1138, pp. 528–541, 2019.
22. G. Ju and Y. Li, A review on network traffic monitoring technology and its application, *China Academic Journal Electronic Publishing House*, Vol. 7; pp. 86–88, 2011.
23. B. O. Rothbaum, E. A. Meadows, P. Resick, and D. W. Foy, *Cognitive-Behavioral Therapy*, Guilford Press, United States, 2000.
24. M. P. Nichols and R. C. Schwartz, *Family Therapy: Concepts and Methods*, Gardner Press, New York, 1984.
25. A. E. Kazdin and L. A. Wilcoxon, Systematic desensitization and nonspecific treatment effects: A methodological evaluation, *Psychological Bulletin*, Vol. 83; No. 5, pp. 729, 1976.
26. B. F. Skinner, Contrived reinforcement, *The Behavior Analyst*, Vol. 5; No. 1, pp. 3, 1982.

Chapter 5

Cyborg: A Fusion System of Human and Electronic Machinery

5.1 Introduction

Speaking of the Cyborg, the first thing that comes to mind is the science fiction movies, such as "The Matrix", "Ghost in the Shell", and "Happy Hunting". In these movies, people are full of the imagination of Cyborg. For example, humans use Cyborg body to replace body components, which break through the human body's limits and give people superpowers. However, the continuous optimization of the human body may cause the loss of oneself, and human self-awareness may become a power struggle tool. Cyborg is no longer just science fiction now, and it is closer than we imagine. In this chapter, the origin and development of Cyborg are briefly summarized. Besides, a few hot issues of Cyborg are listed as follows: first, the emergence of Cyborg technology has brought a significant impact on morality and ethics. Substantially, there is legal regulation. Some examples and rules from the U.S. and Japan are briefly listed. Second, "whether the implementation of Cyborg's application is suitable for human beings or not?" is a hot issue discussed by some scholars. The last part of this chapter analyzes what attitude should be adopted to welcome the arrival of Cyborg.

5.2 The Origin of Cyborg

Since George Devor invented the world's first programmable robot in 1954, people have spent much time and financial resources researching mechanical automation

DOI: 10.1201/9781003257387-5

45

technology and made significant progress. For example, industrial robots have been put into industrial labor to liberate much productivity. Humans are no longer satisfied that robots only look like humans. Instead, they want the robots to have human behavior and thought. In the 1960s, humans began to study humanoid robots and wanted to create mechanical systems similar to humans in terms of appearance, behavior, and thought. Until the 1970s, people added visual and auditory functions to humanoid robots. In the 1990s, humanoid robots focused on analyzing the human brain and imitating human behavior and thought. Although brain science is quite advanced, it is almost impossible to restore the human brain and nervous system. The humanoid robot ASIMO was born in 2000, and it took 20 years to "learn" to walk like a human. However, Honda Motor Co., Ltd.[1] abandoned the iteration of ASIMO due to its enormous cost and extremely low practicality in 2018.

During the study on making robots more like humans, the researchers find that the human brain is more intelligent than artificial intelligence (AI). As a result, some people have changed their manufacturing humanoid robot strategy and wanted to use human brains instead of AI to make humanoid robots. In the 1940s, the information transmission theory between organisms and machines emerged, laying an ideological foundation for another possible path to creating robots. In the 1960s, some scientists merged the human nervous system with machines, creating the concept "Cyborg". This book supposed that the research and development of robots are an attempt to equip machines with a human-like nervous system. In that case, Cyborg technology attempts to add machine parts to the human nervous system. The thoughts and practices of Cyborg continue to impact the inherent definition of "person" and promote the diversified development of culture and technology.

5.3 Cyborg Development History

With the development of information technology, the Cyborg is continually evolving from the perspective of theory and application. The Cyborg development history is divided into three stages according to the Cyborg development characteristics and integration with people [1] (see Table 5.1).

5.3.1 Cyborg: Combination of Cybernetics and Organism

In 1948, Norbert Wiener published "*Cybernetics: The Science of Control and Communication in Animals and Machines*", which marked the official birth of this discipline of the information transmission theory between organisms and machines. Cybernetics laid the foundation for the development of cyborgs. Besides, Wiener combined it with the emerging computer field to form a new interdisciplinary system approach [2], aiming to realize the information interaction of systems at all

---

[1] https://www.honda.com/

Table 5.1 Cyborg Development History

Stage	Tightness	Characteristic	Interface Location	Application
The first stage	Machines and biological organisms are independent of each other	The organism itself has not been invaded or implanted	External to the human body	Google glasses; prosthetic body
The second stage	A system has been formed between the machine and the biological organism without changing the mind	Breakthrough the skin barrier of the organism and realize the functions of the tissues, organs, and systems of the organism	Inside the human body	Mechanical heart, artificial lung, artificial retina, optic nerve chip, etc.
The third stage	The machine is a connection between the brain and the nervous system of a biological organism, which can change cognition, feelings, and emotions	Regulate and influence people's minds and give people new understanding, feelings, and emotions	Inside the human body	IBM brain-inspired Chip[3]

[3] https://www.research.ibm.com/articles/brain-chip.shtml

levels, especially between organisms and machine components. In the 1960s, two NASA scientists, Manfred Clynes and Nathan S. Kline, came up with the cyborg concept that is a combination of cybernetics and organisms while studying astronauts' space survival. They believed that the human body could operate on control and feedback like a machine. Therefore, the human body can be combined with the device to realize the possibility of an automated human-machine system [3].

In the 25 years after its birth, Cyborg has not received widespread attention from academia, except for being used in science fiction works. In 1985, Donna Haraway published her famous essay *"A Cyborg Manifesto: Science, Technology, and Socialist Feminism in the Late Twentieth Century"* [4]. She believed that Cyborg was able to arouse repercussions in the field of international humanities and social sciences, and Cyborg is a controlled organism, a mixture of machines and living organisms, a social reality product, and fiction.

In 1988, Kenneth Flamm took the lead in linking the economy with Cyborg in his book *"Creating the Computer: Government, Industry, and High Technology"* and determined the origin of the technology essential to computer creation. Cyborg technology trends and national policies are linked to each other, affecting the computer industry development. In 1992, American Anthropological Association (AAA) annual meeting was held in San Francisco. Several scholars proposed Cyborg anthropology, increasing the attention of cultural anthropologists to cyborgs [5].

In 1995, Andy Pickering applied Cyborg to computer development and industrial organizations [6]. He believed that the origin of Cyborg objects and science was attributed to World War II, stabilizing and expanding humanity's boundaries in different ways. Andy classified the development of Cyborg into three levels: the extensive hybridization of science and military in World War II; the birth and subsequent evolution of electronic objects and science in World War II; and the cyborgization of industry. In 1996, Paul Edwards conducted the first comprehensive investigation of the influence of the military and Cyborg. Ian Hacking linked cyborgs with Georges Canguilhem and Michel Foucault's philosophy in 1998 [7], connecting Cyborg with science and society. Georges Canguilhem believed that all tools and machines are extensions of the body and part of life itself [8]. Michel Foucault was passionate about the relationship between knowledge and social power [9].

5.3.2 Cyborg Science and Technology: Man-Machine Hybrid

In 1995, Chris Gray and others had already seen the clues of Cyborg in the field of biotechnology [10]. They thought that older adults with pacemakers, people with disabilities equipped with electromyographic arms, and people whose immune systems have been edited by vaccination are Cyborg in the technical sense. In the Canguilhem meeting held in 1996, it was heard that a bioengineer had installed a computer chip on the back of a blind person's head, which gave the blind person a preliminary vision [11]. The meeting pointed out that in the next 30 years, the human brain may become a common phenomenon as a computer, which will provide people with unexpected forms of communication and computer-driven memories. In 1997, Frank Biocca proposed the Cyborg Dilemma [12]. He believed that the pursuit of the physical existence of short-distance communication promotes the close coupling between the body and the computer interface. Therefore, interface sensors and effectors have been increasingly mapped to the human body's sensory and motion systems in virtual reality and augmented reality, forming a cyborg dilemma.

Later, some scholars continued to deepen and refine the concept of Cyborg. In 2000, Chris Gray defined Cyborg in his book *"Cyborg Citizen: Politics in the Posthuman Age"* as follows: A self-regulating organism that mixes natural and artificial things in the same system [13]. Any organic matter/system that combines evolution, creation, animate, and inanimate is a Cyborg technology. In 2001, Andy Clark pointed out in *"natural-born cyborgs"* that humans can freely use tools to extend the body [14]. Because of the human brain's plasticity, new devices will be continuously absorbed and adapted by our body and become a part of the body. In 2002, the book *"Machine Dreams: Economics Becomes a Cyborg Science"* mentioned that computer technology development embodies the Cyborg technology of novel interaction between humans and machines [15].

All in all, when researchers explore the logic of the complex system of cyborgs, they need to find a way out of cyborg research in uncertainty and chaos. As integrating technology, physiology, and the external environment, humans and society's relationships will also change. The proposal of Cyborg Urbanization in 2003 exposed the contradiction between technology and politics [16]. People use the potential of Cyborg Urbanization to mobilize continued political prominence in the public sphere. In 2006, Swyngedouw believed that the modern city is regarded as integrating society and nature, resulting in a unique Cyborg Urbanization. That opens up theoretical and practical possibilities for creating the environment humans want to live in [17].

Man-machine Hybrid has made significant progress not only in theory but also in application. For example, Twitter is a new type of web partial automation application in Cyborg Urbanization. The program derives a Cyborg between humans and robots [18]. A legitimate Cyborg or bot generates a large number of well-meaning tweets, while a malicious bot or Cyborg spreads spam or malicious content. Technological development has reached a stage in which Cyborg began to intervene in human nature. Cyborg's intentions have been extended to the field of technology and human technology mixtures [19].

5.3.3 Cyborg Application

With the development of science and technology, some Cyborg ideas have become a reality. This book lists several typical applications about that. Cochlear implant is an early Cyborg application that converts sound into electrical stimulation. The electrodes implanted in the body stimulate the auditory nerve and make the patient "hear" the sound. In 1957, Djourno and Eyries in France first implanted electrodes into a completely deaf patient's cochlea, which enabled the patient to perceive ambient sounds [20]. The exoskeleton is a wearable mechanical device that cooperates with the human body's nerve endings to assist human limbs' movement, like the armor of Iron Man, providing superhuman strength. Cyberdyne, the Japanese company, developed the Hybrid Assistive Limb in 2004, which is the world's first practical exoskeleton device. It is said that it increased the body's muscle strength by more than ten times. In 2013, scientists used shrimp to simulate human blood circulation's fluid system to power electronic devices, bringing hope to implanted electronic medical devices in the future [21]. To cure traumatic and congenital hand amputations or reductions and reduce treatment costs, in 2015, scientists proposed a low-cost three-dimensional printed prosthetic hand for the treatment of upper-limb reduction children. Furthermore, they proposed a remote installation method of the prosthesis [22].

With the development of Cyborg technology, scientists began to do some more fine-grained applications and research. In 2016, Remora appeared. It is a system for designing interactive subcutaneous devices. Its development is mainly focused on battery and power management, and functions [23]. In 2019, some researchers realized the creation of Cyborg organs. In the process of organ formation, they used cell-cell gravity to assemble soft and stretchable networked nanoelectronic devices in three dimensions throughout the organoid [24]. Musk released the latest brain-computer interface system developed by Neuralink in July 2019. He describes the working principle and implementation details of the brain-computer interface system in [25].

5.4 Laws about Cyborg

The development of Cyborgs has brought a series of challenges to traditional laws. According to the current technological development, civil subjects will no longer be natural persons in the future. There will be other "non-persons", including Cyborg. Traditional civil law is based on the legal personality theory of biology and psychology, so it is based on the subject's will and rational personality. What is the basis of Cyborg's law? At a conference in 2019, journalists asked Angela Merkel whether robots should have rights. She asked rhetorically that the right to electricity or regular maintenance. If robots have independent rights, can they sue the household head for low maintenance or request power supply? Therefore, humans should consider whether Cyborgs should have the same rights and personalities. This is already a recognized right in Japanese and American companies. Although it sounds good in theory, the right only makes sense when it is claimed. If Cyborg makes independent judgments of things without human intervention, society may become different, so we need to redefine the rights of Cyborg [26].

5.4.1 United States

In June 2014, the Supreme Court ruled in Riley v. California that police cannot search the data on mobile phones seized during the arrest without a search warrant [27]. This may be the first time that the Supreme Court has explicitly considered Cyborg in the "Case Law" – indeed, this is a metaphor. In 2011, Tim Wu, a law professor at Columbia University, believed that we had reached the very beginning of a thorough understanding of the Cyborg law to augment human law. Human beings have the right to retain a certain degree of domination over their bodies. Our statutes can directly or indirectly protect people's rights to use specific machines. However, our law does not recognize the rights of the device itself. The law also does not recognize Cyborg, a hybrid that adds machine functions and capabilities to the human body and consciousness.

1) Robots must serve humanity.

2) Robots must not kill or harm humans.

3) A robot must call its human creator "father".

4) A robot can make anything except money.

5) Robots may not go abroad without permission.

6) Male and female robots may not change their genders.

7) Robots may not change their face to become a different robot.

8) A robot created as an adult may not become a child.

9) A robot may not reassemble a robot that has been disassembled by a human.

10) Robots shall not destroy human homes or tools.

Figure 5.1   The privacy principles of the Organization for Economic Cooperation and Development (OECD).

5.4.2 Japan

Japan's research on Cyborg applications and technology is in a leading position and does much work on humanoid robots. However, there are very few laws on the Cyborg. Keio University professor Shinpo Fumio proposed ten principles of robotics law in 2015,[2] citing the privacy principles of the Organization for Economic Cooperation and Development (OECD) (see Figure 5.1):

Countries worldwide have not yet started to formulate Cyborg laws, and more efforts are needed. If we make laws about Cyborg as a particular subject, we should consider the following points:

- Ensuring that people possess the subject consciousness
- Ensuring the confidentiality of the privacy of humans, Cyborg, and machines
- Providing a responsible system for the implementation of Cyborg management and power.

5.5 Discussion: Can Cyborg make us better?

In 1988, Hans Moravec, in his book *"Children of the Mind"*, believed that humans could scan and upload their thoughts digitally and transfer their consciousness to the computer with the power of AI [28]. In the future, network progress and

---

[2] https://www.japantimes.co.jp/community/2019/03/06/issues/robot-rights-asimov-tezuka/

network interaction will become more rapid. Cyborg's ability to establish neural signal connections and realize brain-brain induction or the traditionally so-called psychological induction is no longer entirely science fiction [29]. Cyborg, which has been transformed by its nervous system, will acquire knowledge quickly. Besides, memory degenerative diseases and depression will no longer exist. Donna Haraway's Cyborg Manifesto also pointed out that Cyborg technology can turn everyone into a mixed subject of machines and organisms, placing the opposed initially people in the same identity. Thus, inequality will disappear.

However, more people have reservations about this. Susan Schneider, a philosophy and cognitive science professor at the University of Connecticut, named the merger of Cyborg and AI in *"The Suicide of the Human Mind"*. She believed that the deep integration of humans and machines is facing technical obstacles and urgent philosophical dilemmas. If we radically change our memory or character, the enhancement of human–computer integration is very insecure [30]. In 2017, *"Understanding Human Technogenesis: Human Development in the Post-Genomic World"* linked Cyborg with religion and defined Cyborg's most fundamental values [31]. Sharma believed that a powerful Cyborg that can reshape the current system would bring possible evil consequences for liberal democracy and politics. Furthermore, Hawking believes that the rich will one day use gene-editing technology to modify the human DNA and create a superman. Cyborgs have a more assertive personality and a higher IQ than the existing human body, which will cause humans to face a more profound division.

The development of Cyborg technology has brought significant challenges to ethics, morality, social, and political systems. Different scholars have different opinions. If Cyborgs' nature is to subvert humanity, then humans must obtain breakthrough technologies to create life. The Cyborg market will be a vast new industry, with essential impacts on industry and society. Given the potential changes involved in Cyborg creation, ethics must become the cornerstone of Cyborg marketing decisions. Ethics will be an essential factor in the buyer's decision [32].

Imagine using Cyborg technology to mechanically replace parts of our body, leaving only the brain's neurons. Are "we" still us? Under the temptation of superhuman energy, we need to be in awe of the human body itself and adhere to the principle of nonabuse of technology, which is the appropriate solution for applying Cyborg.

References

1. M. Tegmark, *Life 3.0: Being Human in the Age of Artificial Intelligence*, Knopf, Germany, 2017.
2. P. Mirowski, *Machine Dreams: Economics becomes a Cyborg Science*, Cambridge University Press, UK, 2002.
3. P. Galison, The ontology of the enemy: Norbert Wiener and the cybernetic vision, *Critical Inquiry*, Vol. 21; No. 1, pp. 228–266, 1994.

4. D. Haraway, A Cyborg Manifesto, In *Cultural Theory: An Anthology*, I. Szeman, T. Kaposy (eds), Wiley-Blackwell, New Jersey, 2010.

5. G. L. Downey, J. Dumit, and S. Williams, Cyborg anthropology, *Cultural Anthropology*, Vol. 10; No. 2, pp. 264–269, 1995.

6. A. Pickering, Cyborg history and the World War II regime, *Perspectives on Science*, Vol. 3; No. 1, pp. 1–48, 1995.

7. I. Hacking, Canguilhem amid the cyborgs, *Economy and Society*, Vol. 27; No. 2/3, pp. 202–216, 1998.

8. D. Lecourt, *Georges Canguilhem*, Presses universitaires de France, Paris, 2008.

9. M. Foucault, *Power: The Essential Works of Michel Foucault 1954–1984*, Penguin, UK, 2019.

10. C. H. Gray, S. Mentor, and H. J. Figueroa-Sarriera, Cyborgology: Constructing the knowledge of cybernetic organisms, In *The Cyborg Handbook*, C. H. Gray, S. Mentor, H. Figueroa-Sarriera (eds), Routledge, UK, pp. 1–14, 1995.

11. N. Nuttall and N. Hawkes, Computer implant gives sight to the blind, *The Times, 14 September*, Vol. 8, pp. 1–1, 1996.

12. F. Biocca, The cyborg's dilemma: Progressive embodiment in virtual environments, *Journal of Computer-Mediated Communication*, Vol. 3; No. 2, JCMC324, 1997.

13. C. H. Gray, Cyborg citizen: Politics in the posthuman age, Routledge, UK, 2000.

14. A. Clark, Natural-born cyborgs? *International Conference on Cognitive Technology*. Springer, Berlin, Heidelberg, pp. 17–24, 2001.

15. P. Mirowski, *Machine Dreams: Economics becomes a Cyborg Science*, Cambridge University Press, UK, 2002.

16. M. Gandy, Cyborg urbanization: Complexity and monstrosity in the contemporary city, *International Journal of Urban and Regional Research*, Vol. 29; No. 1, pp. 26–49, 2005.

17. E. Swyngedouw, Circulations and metabolisms: (hybrid) Natures and (cyborg) cities, *Science as Culture*, Vol. 15; No. 2, pp. 105–121, 2006.

18. Z. Chu, S. Gianvecchio, H. Wang, and S. Jajodia, Who is tweeting on Twitter: Human, bot, or Cyborg? *Proceedings of the 26th Annual Computer Security Applications Conference*, pp. 21–30, 2010.

19. P. P. Verbeek, Cyborg intentionality: Rethinking the phenomenology of human-technology relations, *Phenomenology and the Cognitive Sciences*, Vol. 7; No. 3, pp. 387–395, 2008.

20. M. D. Eisen, Djourno, Eyries, and the first implanted electrical neural stimulator to restore hearing, *Otology & Neurotology*, Vol. 24; No. 3, pp. 500–506, 2003.

21. K. MacVittie, J. Halámek, L. Halámková, M. Southcott, W. D. Jemison, R. Lobel, and E. Katz, From "cyborg" lobsters to a pacemaker powered by implantable biofuel cells, *Energy & Environmental Science*, Vol. 6; No. 1, pp. 81–86, 2013.

22. J. Zuniga, D. Katsavelis, J. Peck, J. Stollberg, M. Petrykowski, A. Carson, and C. Fernandez, Cyborg beast: A low-cost 3D-printed prosthetic hand for children with upper-limb differences, *BMC Research Notes*, Vol. 8; No. 1, pp. 1–9, 2015.

23. P. Strohmeier, C. Honnet, and V. S. Cyborg, Developing an ecosystem for interactive electronic implants, *Conference on Biomimetic and Biohybrid Systems*. Springer, Cham, pp. 518–525, 2016.

24. Q. Li, K. Nan, P. L. Floch, Z. Lin, H. Sheng, T. S. Blum, and J. Liu, Cyborg organoids: Implantation of nanoelectronics via organogenesis for tissue-wide electrophysiology, *Nano Letters*, USA, Vol. 19; No. 8, pp. 5781–5789, 2019.

25. B. Wittes and J. Chong, *Our Cyborg Future: Law and Policy Implications*, Center for Technology Innovation at Brookings, 2014.

26. E. Musk, An integrated brain-machine interface platform with thousands of channels, *Journal of medical Internet research*, Vol. 21; No. 10, pp. 16194, 2019.

27. J. R. Carvalko, Law and Policy in an era of cyborg-assisted-life, *2013 IEEE International Symposium on Technology and Society (ISTAS): Social Implications of Wearable Computing and Augmediated Reality in Everyday Life*, Toronto, ON, Canada, pp. 204–215, 2013.

28. H. Moravec, *Mind Children: The Future of Robot and Human Intelligence*, Harvard University Press, United States, 1988.

29. S. Schneider, *Future Minds: Transhumanism, Cognitive Enhancement and the Nature of Persons*, Neuroethics Publications, Vol. 37; 2008.

30. I. Babelon, A. Ståhle, and B. Balfors, Toward Cyborg PPGIS: Exploring sociotechnical requirements for the use of web-based PPGIS in two municipal planning cases, Stockholm region, Sweden, *Journal of Environmental Planning and Management*, Vol. 60; No. 8, pp. 1366–1390, 2017.

31. D. Sharma, Understanding human technogenesis: Human development in the postgenomic world, *Genomics, Society and Policy*, Vol. 4; No. 3, pp. 89–102, 2008.

32. J. Pelegrín-Borondo, M. Arias-Oliva, K. Murata, et al., Does ethical judgment determine the decision to become a cyborg? *Journal of Business Ethics*, Vol. 161; No. 1, pp. 5–17, 2020.

Chapter 6

The Brief History of Digital Twin Research

6.1 Introduction

It is essential to establish the digital model of objects in many fields, such as industrial manufacturing. The related technology is called Digital Twin, which is an epoch-making technology. The most critical significance of Digital Twin is that it can map the physical data in the physical space into cyberspace. With this mapping, Digital Twin can track and feedback product data at any stage of the whole life cycle, promoting digitization and informatization in industrial manufacturing. Therefore, people began to research the simulation, analysis, data accumulation, data mining, and other Digital Twin related technologies.

In the next section, the emergence of Digital Twin is reviewed. On this basis, this chapter explores the evolution of the Digital Twin concept after the emergence of related conditions and various enterprises and countries put forward their strategies. Then, the practical application of Digital Twin is reviewed in recent years. Finally, the existing problems and development trends are summarized.

6.2 The Emergence of Digital Twin

Digital Twins appeared in the early 21st century. As the American Apollo 13 flew off the Earth in 2010, an oxygen tank in its living quarters exploded. The ground mission control center combines information from all sources to diagnose the problem quickly and accurately. The astronauts were transferred to the lunar module before the oxygen supply in the living quarters ultimately failed. A key to accomplishing

DOI: 10.1201/9781003257387-6

all these tasks is that National Aeronautics and Space Administration (NASA) has a complete and high-quality ground simulation model. Except for the crew, cockpit, and mission console, everything else in the living cabin is digitally simulated during simulation training, representing an early Digital Twin form. Later, NASA proposed Digital Twin in the Area 11 technology roadmap released in 2010: "Digital Twin, it is a kind of integration of various physical quantities, a variety of spatial scale of vehicle or system simulation, the simulation using the physical model of the most effective, sensors, data update, the history of flight, and so on, to simulate the image object corresponding to the craft of twin survival state".[1]

NASA has been working on the Digital Twin, and there are still some doubts whether NASA is the first to propose the concept. The reason is as follows: in 2002, Michael Grieves first proposed the conceptual model of Product Lifecycle Management (PLM). This model maps information from the physical space to the virtual space through data streams, an early Digital Twin form [1]. In [2], Michael Grieve first proposed the concept of Digital Twin. In 2014, Michael Grieves wrote another white paper [3], in which he attributed the Digital Twin to him, and John Vickers worked with Michael. Michael Grieve also claimed in [4] that he was the first person to propose Digital Twin. Although there are ambiguities in the industry regarding who first proposed Digital Twin, Michael Grieves' contribution to Digital Twin is undeniable.

6.3 The History of Digital Twin Concept: Based on Ideas and Technology

The further development of Digital Twin is based on the research of Digital Thread [5] technology carried out in the U.S. in 2003. The Digital Thread first arose in the F-35 JSF project of the U.S. Air Force and Lockheed Martin. And it refers to the F-35's 3D digital design, which replaced traditional paper blueprints.[2] The Digital Thread results from integration with intelligent manufacturing systems, digital measurement and inspection systems, and Cyber-Physical Systems (CPS) [6].

In addition to products, production systems (production equipment, production lines) and maintenance systems also need to establish a Digital Twin. In 2012, the American National Institute of Standards and Technology put forward Model-Based Definition (MBD) [7], realizing simulation and analysis throughout the entire product life cycle to create digital models. The tremendous significance of MBD changes the traditional conceptual model to the 3D digital models, represents a deeper integration of design and manufacturing.

With the advent of Digital Thread and MBD, the technical conditions of Digital Twin have been continuously improved. In addition to the previously mentioned

---

[1] http://www.clii.com.cn/lhrh/hyxx/202006/t20200617_3945076.html
[2] https://baike.baidu.com/item/%E6%95%B0%E5%AD%97%E5%AD%AA%E7%94%9F/22197545?fr=aladdin

technical conditions, another essential condition for realizing Digital Twin, namely a universal definition of Digital Twin, also emerged. In 2012, Edward Glaessgen and David Stargel [8] came up with a standard definition of Digital Twin: "A Digital Twin is an integrated multiphysics, multiscale, probabilistic simulation of an as-built vehicle or system that uses the best available physical models, sensor updates, fleet history, e.g., to mirror the life of its corresponding flying twin".

Digital Twin still looked like a very surreal concept before 2013, which is hard to implement. Both NASA and Michael Grieves' applications involve Digital Twin prototypes. Still, the problems they solved are limited to giving Digital Twin a definition, which cannot lead to concrete applications for Digital Twin. Faced with this situation, researchers began to study related technologies. By 2013, all the supporting technologies needed for Digital Twin have been implemented, such as multiphysical scale and multiphysical quantity modeling, structured health management, and high-performance computing. However, Digital Twin requires implementing these technologies and integrating the complementary technologies into a model by experts in various fields applied to specific scenarios [9]. Therefore, it is natural for us to think about implementing Digital Twin in stages is a viable solution.

In 2013, the Air Force Research Laboratory released Spiral 117 with General Electric's cooperation (GE). Digital Twin has been applied in an experiment on recognizing virtual entities based on the US Air Force's F-15 testbed and related technologies [8]. GE regarded it as an essential concept for the industrial Internet and analyzed big data to gain a comprehensive understanding of machines' working way in the physical world. For example, the workshop head gets a phone call telling factory director that the factory has some assembly parts problems. However, the caller was not an employee but the turbine's Digital Twin. Colin Parris thought that this caller is a digital replica of a machine built using artificial intelligence (AI) algorithms to see and act like a human. GE's efforts make people see the achieving possibility of Digital Twin and lay a foundation for other applications.[3] Since then, many leading companies have followed GE with their Digital Twin scenarios, expanding the application scope of Digital Twin. By this time, theoretical research on Digital Twin was still in its infancy. To prompt the practical application of Digital Twin, relevant personnel need to do further research on it, enabling the improvement and evolution of its definition, as shown in Table 6.1.

6.4 The Strategies of Digital Twin

Many enterprises have put forward their own Digital Twin strategy following GE to cope with the digital manufacturing industry's rapid development. For example, Siemens introduced its digital system in 2013 to differentiate from Germany's Industry 4.0 [17]. On behalf of Autodesk, a software supplier of engineering construction, it

---

[3] https://www.sohu.com/a/376858158_120521462

Table 6.1   The Evolution of the Definition of Digital Twin after 2013

Time	Definition	Key Points
2013	The coupled model is a digital twin of the real machine that operates in the cloud platform and simulates the health condition with an integrated knowledge from both data driven analytical algorithms as well as other available physical knowledge [10].	Analytical algorithms
2014	Digital Twin is a life management and certification paradigm whereby model and simulations consist of as-built vehicle state, as-experienced loads and environments, and other vehicle-specific history to enable high-fidelity modeling of individual aerospace vehicles throughout their service lives [11].	Fidelity modeling
2015	Very realistic models of the current state of the process and their behaviors in interaction with their environment in the real world – typically called the Digital Twin [12].	Realistic model
2016	Digital Twin is virtual substitutes of real-world objects consisting of virtual representations and communication capabilities, making up smart objects acting as intelligent nodes inside the Internet of things and services [13].	Virtual substitutes
2017	Faster optimization algorithms, increased computer power and amount of available data, can leverage the area of simulation toward real-time control and optimization of products and production systems – a concept often referred to as a Digital Twin [14].	Real-time control and optimization
2018	Digital Twin is essentially a unique living model of the physical system with the support of enabling technologies including Multiphysics simulation, machine learning, AR/VR and cloud service, etc. [15].	Living model
2019	A digital twin is a virtual instance of a physical system (twin) continually updated with the latter's performance, maintenance, and health status data throughout the physical system's life cycle [16].	Updated virtual instance

proposed to apply Digital Twin technology to the construction of infrastructures, such as buildings and factories, and to take the whole life cycle and infrastructure of buildings as a product of pipes. In 2013, the U.S. Air Force published a Global Vision technology planning document, in which digital lines and Digital Twin were identified as game-changing opportunities. In 2014, Lockheed did much forward-looking work on Digital Twin applications. More importantly, it proposed the digital transformation strategy, which formed Digital Tapestry's solution [18].

After 2015, many countries have put forward manufacturing transformation strategies at the national level. In May 2015, the State Council of China issued the strategic document "Made in China 2025" [19], a plan of action for the first decade of China's digital manufacturing strategy. In the same year, the Modi government put forward initiatives aiming to lead the country's future with "Made in India" [20] and "Digital India" [21]. In 2016, the U.S. successively released three reports: "Artificial Intelligence Research and Development and National Strategic Plan" [22], "National Strategic Plan for Artificial Intelligence Research and Development" [23], and "Artificial Intelligence, Automation, and Economy" [23], which thoroughly explained the development plan of AI in the U.S., and the educational application of AI technology was one of the contents of the report. The Digital Economy Plan of the Russian Federation, officially approved by the government of the Russian Federation in 2017, provides a roadmap for the digital economy development in Russia [24]. In 2018, the UK's Industrial Strategy: Action in the Field of AI proposed to invest £406 million in skills development, with a focus on math, digital, and technical education, to ensure Britain is at the forefront of the digital manufacturing industry and nurture relevant professionals [25,26].

6.5 The Applications of Digital Twin

The development of Digital Twin promotes digital applications. It is applied from low to a high level, such as Data modeling for personal information, Digital Factory, Digital Twin City, Digital Earth, and Parallel World.

6.5.1 Personal Information Modeling

Mapping citizens' personal information into the virtual space, collating, and maintaining are critical to improving social governance's efficiency in the booming era of Digital Twin. At present, there are two typical specific applications of digital medical treatment and public security information.

The electronic medical record is a significant way for citizens to digitize medical information. In 1945, Vannevar Bush proposed Life Log [27], namely, the extensive use of intelligent equipment, full time to record the individual life characteristics, forming many separate information databases. America's Defense Advanced Research Projects Agency has also launched a Life Log study to capture and store human experience to develop intelligent robots' methods. They hope to record a person's entire life experience to create a database system of human life [28]. The precursor to electronic medical records before the advent of Digital Twin is Life Log which provides the basis for the current digital modeling of individual medical records [29]. Another evolution of electronic medical records is Gordon Bell's Memory Bank. Gordon Bell recorded information in his Memory Bank about his diet and exercise, as well as the number and symptoms of angina attacks, so doctors could better understand his body when they underwent heart bypass surgery. After that, The Phoenix Partnership (TPP) was established in 1997. It was based on electronic medical records and related medical and health information software development, production, sales, and after-sales service. At this time, electronic medical records as complete public goods appeared in people's sight. By 2020, TPP was the leading enterprise in the UK information technology service industry with electronic medical records[4]. With the emergence and development of the electronic medical record, doctors can make more intuitive judgments about the patients' condition based on their various information in the cyberspace model. The appearance of electronic medical records began a new round of competition, from which the digitization of medical records about citizens entered a period of gradual development. It is foreseeable that more information about patients in the healthcare system will be stored in the clinical system's cyberspace in citizens' twins.

The establishment of the citizen data model is the primary way of public security information and public security data fusion and sharing. The citizen data model contains much privacy, such as name, ID number, contact information, address, an account password, property status, and whereabouts track. Most of this information can be linked to a unique ID number. Analyzing the citizen data can improve the capability of precision strikes and dynamic control. Using a citizen's ID number, the Police Cloud system can track a person's whereabouts. Besides, the Police Cloud system can uncover invisible links between people and events to the police and alert police officers to unusual activities. For example, someone regularly stays at a local hotel despite having a local residence. The police system is better as the continuous development of Digital Twin, making the police system has more diversified ways to modeling the citizen information.

6.5.2 Digital Factory and Digital Twin City

In today's fierce market competition, manufacturing enterprises found that they face considerable challenges such as cost, quality, e.g., a design mistake can lead to the demise of an entire enterprise. To avoid catastrophic consequences, manufacturing enterprises need to find ways to reflect production results in the production process directly. This reflection is essentially mapping the information of physical products into cyberspace. Digital Factory technology is effective in solving such problems. It is necessary for industrial manufacturing to apply Digital Twin according to its definition. The implementation of technology is inseparable from the support of the related ideas. Michael Grieves formally proposed the complete concept of PLM in 2011 [2]. PLM is the cornerstone of Digital Factory according to the relationship between Digital Factory and Digital Twin. And the development of the digital factory is highly consistent with the development of Digital Twin.

---

[4] https://www.tpp-asia.com/enterprise

Companies, such as Alstom, Hyundai Heavy Industries, and China Railway Rolling Stock Corporation, put forward Digital Factory strategies. The acuteness impact of the outbreak COVID-19 virus on traditional manufacturing enterprises reminded large manufacturing enterprises to go ahead with these strategies in 2020 and be firmer in the direction of digital development and the era of Digital Twin.

With the continuous improvement and update of Digital Twin, people found that the Digital Twin theoretical and technological framework can be extended to Digital Twin City. Building Information Modeling (BIM) [30] is the germ of Digital Twin city. From BIM to City Information Modeling (CIM) [31] to Digital Twin, Digital City is developing rapidly in Digital Twin's footsteps. Autodesk first proposed BIM in 2002, which can use digital technology to build a 3D virtual model of a construction project. The virtual model provides a complete and consistent construction project information library for the model. CIM is a BIM city analogy, and it is a system of city elements represented by symbols in the 2D space and the 3D space. What's more, CIM is conceived as a 3D expansion of GIS (3DIS or 3D information system), and it enriches the level and scale of the model view [32].

6.5.3 Digital Twin Earth and Parallel World

In 1992, Vice President Al Gore of the U.S. proposed Digital Earth (DE) from ecological and global climate change, which did not attract attention. The main problem in implementing this concept in the 1990s was the lack of Conditions of Implementation.[5] To solve this problem, progress needs to be gain in observation, computation, and storage. After the corresponding technology got rapid progress, several online map services (Google map) and desktop virtual earth (Google earth) also followed, making the DE may become a reality [33].

In 1998, the International Telecommunication Union released a Digital Earth report at a conference organized by the Organization for International Economic Cooperation and Development. At that time, the U.S. is still the strongest country for Digital Earth. Besides, China announced the International Digital Earth Association's establishment in 2006. In the last decade, countries and companies involved in the digital globe have improved their capabilities to monitor and model Earth entities. In 2007, Digital Globe's *WorldView-1* remote sensing satellite was successfully launched aboard using a *Boeing Delta II 7920* rocket from Vandenberg Air Force Base in California. By 2016, the company had increased the number of Earth-observing satellites to five, and some Digital Earth strategies support the Digital Earth development. As mentioned earlier, IBM introduced its Smart Earth strategy in 2008, emphasizing that physical and information infrastructure should not be built separately but as a unified smart infrastructure [34]. European Commission (EC) dedicated one of its seven flagship initiatives to the Digital Agenda, which was the first political initiative to embed the DE concept

---

[5] http://www.ceode.cas.cn/qysm/ghzl/200807/t20080705_2371222.html

in geopolitical dates. EC released the INSPiRE protocol [35] that required uniform standards in 2015. According to Roscosmos' news service, Roscosmos began to regularly update the global terrestrial digital model under the Digital Earth project framework in 2017. Like GE's Predix platform for Digital Twin, Alibaba Cloud Computing Co. Ltd released the Digital Earth Engine at Alibaba Cloud Guangdong Summit in 2019. As a platform to support the Digital Earth development, Alibaba Cloud provides open image data sets, remote sensing capabilities, rich API interfaces, etc. Other companies and scholars can also use the platform to conduct their local research on the digital globe. The challenges posed by DE are multifaceted, especially in the fields of computers and communications.[6]

Parallel World is another fantasy application of Digital Twin. Popper put forward the concept of the Third World, namely the early form of Parallel World, in [36] published in 1972. The Third World refers to the product of human spiritual activities and related objects. If relevant personnel want to establish The Third World, they still need to dig deeper and make Popper's full use. Wang proposed Parallel System in 2004, an exploration to Popper [37]. It refers to the system composed of a system in reality and the corresponding system in cyberspace. In the same year, Wang proposed a vision of the future society, in which everyone would be born as an individual in the physical space. Simultaneously, there would be the one you, and perhaps more than one you, in cyberspace. In 2015, Wang emphasized the future society, beginning with one-to-one virtual reality, then one-to-many, multi-to-one, and finally multi-to-many, forms a Parallel World where virtual reality interacts, interpenetrates, and interests [38]. In 2019, Wang et al. [39] first focused on Parallel City and used Parallel City's points to service the ordinary world. Parallel City consists of a real city and an equivalent artificial city. The artificial city represents a real city computer model and simple digital representation. In the same year, Alibaba released a new product in the urban brain – Digital Parallel World at the Global Artificial Intelligence Product Application Expo held in Suzhou, China. As a Parallel World product, the concept proposed by Ali DAMO Academy also stays on city governance. To truly complete the digital parallel world, the related technology and the basic theory need to be further improved.

6.6 Development Summary

6.6.1 The Current State of Digital Twin

Digital Twin adds great significance to the digital age. More and more attention is focused on it. From 2011 to 2020, a total of 3,880 Digital Twin papers have been published. Figure 6.1 (data from the Scopus database as of December 31,

---

[6] http://www.ceode.cas.cn/qysm/ghzl/200807/t20080705_2371222.html

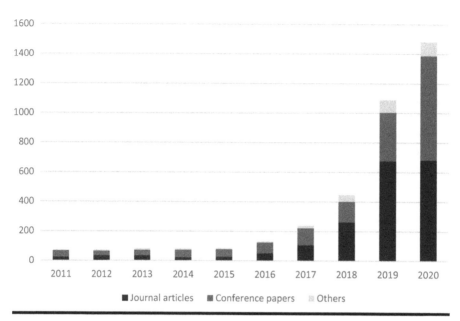

Figure 6.1   Annual chart of the number of digital twin literature from 2011 to 2020.

2020) shows the annual publication of various literature types during the specific period, including journal articles, conference papers, and other kinds of literature. From the analysis of the number of published literatures, the overall trend is increasing. Few Digital Twin works of literature were published from 2011 to 2015. From 2016 to 2019, the number of Digital Twin literature published entered a rapid growth period. The number of Digital Twin papers is expected to overgrow in the coming years.

Besides, according to the statistics of the distribution of published articles, conference papers are the main publications. Still, journal papers show a noticeable growth trend in recent years. This change shows that the current research on Digital Twin is more and more in-depth, more and more systematic.

However, there are some problems to be solved in Digital Twin as follows: (a) With the gradual development of Digital Twin application scenarios, there is a lack of high-fidelity models for simulation and virtual testing in specific applications. (b) Compared with our vision for Digital Twin, Digital Twin is unsatisfactory in concrete applications because the closed-loop synchronization established between the physical and digital worlds is still not good enough. (c) The analog and emulation technologies used by Digital Twin have security risks in terms of privacy. For example, people with ulterior motives could use RF location technology [40] to track the Digital Twin user's location. (d) In some fields, people are more likely to trust the manual transference results, even when Digital Twin is better.

6.6.2 The Trends for Digital Twin

Although Digital Twin still has some problems, Digital Twin's development is undoubtedly approaching solving these problems. The trends for Digital Twins can be highlighted as follows: (a) The most obvious trend is modeling technology toward improving the efficiency and accuracy of modeling. Furthermore, the continuous improvement of the modeling technology cannot be separated from the collaboration of some related technology such as geometry, simulation, and data. (b) Digital Twin is moving in the direction of closed-loop optimization, in which real objects interact with virtual objects. This interaction superimposes the feedback control function based on intelligent decisions to realize the full closed-loop optimization based on data self-execution. (c) Messages sent from the virtual world to the physical world gradually adopt more sophisticated encryption methods. Information encryption, anonymity, channel coding, and secure routing have been applied to the transmission of information in Digital Twin. (d) The deep combination of Digital Twin and network constructs its new application mechanism and application ecosystem, gradually integrating Digital Twin into people's daily life.

References

1. M. Grieves, *Product Lifecycle Management: Driving the Next Generation of Lean Thinking: Driving the Next Generation of Lean Thinking: Driving the Next Generation of Lean Thinking*, McGraw Hill Professional, United States, 2005.
2. M. Grieves, *Virtually Perfect: Driving Innovative and Lean Products through Product Lifecycle Management*, Space Coast Press, Merritt Island, Fl, 2011.
3. M. Grieves, Digital twin: Manufacturing excellence through virtual factory replication, *White Paper*, Vol. 1; pp. 1–7, 2014.
4. M. Grieves and J. Vickers, Digital twin: Mitigating unpredictable, undesirable emergent behavior in complex systems, In: Kahlen F. J., Flumerfelt S., and Alves A. (eds), *Transdisciplinary Perspectives on Complex Systems*, Springer, Cham, pp. 85–113, 2017.
5. T. Hedberg, J. Lubell, L. Fischer, L. Maggiano, and A. B. Feeney, Testing the digital thread in support of model-based manufacturing and inspection, *Journal of Computing and Information Science in Engineering*, Vol. 16; No. 2, pp. 021001, 2016.
6. J. Lee, B. Bagheri, and H. A. Kao, A cyber-physical systems architecture for Industry 4.0-based manufacturing systems, *Manufacturing Letters*, Vol. 3; pp. 18–23, 2015.
7. V. Quintana, L. Rivest, R. Pellerin, F. Venne, and F. Kheddouci, Will model-based definition replace engineering drawings throughout the product lifecycle? A global perspective from aerospace industry, *Computers in Industry*, Vol. 61; No. 5, pp. 497–508, 2010.
8. E. Glaessgen and D. Stargel, The digital twin paradigm for future NASA and US Air Force vehicles, *53rd AIAA/ASME/ASCE/AHS/ASC Structures, Structural Dynamics and Materials Conference 20th AIAA/ASME/AHS Adaptive Structures Conference 14th AIAA*, pp. 1818, 2012.
9. Y. Yong, S. Fan, and G. Peng, Application of digital twin model in product configuration management, *Aeronautical Manufacturing Technology*, Vol. 60; No. 7, pp. 41–45, 2017.

10. E. Negri, L. Fumagalli, and M. Macchi, A review of the roles of digital twin in cps-based production systems, *Procedia Manufacturing*, Vol. 11; pp. 939–948, 2017.
11. F. Tao, J. Cheng, Q. Qi, M. Zhang, H. Zhang, and F. Sui, Digital twin-driven product design, manufacturing and service with big data, *The International Journal of Advanced Manufacturing Technology*, Vol. 94; pp. 3563–3576, 2018.
12. R. Rosen, G. V. Wichert, L. George, and K. D. Bettenhausen, About the importance of autonomy and digital twins for the future of manufacturing, *IFAC-PapersOnLine*, Vol. 48; No. 3, pp. 567–572, 2015.
13. M. Schluse and J. Rossmann, From simulation to experimentable digital twins: Simulation-based development and operation of complex technical systems, *2016 IEEE International Symposium on Systems Engineering (ISSE)*, IEEE, pp. 1–6, 2016.
14. R. Söderberg, K. Wärmefjord, J. S. Carlson, and L. Lindkvist, Toward a Digital Twin for real-time geometry assurance in individualized production, *CIRP Annals*, Vol. 66; No. 1, pp. 137–140, 2017.
15. J. Wang, L. Ye, R. X. Gao, C. Li, and L. Zhang, Digital Twin for rotating machinery fault diagnosis in smart manufacturing, *International Journal of Production Research*, Vol. 57; No. 12, pp. 3920–3934, 2019.
16. A. M. Madni, C. C. Madni, and S. D. Lucero, Leveraging digital twin technology in model-based systems engineering, *Systems*, Vol. 7; No. 1, pp. 7, 2019.
17. H. Lasi, P. Fettke, H. G. Kemper, T. Feld, and M. Hoffmann, Industry 4.0, *Business & Information Systems Engineering*, Vol. 6; No. 4, pp. 239–242, 2014.
18. C. Rother, S. Kumar, V. Kolmogorov, and A. Blake, Digital tapestry [automatic image synthesis], *2005 IEEE Computer Society Conference on Computer Vision and Pattern Recognition (CVPR'05)*, Vol. 1; pp. 589–596, 2005.
19. Z. He and H. Pan, German "Industry 4.0" and "Made in China 2025", *Journal of Changsha University of Science and Technology (Social Science Edition)*, Vol. 30; No. 3, pp. 103–110, 2015.
20. S. Bhaskaran, *Made in India: Decolonizations, Queer Sexualities, Trans/National Projects*, Palgrave Macmillan, New York, 2004.
21. P. N. Thomas, *Digital India: Understanding Information, Communication and Social Change*, SAGE Publications, United States, 2012.
22. L. E. Parker, Creation of the national artificial intelligence research and development strategic plan, *AI Magazine*, Vol. 39, No. 2, pp. 25–32, 2018.
23. D. Acemoglu and R. Pascual, Artificial intelligence, automation and work, No. w24196. National Bureau of Economic Research, 2018.
24. V. V. Tarakanov, A. O. Inshakova, and V. V. Dolinskaya, Information society, digital economy and law, In: Popkova E. (eds), *Ubiquitous Computing and the Internet of Things: Prerequisites for the Development of ICT. Studies in Computational Intelligence*, Springer, Cham, Vol. 826; pp. 3–15, 2019.
25. H. Wendy and J. Pesenti, *Growing the Artificial Intelligence Industry in the UK*, Department for Digital, Culture, Media & Sport and Department for Business, Energy & Industrial Strategy, Part of the Industrial Strategy UK and the Commonwealth, UK, 2017.
26. C. Cath, S. Wachter, B. Mittelstadt, M. Taddeo, and L. Floridi, Artificial intelligence and the 'good society': The US, EU, and UK approach, *Science and Engineering Ethics*, Vol. 24; pp. 505–528, 2018.
27. R. Harrison and B. Wellman, *Networked: The New Social Operating System*. Vol. 419, MIT Press, Cambridge, MA, 2012.

28. R. Rawassizadeh, M. Tomitsch, K. Wac, and A. M. Tjoa, UbiqLog: A generic mobile phone-based life-log framework, *Personal and Ubiquitous Computing*, Vol. 17; No. 4, pp. 621–637, 2013.
29. M. Kushima, T. Yamazaki, and K. Araki, Text data mining of the nursing care life log from electronic medical record, *The International Multi Conference of Engineers and Computer Scientists (IMECS 2019)*, Hong Kong, 2019.
30. C. M. Eastman, C. Eastman, P. Teicholz, R. Sacks, and K. Liston, *BIM Handbook: A Guide to Building Information Modeling for Owners, Managers, Designers, Engineers, and Contractors*, John Wiley & Sons, United States, 2011.
31. T. Stojanovski, City information modeling (CIM) and urbanism: Blocks, connections, territories, people and situations, *Proceedings of the Symposium on Simulation for Architecture & Urban Design*, pp. 1–8, 2013.
32. A. Amorim, Discutindo city information modeling (CIM) E conceitoscorrelatos, *Gestão & Tecnologia De Projetos*, Vol. 10; No. 2, pp. 87–100, 2015.
33. M. Ehlers, P. Woodgate, A. Annoni, and S. Schade, Advancing digital earth: Beyond the next generation, *Proceedings of the National Academy of Sciences*, Vol. 109; No. 28, pp. 11088–11094, 2012.
34. D. Li, Y. Yuan, Z. Shao, and L. Wang, From digital earth to smart earth, *Chinese Science Bulletin*, Vol. 59; No. 8, pp. 722–733, 2014.
35. F. Coyer, A. Gardner, A. Doubrovsky, R. Cole, F. M. Ryan, C. Allen, and G. McNamara, Reducing pressure injuries in critically ill patients by using a patient skin integrity care bundle (Inspire), *American Journal of Critical Care*, Vol. 24; No. 3, pp. 199–209, 2015.
36. K. R. Popper, *Objective Knowledge*, Oxford University Press, United States, Vol. 360, 1972.
37. F. Wang, A new approach to the management and control of complex systems, *Journal of Control and Decision Science*, Vol. 19; No. 5, pp.485–489, 2004.
38. F. Wang, *On the Coming Fifth Industrial Revolution: "There must be Multiple Parallel You in the Future"*, Southern Weekend, China, 2015 [in Chinese].
39. Y. Lv, F. Wang, Y. Zhang, and X. Zhang, Parallel cities with virtual and real interaction: Basic framework, methods and applications, *Journal of Intelligent Science and Technology*, Vol. 1; No. 3, pp. 311–317, 2019.
40. P. P. Swar, On the performance of in-body RF localization techniques, Master Thesis, 2012.

Chapter 7

Psychology and Emotion Research History in Cyberspace

7.1 Introduction

Cyberspace has been penetrating overwhelmingly into both industrial manufacturing and our daily life [1]. Its predominant impacts on psychology and emotion are becoming increasingly obvious for both humans and machines. Emotions such as happiness, sadness, fear, anger, and so forth are mainly shaped by cultural and biological influences [2], while psychology is a relatively complex discipline with both mental and behavioral matters, including cognition, self-personality, attention, intelligence, etc.[1] In cyberspace, the psychology and emotion of individuals are more easily influenced and shaped by various cyber techniques, contents, and sources. This chapter focuses on different subjects in cyberspace and studies the psychological and emotional research history of human, machine, and human–machine relationship, respectively.

7.2 Psychology and Emotion of Humans in Cyberspace

For humans, psychology and emotion research are always on the way. Emerging as the fourth living space for humans, cyberspace and cyber techniques such as virtual reality and social media provide a virtual environment where humans could meet, negotiate,

---

[1] https://en.wikipedia.org/wiki/Psychology

DOI: 10.1201/9781003257387-7

Table 7.1 Typical Emotion Models for Reference

Year	Name	Content
1980	Plutchik's wheel of emotions [5]	Plutchik designed a paradigm of "Wheel of Emotions" which contains 8 basic emotions (joy and sadness; anger and fear; trust and disgust; surprise and anticipation) standing oppositely in the wheel.
1987	Parrott's emotions by groups [6]	A tree-structured list of emotions ranged from joy, love, surprise, sadness, anger to fear, with 26 secondary emotions, and more than 100 tertiary emotions.
1988	The OCC model [7]	The OCC model was proposed according to the hierarchical branches of consequences of events, actions of agents, and aspects of objects. In this model, there are 22 emotions.
1996	Pleasure-Arousal-Dominance (PAD) Emotional State Model [8]	A three-dimensional model of pleasure, arousal, and dominance ranging from low to high.
2009	Revised OCC model [9]	A disambiguated, inheritance-based hierarchy of emotions of the OCC Model, which identifies the ambiguities existing in the original OCC model.
2012	The Hourglass of Emotions [10]	It contains four affective dimensions of sensitivity, aptitude, pleasantness, and attention, each of which has been divided into six levels.

work, go shopping and entertainments, and are deeply changing the modes and habits of humans, so as to make influence on humans' psychology and emotion status [3]. Meanwhile, the population of Internet, as well as various contents and resources in cyberspace, leads to a series of mental disorders and psychological issues, such as internet addiction, social depression, cybervictimization, and cyberbullying, etc.

According to *Stastics*,[2] the number of Internet users worldwide from 2005 to 2020 increased dramatically, which on the other hand reflects the development tendency of users' psychology and emotion to some extent. Usually, there are no standardized models or criteria for psychological or emotional analysis since they are too subjective. In 2020, Wang provided an overall conclusion for existing emotional classifications [4]. Upon this, we list several popular emotion classifications discussed from the perspective of psychological and affective computing in Table 7.1, most of which were put forward before the 2010s.

---

[2] Source: Statistics, https://www.statista.com/topics/1145/internet-usage-worldwide/

Back to the early 1980s, the Internet was first employed by few specialists and researchers. At that time, online activities were limited to scientific research. Most people felt unfamiliar with Internet and computers and had little enthusiasm and curiosity at all. It is also for this reason that in the early stage of the development of the Internet, too few people used the Internet, and research on psychology and emotion of humans was sporadic.

In the early 1990s, with the development of World Wide Web (WWW), humans noticed the benefits brought by Internet, and participated with various online activities, such as online work, study, and entertainment. At this stage, some scientists noticed the psychological and physical disorders caused by a long-term use of Internet, and in 1996, Dr. Yong initially proposed the concept of Internet addiction and compared its original model with pathological gambling [11]. The Internet Addiction is a kind of mental impairment or disease due to the abuse of computers and Internet, with a series of symptoms in body and mind. For example, users addicted to Internet could not stop checking and surfing the contents online, even when they have no explicit purposes. More seriously, if there is no Internet, he/she would suffer with a strong mental disorder such as depression, sadness, and anxiety.

In the 21st century with the advance in intelligent techniques humans found it more convenient to surf online. As reported by Cisco Internet Annual Report, there will be at least 5.3 billion Internet users around the world until 2023 [12]. More and more people establish strong psychosocial dependency for Internet, social media, and cyberspace, etc. In 2001, scholars had noticed the strong Internet dependency particularly among college students and analyzed six factors found that such dependency is a multifaceted psychological emotion [13]. In 2008, Hilts focused on the motivations and effects of Internet dependency on work productivity in the 21st century and highlighted its impacts on both industry and academia [14]. In 2009, Tencent released a simulated business game named QQ farm, providing a virtual farming environment enabling users to farm and sell products in cyberspace. In the meantime, virtual activities such as keeping pets in the cloud also emerge in time. Besides, the boom of social media has also brought significant impacts; for example, since WeChat was first announced in China in 2011, users have established an increasingly emotional dependency on the Internet and cyberspace, intensifying people's loneliness in real life to a great extent.

However, the long-term addiction of Internet has become increasingly common and serious particularly for adolescents [15]. In addition, new psychological issues such as social depression and phobia emerge, which refers to anxiety or fear for participating in social activities [16]. Since Internet users are used to live alone in virtual cyberspace, they may feel uncomfortable or stressed when communicating with others face to face.

Moreover, cyberbullying has aroused global awareness in recent years. It contains intended psychological violence as traditional bullying, such as posting threats, rumors, and unhealthy messages online [17]. As an important research area in cyber psychology, cyberbullying severely ruins humans' psychological health and makes the cyberspace a dangerous space to some extent. Since the 2010s, some countries have started to formulate relevant laws and regulations to restrict network behaviors, and to create a healthy and harmonious cyber environment [18,19]. In addition, there are many international organizations worldwide that aimed at psychological and emotional research, such as the International Union of Psychological Science (IUPS)[3] founded in 1950 which has more than 100 committees up to now. As can be seen in Table 7.2, we list some typical international organizations worldwide for reference.

In summary, with the popularity of the Internet and cyberspace, humans have experienced vital psychological and emotional changes, moving towards a more healthy and mature future.

7.3 Psychology and Emotion of Machines in Cyberspace

Compared with human beings, machines, another kind of indispensable individuals in cyberspace, also play important roles. The earliest research on psychology and emotion of machines in cyberspace could be traced back to 1995, when the concept of artificial consciousness was put forward [20]. The artificial consciousness, also named machine consciousness, means that human-like consciousness could be synthesized in artificial artifacts. In this section, we classify the development history of psychology and emotions of machines into three phases: the early stage with few emotions, the current phase that could recognize or simulate emotions, and the upcoming phase when machines could have its own psychology.

Taking robot as an example, as shown in Figure 7.1, it was a long period since the 1920s when robots did not own psychology or emotions [21]. At that stage, robots were designed to focus on finishing predefined tasks, such as picking up bottles, writing simple words, etc. Although in the 1970s, humanoid robots appeared and they aimed to simulate humans in appearance and interactions, there were still few robots that could express facial emotions. Due to the technical limitations and the opaque of humans' psychology and emotions, little research focused on psychological or emotional characteristics of machines then.

In the late 1990s, affective computing was proposed, and it referred to the recognition and simulation of humans in computer science, psychology, and cognitive science [22]. Inspired from the new emerging cyber techniques, it enabled robots to recognize, understand, and even simulate humans' emotions. For example, Kismet,[4] invented in 1998, could be regarded as one of the early robots that could understand and own simple emotions. In 2014, SoftBank Robotics published one

---

[3] https://www.iupsys.net/
[4] https://en.wikipedia.org/wiki/Kismet_(robot)

Table 7.2   International Organizations for Psychology and Emotion Research

Countries/ Regions	Organizations
Worldwide	International Association for the Psychology of Religion (IAPR)
	International Association of Applied Psychology (IAAP)
	Society for Research in Child Development (SRCD)
	International Council of Psychologists (ICP)
	International Union of Psychological Science (IUPS)
	Association de Psychologie Scientifique de Langue Francaise (APSLF)
	International Neuropsychological Society (INS)
	International Society for the Study of Behavioral Development (ISSBD)
	International Association for Cross-Cultural Psychology (IACCP)
	International Test Commission (ITC)
	International Society of Comparative Psychology (ISCP)
Asia	Chinese Psychological Society
	Japanese Psychology Association
	Korean Psychological Association
	Singapore Psychological Society (SPS)
Europe	European Association of Social Psychology (EASP)
	European Federation of Psychologists Associations (EFPA)
	European Society for Cognitive Psychology (ESCoP)
	European Association of Work and Organizational Psychology (EAWOP)
America	Canadian Psychological Association (CPA)
	Interamerican Society of Psychology/Sociedad Interamericana de Psicologia (SIP)
	Caribbean Alliance of National Psychological Associations (CANPA)

(Continued)

Table 7.2 (*Continued*)   International Organizations for Psychology and Emotion Research

Countries/ Regions	Organizations
Australia	Australian Psychological Society
ASEAN	ASEAN Regional Union of Psychological Societies (ARUPS)
Arab	Arab Union of Psychological Science (AUPsyS)
IEEE CIS Technical Activities Committee	IEEE Cognitive and Developmental Systems Technical Committee
	Task Force on Developmental Psychology

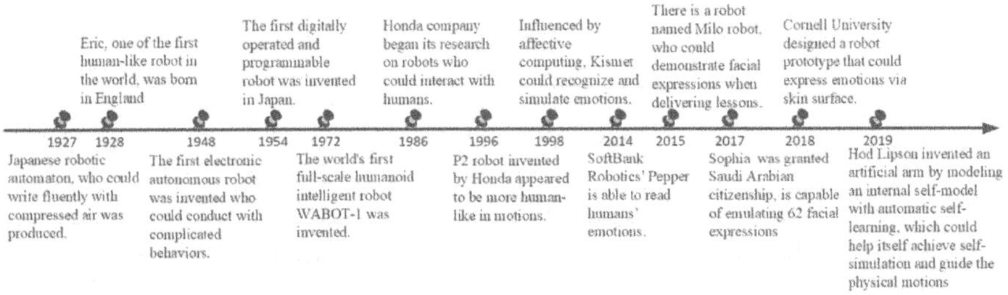

Figure 7.1   Development history of psychology and emotion of robots in cyberspace.

robot named Pepper,[5] who could read humans' emotions. In the next year, Milo robot[6] was invented and aimed at learners with autism, who could demonstrate simple facial expressions automatically when delivering lessons. At that time, robots began to own emotional features as humans, and in 2017, there was a huge leap in the psychological and emotional research of robots, since the world's first robot, Sophia,[7] with human nationality was born. In addition, she owns almost 64 facial expressions, which was a significant advantage compared with other robots.

Up to 2020s, machines in cyberspace possessed emotional features, by simulating and interacting with humans. They could represent specified facial expressions such as happiness, anger, sadness, and fear under appropriate circumstances driven by the internal affective mechanisms and have been widely adopted in applications such as assistant living, healthcare, education, and so on. As for psychological features of machines, some scientists have doubted whether it is possible for machines to own self-consciousness or awareness, to imitate humans in an advanced level.

---

[5] https://en.wikipedia.org/wiki/Pepper_(robot)
[6] https://www.robokind.com/robots4autism/meet-milo
[7] https://www.hansonrobotics.com/sophia/

In 2018, Raja Chatila made an overall discussion of machines' self-awareness and analyzed the issues from five aspects, including the ability of perception, learning, interacting, decision-making, and the cognitive architecture [23]. In 2019, Hod Lipson, a scientist at Columbia University, demonstrated his experiment with an artificial arm by modeling an internal self-model with automatic self-learning, which could help itself achieve self-simulation and guide the physical motions [24].

To be honest, the related research with regarding to psychological characteristics of machines in cyberspace such as cognition, awareness, and consciousness are still far cry from owning the similar ones as humans. Soon, with the advances in Artificial Intelligence (AI), brain science, and neuroscience, it is possible for machines in cyberspace to establish psychological and emotional systems as well, and moreover, machines may also be influenced with psychological and mental disorders such as addiction, bullying, depression, and so forth [25].

7.4 Psychology and Emotion Development in Human–Machine Relationship

Apart from the psychology and emotion research of humans and machines, it is also interesting and promising to study the psychology and emotion development in human–machine relationship. To provide a clear illustration, we describe human–machine relationship as interaction, collaboration, and integration, in which interaction is regarded as the initial stage for human–machine relationship, collaboration is established upon the basis of interaction, and integration would be the development direction for human–machine relationship soon.

As mentioned above, human–machine interaction, the initial stage in human–machine relationship, mainly refers to the interactive communications between humans and machines, ranging from simple keyboard input to advanced body gestures. In early 1970s, researchers at Palo Alto Research Center noticed the possibilities of psychological theories in the interactions with computers. Following that in 1983, Card provided an overall introduction to the cognitive psychology of human–machine interaction, to lay scientific foundations for applying relevant psychological theories in human–machine relationship [26]. Later, a new research area named human factor engineering which considered more human factors in designing the interaction between humans and machines was proposed in both North America and Europe, and it recommended to understanding humans as actors, so that more human factors would help when designing systems [27]. In 1999, Ogata and his colleagues carried out emotional research of robots and evaluated humans' impressions on them [28]. Since then, scientists began to focus on the psychological evaluations in human–machine relationship, and in 2001, Kanda from Kyoto University continued to study humans' attitudes to gaze control of robots, with psychological methods, semantic differential methods as well as factor analysis [29].

At this stage, for humans, machines were regarded as artificial tools that were born to provide humans with services and conveniency, and existing research mainly focus on humans' psychological responses to machines, so as to evaluate its functions.

Afterward, with the advances in cognitive computing and AI, machines play an increasingly significant role in daily life and industrial manufacturing. In addition to the simple information interaction, more complicated tasks require humans and machines to handle together, similar like common partners. In 2008, when Bauer made an overview of human–robot collaboration, he emphasized that humans and robots should hold complementary skills and were mutually accountable [30]. In 2017, with the development of social robots, scientist noticed the significance of social psychology in the collaboration between humans and robots [31]. In 2018, Cangelosi initially introduced the interdisciplinary approach named Developmental Robotics, which was inspired from the child and cognitive psychology [32]. During the collaboration between humans and machines, humans gradually build up dependence and trust on machines, to achieve mutual goals. Moreover, many of them even start to create various virtual characters or find another "him/her" in virtual environment for establishing emotional sustenance. Visible changes have taken place regarding humans' psychological attitudes to machines, such as equality and respect, and even "solid" emotional resonance or connections with machines.

The advanced relationship between humans and machines which we envision may be a high-level integration in the upcoming 2020s. It represents a stage where machines own psychological and emotional states like humans and hold almost equal positions in relationships. Concepts such as Cyborg and Digital twins could be regarded as the first step toward further integration. In 1960s, Cyborg was first introduced. In 1980s, Haraway highlighted Cyborg as a hybrid composition of organisms and machines, and it provided possibilities for the seamless combination and integration of humans and machines [33]. Digital Twin refers to the virtual avatars in cyberspace, which has a corresponding mapping from individuals, procedures, and systems in physical space [34]. They would all serve as fundamental techniques in achieving the seamless integration, for example, in helping optimize the brain–machine interfaces and achieving comprehensive communications. More development histories of Cyborg and Digital Twin could be seen in Chapters 5 and 6. Under such hybrid circumstances, it is possible for both humans and machines to establish synchronous and bi-directional psychologies and emotions, and at that time, more legal and moral issues need to be discussed further.

7.5 Conclusion

This chapter provides an overall psychology and emotion research history in cyberspace from the perspectives of humans, machines, human–machine relationships, respectively. As time goes on, no matter whether it is for humans, machines, or human–machine relationships, psychological and emotional research has experienced an evolution from budding growing to maturity. Cyberspace needs to establish a complete and strong psychological and emotional system in the coming years, to create a healthy and upward cyber living space.

References

1. H. Ning, X. Ye, M. A. Bouras, D. Wei, and M. Daneshmand, General cyberspace: Cyberspace and cyber-enabled spaces, *IEEE Internet of Things Journal*, Vol. 5; No. 3, pp. 1843–1856, 2018.
2. P. Ekman and R. J. Davidson, *The Nature of Emotion: Fundamental Questions*, Oxford University Press, United States, 1994.
3. Á. J. Gordo-López, and I. Parker, *Cyberpsychology*, Taylor & Francis, United States, 1999.
4. Z. Wang, S. B. Ho, and E. Cambria, A review of emotion sensing: Categorization models and algorithms, *Multimedia Tools and Applications*, Vol. 79; No. 47, pp. 35553–35582, 2020.
5. D. Chafale and A. Pimpalkar, Review on developing corpora for sentiment analysis using Plutchik's wheel of emotions with fuzzy logic, *International Journal of Computer Sciences and Engineering*, Vol. 2; No. 10, pp. 14–18, 2014.
6. P. Shaver, J. Schwartz, and D. Kirson, Emotion knowledge: Further exploration of a prototype approach, *Journal of Personality and Social Psychology*, Vol. 52; No. 6, pp. 1061–1086, 1987.
7. A. Ortony, G. L. Clore, and A. Collins, *The Cognitive Structure of Emotions*, Cambridge University press, UK, 1990.
8. A. Mehrabian, Pleasure-arousal-dominance: A general framework for describing and measuring individual differences in temperament, *Current Psychology*, Vol. 14; No. 4, pp.261–292, 1996.
9. B. R. Steunebrink, M. Dastani, and J. J. C. Meyer, The OCC model revisited, *Proc. of the 4th Workshop on Emotion and Computing*, 2009.
10. E. Cambria, A. Livingstone, and A. Hussain, *The Hourglass of Emotions*, In: Esposito A., Esposito A.M., Vinciarelli A., Hoffmann R., Müller V.C. (eds), *Cognitive Behavioural Systems*, Lecture Notes in Computer Science, Springer, Berlin, Heidelberg, Vol. 7403, 2012.
11. K. S. Young, Internet addiction: The emergence of a new clinical disorder, *Cyberpsychology & Behavior*, Vol. 1; No. 3, pp. 237–244, 1998.
12. Cisco Annual Internet Report (2018–2023) White Paper, https://www.cisco.com/c/en/us/solutions/collateral/executive-perspectives/annual-internet-report/white-paper-c11-741490.html [Accessed January 12, 2021].
13. W. Wang, Internet dependency and psychosocial maturity among college students, *International Journal of Human-Computer Studies*, Vol. 55; No. 6, pp. 919–938, 2001.
14. M. L. Hilts, Internet dependency, motivations for internet use and their effect on work productivity: The 21st century addiction, Thesis, Rochester Institute of Technology, 2008.
15. M. Shaw and DW. Black, Internet addiction, *CNS Drugs*, Vol. 22; No. 5, pp. 353–365, 2008.
16. H. T. Wei, M. H. Chen, and P. C. Huang, The association between online gaming, social phobia, and depression: An internet survey, *BMC Psychiatry*, Vol. 12; No. 1, pp. 1–7, 2012.

17. F. Dehue, C. Bolman, and T. Völlink, Cyberbullying: Youngsters' experiences and parental perception, *Cyber Psychology & Behavior*, Vol. 11; No. 2, pp. 217–223, 2008.

18. A. V. King, Constitutionality of cyberbullying laws: Keeping the online playground safe for both teens and free speech, *Vand. L. Rev*, Vol. 63; pp. 845, 2010.

19. J. L. Williams, Teens, sexts & cyberspace: The constitutional implications of current sexting & cyberbullying laws, *William & Mary Bill of Rights Journal*, Vol. 20; pp. 1017, 2011.

20. I. Aleksander, Artificial neuroconsciousness an update, In: J. Mira, F. Sandoval (eds), *From Natural to Artificial Neural Computation, International Workshop on Artificial Neural Networks*, Lecture Notes in Computer Science, Springer, Berlin, Heidelberg, Vol. 930, pp. 566–583, 1995.

21. X. Cai, H. Ning, S. Dhelim, R. Zhou, T. Zhang, Y. Xu, and Y. Wan, Robot and its living space: A roadmap for robot development based on the view of living space, *Digital Communications and Networks*, 2020, https://doi.org/10.1016/j.dcan.2020.12.001.

22. R. W. Picard, Affective Computing for HCI, *HCI*, Vol. 1; pp. 829–833, 1999.

23. R. Chatila, E. Renaudo, and M. Andries, Toward self-aware robots, *Frontiers in Robotics and AI*, Vol. 5; pp. 88, 2018.

24. R. Kwiatkowski and H. Lipson, Task-agnostic self-modeling machines, *Science Robotics*, Vol. 4; No. 26, pp. 4, 2019.

25. H. Ning and F. Shi, Could robots be regarded as humans in future, *arXive-print*, arXiv: 2012.05054, 2020.

26. S. K. Card, T. P. Moran, and A. Newell, *The Psychology of Human-Computer Interaction*, CRC Press, United States, 1983.

27. L. J. Bannon, From human factors to human actors: The role of psychology and human-computer interaction studies in system design, *Readings in Human–Computer Interaction*, Morgan Kaufmann, pp. 205–214, 1995.

28. T. Ogata and S. Sugano, Emotional communication between humans and the autonomous robot which has the emotion model, *Proceedings 1999 IEEE International Conference on Robotics and Automation*, Vol. 4; pp. 3177–3182, 1999.

29. T. Kanda, H. Ishiguro, and T. Ishida, Psychological analysis on human-robot interaction, *Proceedings 2001 IEEE International Conference on Robotics and Automation*, Vol. 4; pp. 4166–4173, 2001.

30. A. Bauer, D. Wollherr, and M. Buss, Human–robot collaboration: A survey, *International Journal of Humanoid Robotics*, Vol. 5; No. 1, pp. 47–66, 2008.

31. J. Bütepage and D. Kragic, Human-robot collaboration: From psychology to social robotics, arXiv preprint, arXiv: 1705.10146, 2017.

32. A. Cangelosi and M. Schlesinger, From babies to robots: The contribution of developmental robotics to developmental psychology, *Child Development Perspectives*, Vol. 12; No. 3, pp. 183–188, 2018.

33. D. Haraway, A manifesto for cyborgs: Science, technology, and socialist feminism in the 1980s, *Australian Feminist Studies*, Vol. 2; No. 4, pp. 1–42, 1987.

34. S. Boschert and R. Rosen, Digital Twin—The Simulation Aspect, In: *Mechatronic Futures: Challenges and Solutions for Mechatronic Systems and their Designers*, P. Hehenberger, D. Bradley (eds), Springer International Publishing, Cham, pp. 59–74, 2016.

Chapter 8

The History of Gender Research in Cyberspace

8.1 Introduction

Gender refers to a series of characteristics of masculinity and femininity that is constructed by societies or cultures.[1] As a social construct, gender, different from sex as a kind of biological construct, is defined differently in societies and cultures. It represents people's expectations of male and female roles in their respective societies and cultures [1]. In real life, such gender roles are most directly reflected in a person's physical characteristics and behavior. When encountering a person, people will compare the person's physical characteristics and behavior with the culturally constructed expectations of gender categories and draw preliminary conclusions about his/her gender.[2] Therefore, physical characteristics and behavior are the main ways to distinguish genders in real life.

With the emergence of cyberspace, in Computer Media Communication (CMC), the body cannot be seen, and the physical existence and characteristics are not obvious. People can see only virtual characters. Therefore, what gender would be like in cyberspace has aroused a lot of people's thinking. In the early days of cyberspace, many people who had long been involved in network believed that cyberspace would become more egalitarian than the real world, in which characteristics such as gender that are classified based on physical bodies would be meaningless, and gender-based inequality would no longer exist [2]. This idea expresses the early people's hypothesis that there is no gender division in cyberspace, and also expresses people's expectations for gender equality in cyberspace, which seems

---

[1] https://www.who.int/health-topics/gender#tab=tab_1
[2] https://thalis.math.upatras.gr/~mboudour/articles/gender@cyberspace.html

DOI: 10.1201/9781003257387-8

difficult to be achieved in real life. In response to this view, an increasing number of scholars have begun to research the gender of humans in cyberspace. In addition, with machines, especially robots, gradually penetrating people's lives, the gender issue of machines has also aroused many scholars' discussions. This chapter focuses on the history of the research of human and machine gender in cyberspace.

8.2 Gender Research for Humans in Cyberspace

As mentioned above, in the early days of the Internet, people were full of expectations for cyberspace. However, this early utopian view was quickly changed. As early as 1992, Bruckman has presented identity and gender in the text-only environment of multiuser dungeon (MUD) [3], which showed that gender exists in cyberspace. In addition, scholars also pointed out that gender in cyberspace is an enacted, multiple, and fluid behavior [4], and gender-based discriminations still have persisted online [5]. Indeed, in this virtual world where no one knows who you are, people can "computer disguise" [6] to describe themselves and their gender in any way they like, whose cost is only using keystrokes and mouse clicks, and the next thing to consider is how to perform this role well. Similarly, if people have the time and energy to create, they can also perform multiple genders on the Internet and modify them at will. However, the most important reason why people can construct their gender so quickly is the convenient method of gender presentation in cyberspace.

In the early days of the Internet, people communicated in text-only social environments such as LambdaMOO, chatrooms, and MUD. It was common for users to invent nicknames and imagined personas. People could present their gender information depending on only one character [2,3]. In addition, one's identity and gender can also be expressed in some positions of the e-mail [7].

Nowadays, with the development of various applications on the Internet, there are more and more ways to present one's gender in cyberspace. In some social popular platforms such as Facebook and Twitter, people tend to present their identity and gender on these sites through their username, photographs, website, and other information about themselves [8]. In video games, especially massive multiplayer online role-playing games (MMORPG) (e.g., World of Warcraft, Final Fantasy, etc.), players can customize the faces, dresses, and actions of their virtual game characters, enabling players to show a masculine or feminine temperament [9].

Based on the gender constructed by people in cyberspace, scholars began to carry out a series of other researches on gender in cyberspace, including gender differences, gender swapping, gender prediction, etc.

8.2.1 Gender Differences in Cyberspace

Although gender differences in cyberspace have existed since the birth of the Internet, research on gender differences in cyberspace is relatively later. Because, in the early days of the Internet, the Internet was mainly developed by male scientists, mathematicians, highly skilled computer hackers, and few female participation [10].

With the continuous popularization of the Internet, women began to have widespread participation in online activities, and they gradually began to form two groups with men, but women still accounted for a minority. According to research [10] in 1996, nearly two-thirds of Internet users were males, accounting for 77% of total online time. At this time, most women had just come into contact with the Internet, while most men had been involved on the Internet for a long time. Therefore, gender differences in cyberspace during this period were mainly reflected in Internet attitudes, Internet use, and linguistic differences (It is the main method of predicting the real gender in cyberspace. The research on it will be explained later).

In the early days of the Internet, the main reason for the huge gap in the number of men and women Internet users was gender differences in attitudes and use of the Internet. In 1986, a study by Gilroy et al. showed that men were more relaxed when using a computer, while women were more anxious [11]. Similarly, the researchers found that men were more likely than women to use computers [12]. In 1997, another study also had found that men were more competent than women in most aspects of using the computer [13]. Although many of these studies were based on attitudes and use of computers, the same holds for the Internet. These early gender differences in use and attitudes are largely due to gender biases and stereotypes [10]. At that time, most people believed that the Internet was a highly technical male domain, and women who were slow to accept technology were not suitable for this field, which made the resistance of most women to the Internet. This stereotype also directly led to most of the software applications at the time were mainly aimed at men. For example, most children's computer games favor action, adventure, violence, and competition with male themes; only 23%–33% of computer games were sold to girls [10,14].

In the mid-1990s, the number of women using the Internet was significantly lower than men. But by the early 21st century, the gap in the number of Internet users was decreasing between genders, and the proportion of women among Internet users was steadily increasing, but the frequency and intensity of women using the Internet remained low [15]. Nowadays, the ratio of men and women on the Internet is almost evenly balanced in number, frequency, and intensity. Figure 8.1[3] indicates the ratio of American Internet users' number between men and women in the past 20 years. Meanwhile, since the beginning of the 21st century, there has been a general acceptance of attitudes toward the Internet and an increasing amount of people's online behavior. Scholars' research has gradually shifted from gender differences in Internet attitudes and uses to gender differences in online behavior. These gender differences in behavior are manifested in many aspects of the Internet, such as social media, online games, online dating, etc.

---

[3] https://www.statista.com/statistics/184415/percentage-of-us-adults-who-are-internet-users-by-gender/

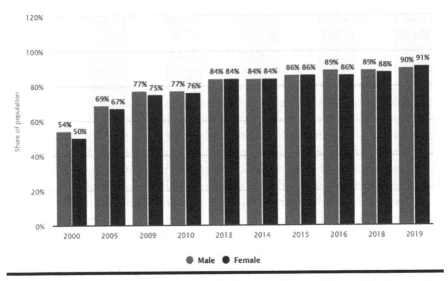

Figure 8.1 Internet usage penetration in the U.S. from 2000 to 2019, by gender.

Online social networking is the main online activity of most people, especially on some social platforms; different genders will show great differences. In 2009, Carstensen discussed the gender differences in blogs and found that the percentage of female authors was much higher than that of male authors, but most women wrote personal blogs while adult men wrote news-oriented blogs on "political" issues, resulting in a majority of the most-read bloggers being male. The main reason for this was the social stereotype that women are less suited to talking about politics [16]. In another 2012 study, Thompson et al. have researched the use of Facebook found that women were more likely than men to experience anxiety and depression, and this difference in anxiety and stress will directly lead to differences in the use of social media between genders [17]. In 2017, Biernatowska et al. found that women were more likely to indulge in Facebook than men [18].

In addition, online gaming is also a good place to research gender differences. In 2008, DiGiuseppe et al. explored characters in *World of Warcraft*. They found that consistent with stereotypes, women tended to choose ancillary occupations, while men were more likely to play melee warriors [19].

With the increasing social interaction in cyberspace, people tend to look for partners on the Internet. Interestingly, there are also gender differences in online dating behavior. In 2016, Abramova et al. made a comprehensive review from six aspects, namely, motivation, preferences, disclosure, misrepresentation, interaction, and outcome [20]. It is worth noting that both men and women were likely to distort their information online (e.g., women tended to underreport their weight and age, while men tended to emphasize personal interests and assets) to find a better match, which also reflected the differences in the preferences of men and women in online dating.

Briefly, gender differences in cyberspace are mostly caused by gender stereo-types. This stereotype can invisibly affect the use of the Internet or the behavior of different genders on the Internet. While restraining people in the network, this stereotype will also bring some gender prejudice and discrimination.

8.2.2 Gender Swapping Behavior in Cyberspace

Gender swapping (or Gender switching) is the behavior of Internet users who present gender in cyberspace differently from their real-life gender [21]. Scholars occasionally discovered this interesting phenomenon when studying the gender of humans in cyberspace. This phenomenon is very prominent in virtual social environments.

The results of early research are mostly negative. In 1993, Bruckman designed a pioneering case study in which a male MUD player adopted a female character and then observed his behavior on the Internet. The research had found that men who logged into MUD as female characters exhibited suggestive sexual behavior, which further encouraged players to engage in such sexual advances [21]. In the same year, Rheingold described online gender swapping behavior as gender deception in *The Virtual Community*. By using the example of Sue and Joan, Rheingold showed that CMC could not resist deception and called for the regulation of the online community to reduce the possibility of such deception [22]. Similarly, in 1997, Turkle also linked gender swapping and deception in his book *Life on the screen* [23]. In short, the freedom provided by the early Internet had made gender "problematized" and gender swapping had become a standard topic of online discussion. However, it is surprising that most of the early researches and discussions focused on controversial case, anecdotal data, or critical commentaries about limited data sets [24] and lack of research on women's online gender swapping behavior. As a result, most of the studies are relatively negative.

With the development of advanced information technology, there are more and more forms of communication in cyberspace, and gender swapping behavior on the Internet is becoming more and more common. People's attitude toward gender swapping is gradually neutral, and scholars also begin to explore the reasons for gender swapping with a neutral attitude. In 2004, Suler[4] conducted a comprehensive conceptual study of the possible causes of gender swapping. In 2006, Lee et al. pointed out that modern online games, especially MMORPGs, have high-quality graphical interfaces and encourage players to cooperate, which provided a better platform for gender swapping [25]. Some studies have found that gender swapping was common among both male and female players. In 2008, Hussain and Griffiths reported that 54% of male players and 68% of female players had attempted gender swapping [26]. There were also a series of explorations into the reasons for gender swapping in online games. Research had shown that most players chose a character of the opposite gender not necessarily to express their gender identity, but rather as a strategic choice [27]. For example, the majority of players thought that choosing a female might benefit from

---

[4] http://truecenterpublishing.com/psycyber/genderswap.html

other male players, or just for aesthetic or practical purposes [26–31]. Some players might be out for social purposes since women were easier to add friends [31]. Only a small number of people were looking for a partner because they were homosexual [30]. In 2017, Chou et al. used qualitative research methods to further explore gender exchange behavior to improve the richness of information. A comprehensive summary of the reasons for gender swapping in the game was conducted from six aspects: social interactions, harassment avoidance, gifts, fooling others, fantasy experiences, and playing superior avatars [32]. This research also confirms a large number of previous studies.

8.2.3 Gender Prediction in Cyberspace

The anonymity of the Internet hides people's physical features and strips them of their appearance cues, leaving them to express themselves through virtual information that may or may not be true. However, sometimes due to various reasons (e.g., to prevent identity deception, and gender deception), it is very important to understand the identity of their online conversation partners. This is especially true for gender because gender is the most basic classification of people, which is often linked by different norms, roles, and communication methods [33]. Therefore, how to determine the gender of participants in cyberspace was a problem worthy of research.

In the early text-only communication environment, the language of the interlocutor was the main clue to predict gender. Therefore, a large number of researches relating linguistic differences between the genders on the Internet have emerged. Much research had found differences between genders in language style, language content, and language attitude. For example, women were more likely than men to use emphatic adverbs, questions [34], and compliments [35]. In terms of language attitude, according to the research of Herring in 1994, women's language on the Internet would show an attitude of support and gratitude, while men's language would show an attitude of confrontation [36]. Early studies on gender prediction were also based on these linguistic differences. In 2001, Thomson and Murachver used language style to predict one's gender, and finally compared the predicted gender with the real gender, showing that it was possible to predict a gender by using gender differences in electronic language, and people were sensitive to these differences [37].

With the development of natural language processing technology and artificial intelligence (AI) algorithms, the prediction of gender has become more intelligent and more diverse. In 2011, Pennacchiotti et al. used machine learning to automatically infer a user's identity by leveraging observable information [38]. In 2013, Liu et al. used the users' names as the criterion to infer the users' gender in Twitter, developed a method to obtain the gender tags of Twitter users without analyzing the users' profiles or text contents, and established a large data set of gender tags [39]. In 2015, Merler et al. proposed a way to extract users' information (mainly gender information) from images posted on social media [40]. In 2019, Vicente et al. used multiple information sources including username, user description, tweet content, and profile picture to detect the gender of Twitter users, and the accuracy of detection was further improved [41].

8.3 Gender Research for Machines (Robots) in Cyberspace

In cyberspace, gender is not only a specific attribute of humans but it can also be given to machines by humans and given certain social attributes to machines. The gender of a robot has been considered by people in the early years, and this kind of considerations was mostly reflected in science fiction, movies, and comics. For example, Maria in the film *Metropolis* directed by Fritz Lang in 1927 was the first image of the female robot and one of the first depictions of robots.[5] A cute boy robot image Atom was created by Japanese physician and cartoonist Osamu Tezuka in 1951, and it has become the most famous robot [42].

With the creation of the world's first robot (especially humanoid robots), the discussion about the gender of a robot has gradually moved from literature to real life. Unlike literature, robot gender may contribute to gender inequality in society. Richardson et al. argued that robots were constructed in the image of male and female in patriarchal systems that could be abused by their owners in any way to further intensify gender injustice and inequality, even sexual violence [43]. But many roboticists believed that in a world full of gender norms, gender identities, and gender relations, it was reasonable to assign gender to robots when they were designed [44]. Not only do roboticists tend to assign gender to robots, but also users often try to assign genders to inanimate objects [44].

The question is how to determine the gender of a robot. Different roboticists have different strategies, either model robots as specific women or men, or giving them standardized and stereotypical gendered features. For example, Powers et al. divided the gender of a robot by voice ("feminine" voice and "masculine" voice) and lip color (pink is female, gray is male) [45], and Ishiguro was committed to model robots in real people, the robots he created always had realistic appearances [42]. Based on the previous research, in 2019, Schiebinger provided a comprehensive summary of the gender features of robots, assigning genders to robots based on voice, name, anatomy, color, and character [46,47]. All of these features were reflected in Pepper (a social robot produced by SoftBank of Japan).

8.3.1 Human–Robot Interaction

After entering the 21st century, a large number of robots have begun to be used in people's daily life, including home care, hospital health care, hotel services, entertainment, and teaching, etc. Humans and robots are interacting more and more frequently. Most of these robots have human features mentioned by Londa Schiebinger [46], such as voice and appearance. Therefore, to understand the interaction between robots and humans, a large number of researches on human–robot interaction (HRI) have been conducted, in which gender characteristics are one of

---

[5] https://io9.gizmodo.com/from-maria-to-ava-why-are-so-many-artificial-intellige-1699274487

the most important research contents in the process of HRI. As Jennifer Robertson pointed out, most of the studies on robot gender were related to HRI, more precisely (a) differences in interaction between humans and robots of different genders and (b) differences in interactions between humans of different genders and robots [42]. Although her observations were more than 10 years ago, the situation today looks the same [47].

Gender presentations will affect the interaction between humans. Whether the gender of a robot will affect the HRI has become a question worth thinking about. In 2013, Nomura and Hayata found that people often assigned gender to a robot (even if the robot was neutral), and that gender assignment also affected their behavior toward the robot, such as the number of smiles and the duration of interaction with the robot [48]. In another research, participants were asked to "clean" dust particles from virtual characters. Both male and female participants applied less force to female avatars than to the male avatars. They also used more force on the torso than they did on the face [46]. The above experiments show that people treat robots like humans, and the interaction between humans and robots is affected by the gender of the robot.

In addition, there are some differences in the interaction between people of different genders and robots, among which the most important difference is the attitude of men and women towards robots. According to a 2006 social survey conducted by Nomura et al., women had a more negative attitude toward robots [49]. At the same time, a large number of studies also showed that men were more positive than women about the use of robots in life. In 2009, Kuo et al. found that men were more positive about the use of medical robots in the future [50]. Similarly, in 2012, Lin et al. found that men were more likely to use robots in education. These researches showed that men had a more positive attitude toward robots and were more willing to use them in their daily lives [51]. Another very meaningful question is whether men and women interact more efficiently with robots of the same gender or opposite gender. In order to explore this issue, in 2009, Siegel et al. designed an experiment. Participants donated money to robots of different genders to determine their gender preferences of robots. Experimental results showed that people were more inclined to think robots of the opposite gender more credible [52]. In 2014, in an experiment by Alexander et al., participants were asked to work with robots to solve puzzles. Experimental results also showed that interacting with robots of the opposite gender would make people feel more comfortable and the efficiency of cooperation would be higher [53].

8.3.2 *Stereotypes and Robot Gender*

It is well known that human beings have some stereotypes about gender, and these stereotypes can arouse expectations about other people's roles and behavior when interacting with them. So, does this stereotype exist among robots of different genders?

In order to solve this problem, in 2012, Eyssel et al. designed an experiment about identifying the gender of a robot based on facial features (simple change through hair change). Most participants assumed that the robot with short hair would be male, while the robot with long hair would be female [54]. This experiment suggested that the stereotype, a social bias in humans, also applied to robots. This stereotype can also lead to gender differences in robot careers. In 2014, Tay et al. investigated the impact of robot gender and robot occupational roles. The results suggested that stereotypes would determine the careers of robots of different genders [55], for example, using male robots in security and female robots in medicine.

Although the genders of robots satisfying stereotypes could make them more acceptable, the stereotype is inherently a kind of gender bias. Designing robots that conforms to stereotypes can exacerbate this gender bias and inequality. To avoid this robot stereotype, Schiebinger proposes several options for achieving greater gender equality in robots [46]: (a) challenging current gender stereotypes; (b) designing a customizable robot, users can choose among them; (c) designing "genderless" robots; (d) out of human social relations; (e) designing gender fluid robots; (f) designing a special gender for robots.

8.4 Discussion

No matter in the process of studying the gender of people or machines in cyberspace, it is not difficult for us to find that cyberspace is full of gender inequality. And this inequality will be further expanded by the anonymity, virality, and prohibition of cyberspace, and even evolve into gender-based cyber violence when women participate in online activities [56].

According to a survey conducted by the United Nations in 2015, the prevalence of online violence was higher than offline, because about 73% of women have been exposed to or experienced some form of online violence.[6] This gender-based violence includes the abuse of technology to carry out online aggression, deception or surveillance against women, or negative comments, ridicule, sexual suggestion, and harassment of women when they post content on the Internet, which cause great harm to women. In order to fight against such inequality online and the patriarchy, online feminists have emerged. While the Internet has exacerbated gender inequality, it has also provided feminists with the most appropriate platform for pursuing gender equality, which unites feminists closely. At this time, the Internet is interpreted as a medium, not a technology. They published feminist theories and insights in the medium of the Internet, spreading this concept of gender equality widely [16]. Unfortunately, although the online environment provides opportunities to express

---

[6] http://www2.unwomen.org/-/media/headquarters/attachments/sections/library/publications/2015/cyber_violence_gender%20report.pdf?v=1&d=20150924T151535

and expose feminist ideas, the online environment also provides opportunities to spread responses that maintain the status quo through attacks, censorship, and ridicule. In research, it was found that the phenomenon of distorting feminist perspectives and denying gender discrimination to discredit feminism and perpetuate inequality still existed on the Internet [56]. In addition, stereotypes about robots could also reflect many inequalities against women [55].

Therefore, there is still a long way to go before people can achieve gender equality. Creating a gender-equal world still requires people's joint efforts both online and offline. For this reason, a large number of organizations related to gender equality are constantly striving for gender equality, as shown in Table 8.1.

Table 8.1 Organizations Related to Gender Equality

Organizations	Year	Description
Plan International	1937s	Committed to the promotion of children's rights, especially the equal rights of girls
International Center for Research on Women	1976s	Committed to empower women, advance gender equality and fight poverty in the developing world
Match International Women's Fund	1976s	Committed to match the needs and resources of women around the world
Association for Women's Rights in Development	1982s	Committed to achieving gender equality, sustainable development and women's human rights
International Women's Development Agency	1985s	Committed to address poverty and oppression in developing countries and create positive change for women and their communities
Global Fund for Women	1987s	Committed to fund women's initiatives around the world
Global Fund for Women	1987s	Committed to fund women's initiatives around the world
Women's Refugee Commission	1989s	Committed to improve the lives of displaced women, propose possible solutions, and advocate for policies that benefit women and children
Equality Now	1992s	Committed to the use of law advocacy, protection and promotion of women's rights

(Continued)

Table 8.1   Organizations Related to Gender Equality

Organizations	Year	Description
Women for Women International	1993s	To address the rights of the most marginalized groups of women in countries or regions affected by war and conflict
World Pulse	2003s	Use social media and new technologies to advocate for women's rights and help train and educate women on the use of digital media
UN Women	2010s	Committed to gender equality, women lead, income security, and from all forms of violence

8.5 Conclusion

This chapter mainly introduces the brief history of gender researches in cyberspace. Although cyberspace is a new electronic space, it is still an extension of real space. It only provides humans with new living space from the technical level, and it cannot fundamentally change people's gender relations and gender stereotypes. In real life, gender inequality, especially inequality for women, is also mapped to cyberspace. But at the same time, the Internet also provides a good platform for promoting gender equality and researching gender relations. Therefore, it is necessary to explore the research history of gender in cyberspace.

References

1. J. M. O'Neil, Patterns of gender role conflict and strain: Sexism and fear of femininity in men's lives, *The Personnel and Guidance Journal*, Vol. 60; No. 4, pp. 203–210, 1981.
2. L. Kendall, Meaning and identity in "cyberspace": The performance of gender, class, and race online, *Symbolic Interaction*, Vol. 21; No. 2, pp. 129–153, 1998.
3. A. Bruckman, Identity workshop: Emergent social and psychological phenomena in text-based virtual reality, 1992, http://citeseerx.ist.psu.edu/viewdoc/download; jsessionid=6F4C02A509EAD536755070DA934FB164?doi=10.1.1.124.9888&rep= rep1&type=pdf.
4. M. Flanagan, Navigating the narrative in space: Gender and spatiality in virtual worlds, *Art Journal*, Vol. 59; No. 3, pp. 74–85, 2000.
5. N. McCormick and J. Leonard, Gender and sexuality in the cyberspace frontier, *Women & Therapy*, Vol. 19; No. 4, pp. 109–119, 1996.
6. S. Turkle, Constructions and reconstructions of self in virtual reality: Playing in the MUDs, *Mind, Culture, and Activity*, Vol. 1; No. 3, pp. 158–167, 1994.
7. J. S. Donath, Identity and deception in the virtual community, In: *Communities in Cyberspace*, P. Kollock, M. Smith (eds), Routledge, UK, 1998.

8. S. C. Herring and S. Kapidzic, Teens, gender, and self-presentation in social media, *International Encyclopedia of Social and Behavioral Sciences*, Vol. 2; pp. 1–16, 2015.

9. L. Eklund, Doing gender in cyberspace: The performance of gender by female World of Warcraft players, *Convergence*, Vol. 17; No. 3, pp. 323–342, 2011.

10. J. Morahan-Martin, The gender gap in Internet use: Why men use the Internet more than women—a literature review, *Cyberpsychology & Behavior*, Vol. 1; No. 1, pp. 3–10, 1998.

11. F. D. Gilroy and H. B. Desai, Computer anxiety: Sex, race and age, *International Journal of Man-Machine Studies*, Vol. 25; No. 6, pp. 711–719, 1986.

12. G. Wilder, D. Mackie, and J. Cooper, Gender and computers: Two surveys of computer-related attitudes, *Sex Roles*, Vol. 13; No. 3, pp. 215, 1985.

13. L. Shashaani, Gender differences in computer attitudes and use among college students, *Journal of Educational Computing Research*, Vol. 16; No. 1, pp. 7–51, 1997.

14. M. D. Griffiths, Are computer games bad for children? *The Psychologist: Bulletin of the British Psychological Society*, Vol. 6; pp. 401–407, 1993.

15. H. Ono and M. Zavodny, Gender and the internet, *Social Science Quarterly*, Vol. 84; No. 1, pp. 111–121, 2003.

16. T. Carstensen, Gender Trouble in Web 2.0. Gender perspectives on social network sites, wikis and weblogs, *International Journal of Gender, Science and Technology*, Vol. 1; No. 1, 2009.

17. S. H. Thompson and E. Lougheed, Frazzled by Facebook? An exploratory study of gender differences in social network communication among undergraduate men and women, *College Student Journal*, Vol. 46; No. 1, pp. 88–99, 2012.

18. A. Biernatowska, J. M. Balcerowska, and P. Bereznowski, Gender differences in using facebook—preliminary analysis, In: J. Nyćkowiak and J. Leśny (eds.), *Badania i Rozwój Młodych Naukowców w Polsce – Społeczeństwo: psychologia i socjologia, Poznań, Poland: Młodzi Naukowcy*, pp. 13–18, 2017.

19. N. DiGiuseppe and B. Nardi, Real Genders Choose Fantasy Characters: Class Choice in World of Warcraft, *First Monday*, Vol. 12; No. 5, 2007, https://doi.org/10.5210/fm.v12i5.1831.

20. O. Abramova, A. Baumann, H. Krasnova, and P. Buxmann, Gender differences in online dating: What do we know so far? A systematic literature review, In *2016 49th Hawaii International Conference on System Sciences (HICSS)*, IEEE, Koloa, HI, USA, pp. 3858–3867, 2016.

21. A. Bruckman, Gender swapping on the Internet, *High Noon on the Electronic Frontier: Conceptual Issues in Cyberspace*, P. Ludlow (eds), MIT Press, United States, pp. 317–326, 1996.

22. H. Rheingold, *The Virtual Community: Finding Commection in a Computerized World*, Addison-Wesley Longman Publishing Co., Inc., UK, 1993.

23. S. Turkle, Life on the screen: Identity in the age of the internet, *Literature and History*, Vol. 6; pp. 117–118, 1997.

24. L. D. Roberts and M. R. Parks, The social geography of gender-switching in virtual environments on the internet, *Information, Communication & Society*, Vol. 2; No. 4, pp. 521–540, 1999.

25. J. J. Lee and C. M. Hoadley, Online identity as a leverage point for learning in Massively Multiplayer Online Role Playing Games (MMORPGs), In *Sixth IEEE International Conference on Advanced Learning Technologies (ICALT'06)*, IEEE, Kerkrade, Netherlands, pp. 761–763, 2006.

26. Z. Hussain and M. D. Griffiths, Gender swapping and socializing in cyberspace: An exploratory study, *Cyberpsychology & Behavior*, Vol. 11; No. 1, pp. 47–53, 2008.
27. R. M. Martey, J. Stromer-Galley, J. Banks, J. Wu, and M. Consalvo, The strategic female: Gender-switching and player behavior in online games. Information, *Communication & Society*, Vol. 17; No. 3, pp. 286–300, 2014.
28. M. Boler, Hypes, hopes and actualities: New digital Cartesianism and bodies in cyberspace, *New Media & Society*, Vol. 9; No. 1, pp. 139–168, 2007.
29. N. Yee, Maps of digital desires: Exploring the topography of gender and play in online games, In: *Beyond Barbie and Mortal Kombat: New Perspectives on Gender and Gaming*, Y. B. Kafai, C. Heeter, J. Denner, and J. Y. Sun (eds), The MIT Press, UK, pp. 83–96, 2008.
30. S. Huh and D. Williams, Dude looks like a lady: Gender swapping in an online game. In: W. Bainbridge (eds), *Online Worlds: Convergence of the Real and the Virtual*, Human-Computer Interaction Series, Springer, London, 2010.
31. P. C. H. Paik and C. K. Shi, Playful gender swapping: User attitudes toward gender in MMORPG avatar customization, *Digital Creativity*, Vol. 24; No. 4, pp. 310–326, 2013.
32. Y. J. Chou, S. K. Lo, and C. I. Teng, Reasons for avatar gender swapping by online game players: A qualitative interview-based study, In: *Discrimination and Diversity: Concepts, Methodologies, Tools, and Applications*, Information resources management association, IGI Global, United States, pp. 202–219, 2017.
33. S. C. Herring and A. Martinson, Assessing gender authenticity in computer-mediated language use: Evidence from an identity game, *Journal of Language and Social Psychology*, Vol. 23; No. 4, pp. 424–446, 2004.
34. J. R. McMillan, A. K. Clifton, D. McGrath, and W. S. Gale, Women's language: Uncertainty or interpersonal sensitivity and emotionality? *Sex Roles*, Vol. 3; No. 6, pp. 545–559, 1977.
35. J. Holmes, Paying compliments: A sex-preferential politeness strategy, *Journal of Pragmatics*, Vol. 12; No. 4, pp. 445–465, 1988.
36. S. Herring, Gender differences in computer-mediated communication: Bringing familiar baggage to the new frontier. *American Library Association Annual Convention*, Miami Beach, FL, Vol. 27; 1994.
37. R. Thomson and T. Murachver, Predicting gender from electronic discourse, *British Journal of Social Psychology*, Vol. 40; No. 2, pp. 193–208, 2001.
38. M. Pennacchiotti and A. M. Popescu, A machine learning approach to twitter user classification, In: *Proceedings of the International AAAI Conference on Web and Social Media (ICWSM)*, Barcelona, Catalonia, Spain, Vol. 5; No. 1, pp. 281–288, 2011.
39. W. Liu and D. Ruths, What's in a name? Using first names as features for gender inference in twitter, In *2013 AAAI Spring Symposium Series*, North America, pp. 10–16, 2013.
40. M. Merler, L. Cao, and J. R. Smith, You are what you tweet…pic! Gender prediction based on semantic analysis of social media images, In *2015 IEEE International Conference on Multimedia and Expo (ICME)*, Turin, pp. 1–6, 2015.
41. M. Vicente, F. Batista, and J. P. Carvalho, Gender detection of Twitter users based on multiple information sources, In *Interactions Between Computational Intelligence and Mathematics Part 2*, Springer, Cham, pp. 39–54, 2019.
42. J. Robertson, Gendering humanoid robots: Robo-sexism in Japan, *Body & Society*, Vol. 16; No. 2, pp. 1–36, 2010.

43. A. Cranny-Francis, Is data a toaster? Gender, sex, sexuality and robots, *Palgrave Communications*, Vol. 2; No. 1, pp. 1–6, 2016.

44. J. Carpenter, J. M. Davis, N. Erwin-Stewart, T. R. Lee, J. D. Bransford, and N. Vye, Gender representation and humanoid robots designed for domestic use, *International Journal of Social Robotics*, Vol. 1; No. 3, pp. 261, 2009.

45. A. Powers, A. D. Kramer, S. Lim, J. Kuo, S. L. Lee, and S. Kiesler, Eliciting information from people with a gendered humanoid robot, In *ROMAN 2005. IEEE International Workshop on Robot and Human Interactive Communication*, Nashville, TN, USA, pp. 158–163, 2005.

46. https://web.stanford.edu/dept/HPS/Schiebinger%20AWIS%20Robots%202019.pdf.

47. A. Pillinger, Literature review: Gender and robotics, 2019, http://www.geecco-project. eu/fileadmin/t/geecco/Literatur/neu/Neu_30062020/Literatur_Review_Gender_ and_Robotics.pdf.

48. T. Nomura and K. Hayata, Influences of gender values into interaction with agents: An experiment using a small-sized robot, In: iHAI 2013: 1st international conference on human–agent interaction, Sapporo, Japan, 2013. Online document at: http://hai-conference.net/ ihai2013/proceedings/pdf/I-3-3.pdf.

49. T. Nomura, T. Suzuki, T. Kanda, and K. Kato, Measurement of negative attitudes toward robots, *Interaction Studies*, Vol. 7; No. 3, pp. 437–454, 2006.

50. I. H. Kuo, J. M. Rabindran, E. Broadbent, Y. I. Lee, N. Kerse, R. M. Q. Stafford, and B. A. MacDonald, Age and gender factors in user acceptance of healthcare robots, In *RO-MAN 2009, The 18th IEEE International Symposium on Robot and Human Interactive Communication*, Toyama, Japan, pp. 214–219, 2009.

51. C. H. Lin, E. Z. F. Liu, and Y. Y. Huang, Exploring parents' perceptions towards educational robots: Gender and socio-economic differences, *British Journal of Educational Technology*, Vol. 43; No. 1, pp. 31–34, 2012.

52. M. Siegel, C. Breazeal, and M. I. Norton, Persuasive robotics: The influence of robot gender on human behavior, In *2009 IEEE/RSJ International Conference on Intelligent Robots and Systems*, St. Louis, MO, USA, pp. 2563–2568, 2009.

53. E. Alexander, C. Bank, J. J. Yang, B. Hayes, and B. Scassellati, Asking for help from a gendered robot, *Proceedings of the Annual Meeting of the Cognitive Science Society*, Vol. 36; No. 36, pp. 2333–2338, 2014.

54. F. Eyssel and F. Hegel, (S)he's got the look: Gender stereotyping of robots 1, *Journal of Applied Social Psychology*, Vol. 42; No. 9, pp. 2213–2230, 2012.

55. B. Tay, Y. Jung, and T. Park, When stereotypes meet robots: The double-edge sword of robot gender and personality in human–robot interaction, *Computers in Human Behavior*, Vol. 38; pp. 75–84, 2014.

56. A. J. Rodríguez-Darias and L. Aguilera-Ávila, Gender-based harassment in cyberspace. The case of Pikara magazine, In *Women's Studies International Forum*, Vol. 66; pp. 63–69, 2018.

Chapter 9

Taking a Glimpse through the Future of Cyberethics

9.1 Introduction

Modern information technology improves people's quality of life and changes their traditional notions of life, bringing about profound changes at the cultural level. As information technology complicates the original social relationship, it causes a series of cyberethics issues. Scholars have begun studying cyberethics firstly proposed by Nobert Wiener, trying to connect with emerging technologies with ethics to propose cyberspace principles.

9.2 The Origin and Development of Cyberethics

Cyberethics can be defined as a field of applied ethics that studies the morality, legal, and social issues in the development and use of cyber technology. There are terms similar to cyberethics, including computer ethics and information ethics. According to Spinello and Tavani [1], computer ethics merely studies the ethical issues relating to computer machines and computing professions, while cyberethics is more comprehensive and profound. Besides, compared with cyberethics that specifically studies information pertaining to networks, the term information ethics is too general. Therefore, cyberethics is a more exact term when it comes to the morality, legal, and social issues in cyberspace.

The source of cyberethics problems is social and technical. On the one hand, there are conflicts between network ethics and traditional ethics, so it is challenging to use existing ethical theories to solve network ethics problems. On the other hand,

DOI: 10.1201/9781003257387-9

problems are more likely to happen due to the characteristics of cyberspace and cyber technology, such as anonymity, reproducibility of information, and lack of laws.

9.3 Studies on Cyberethics

Scholars conduct studies on cyberethics, while institutions set regulations and codes to restrain actions in cyberspace.

9.3.1 Scholars

Scholars have been studying cyberethics and its original form, computer ethics, for decades. In the early 1940s, Nobert Wiener proposed computer ethics [1]. After combining the concept of cyberethics with digital computers, he proposed ethical conclusions relating to information and communication technology (ICT) and foresaw social and ethical issues. In 1950, Wiener published the book *The Human Use of Human Beings* [2], establishing himself as the founder of computer theory. In the mid-sixties, Dohn Parker studied cybercrime and unethical online behavior and published *Rules of ethics in information processing*. Since then, he has been devoted to disseminating computer ethics, and it became a hot topic. Parker is the second person after Wiener to make a considerable contribution to computer ethics.

In 1964, Joseph Weizenbaum created a computer project ELIZA. In 1966, he perfectly simulated a psychotherapist with a computer, making many people think that computers can replace humans. To oppose the idea that humans are just machines for processing information, he published his masterpiece *Computer power and human reason* in the early 1970s. His follow-up research has led to many computer theories and projects. In the mid-1970s, Walter Maner began to use the term computer theory to refer to applied ethics to solve the ethical problems spawned by computer technology. He opened in the university a computer theory course that influenced computer theory education in the U.S.

In the 1980s, computer ethics became in the U. S. and the UK a public issue that attracted much attention from scholars. James Moor published *What is computer ethics*; Deborah Johnson publishes *Computer ethics*; in 1987, Terrell Ward Bynum established the "Computation and Social Research Center"; in 1988, the first international conference on computer theory was held; in the 1990s, computer ethics spread to other countries and Simon Rogerson and Bynum established the "Computing and Social Responsibility Center" and held many meetings.

In 1986, Mason [3] divided cyber ethical problems into four types and summarized them with an acronym: PAPA (see Table 9.1).

In 1997, Johnson [4] proposed three characteristics of the network: scope, anonymity, and reproducibility. They lead to the emergence of online problems. He suggested that a principle should be established and that all online forums should make their rules explicit and specify the consequences of any violation.

Table 9.1   PAPA Issues

PAPA	Content
Privacy	What information about one's self or one's associations must a person reveal to others, under what conditions and with what safeguards? What things can people keep to themselves and not be forced to reveal to others?
Accuracy	Who is responsible for the authenticity, fidelity, and accuracy of information? Similarly, who is to be held accountable for errors in information and how can the injured party be compensated?
Property	Who owns information? What are the just and fair prices for its exchange? Who owns the channels, especially the airways, through which information is transmitted? How should access to this scarce resource be allocated?
Accessibility	What information does a person or an organization have a right or a privilege to obtain, under what conditions, and with what safeguards?

Besides, individuals should follow the general principles as follows: know the rules of forums, respect the privacy and property of others, and respect the people who communicate with you.

In 1998, James Moor [5] proposed two characteristics of computer ethics, policy vacuum and conceptual confusion. He thought that they prevent us from judging properly the nature of things online in many cases. More believes that we should respect others' core values (ability and freedom) and look at policies from a proper perspective. In 2000, Brey [6] proposed revealing computer ethics, which is complementary to mainstream computer theories. He believed that revealing computer theory should be multilevel, interdisciplinary, and divided into revealing level, theoretical level, and application level. In 2001, Alison Adam [7,8] believed that feminist ethics could provide a more collectivistic approach to computer ethics. In 2004, Johnson [9] believed that computer ethics issues could be organized according to ethical theories and topics. He divided computer ethics issues into meta-theoretical, methodological issues, and emerging issues.

Computer ethics has also attracted much attention in educational theory. In 2005, Baum [10] discussed network ethics problems in school education, aiming to point out and answer students' and educators' vague network ethics problems. In 2006, Quinn [11] believed that it would be beneficial to teach computer theories in a computer science course. He enumerated the topics that the computer ethics course could cover and made suggestions for the course. In 2008, Maslin Masrom and Zuraini Ismail [12] investigated some college students' computer theory and security awareness. He found that the computer ethics awareness of computer majors was slightly higher than that of other majors. In 2009, Kuzu [13] surveyed computer ethics issues. Participants were ICT students and practitioners. The research content is to allow participants to put forward the sources and solutions of computer theory problems.

More and more social issues are driving scholars to study computer ethics. In 2010, Spinello [14] examined the social costs and ethical issues caused by the technology supported by cyberspace and stimulated readers to rethink cyber governance. He focused on four areas: content control, freedom of speech, intellectual property rights, privacy, and security. In 2011, Pusey and Sadera [15] tested whether teachers are aware of their ability to model and teach online ethics knowledge. They have concluded that teachers have limited knowledge of network ethics and suggested that teachers raise their ethical awareness in the teaching process. In 2012, Norshidah Mohamed, Nor Shahriza Abdul Karim, and Ramlah Hussein [12] studied the relationship between personal characteristics (gender, religion, organization level) and computer ethics use. The research would make people more aware of computer abuse and provide preventive measures. In 2014, Kizza through a study of the relationship between cybersecurity and cyberethics discussed cyber vandalism, cybercrime, cyberspace infrastructure, information security protocols, etc.

9.3.2 Institutions

Institutions worldwide will convene relevant associations to study online ethics and formulate a series of rules to regulate online behavior.

Much current thinking on informational privacy issues is based on the Code of Fair Information Practices, developed by the U. S. Deptartment of Health and Education in 1973. It is based on five principles outlining the requirements for records keeping systems (see Figure 9.1):

In January 1989, the Internet Architecture Board (IAB) in RFC 1087 defined the following activities as unethical and unacceptable (see Figure 9.2):

1)There must be no personal data record-keeping systems whose very existence is secret.

2)There must be a way for a person to find out what information about the person is in a record and how it is used.

3)There must be a way for a person to prevent information about the person that was obtained for one purpose from being used or made available for other purposes without the person's consent.

4)There must be a way for a person to correct or amend a record of identifiable information about the person.

5)Any organization creating, maintaining, using, or disseminating records of identifiable personal data must assure the data's reliability for their intended use and must take precautions to prevent misuses of the data.

Figure 9.1 The code of fair information practices.

1)Seeks to gain unauthorized access to the resources of the Internet.

2)Wastes resources (people, capacity, computer) through such actions.

3)Destroys the integrity of computer-based information, or

4)Compromises the privacy of users.

Figure 9.2   The Internet Architecture Board (IAB) in RFC 1087.

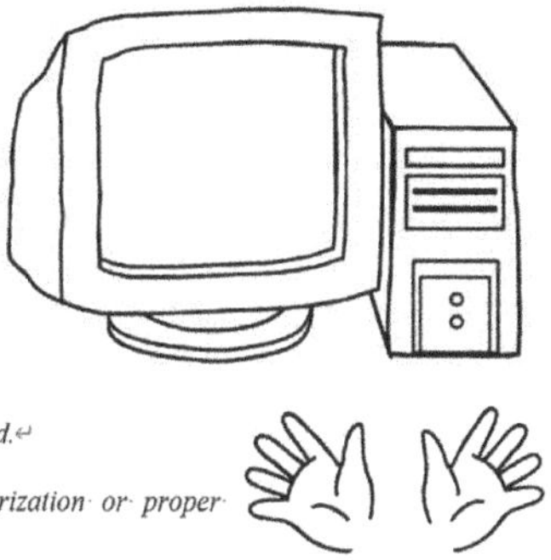

1) Thou shalt not use a computer to harm other people.

2)Thou shalt not interfere with other people's computer work.

3)Thou shalt not snoop around in other people's computer files.

4)Thou shalt not use a computer to steal.

5)Thou shalt not use a computer to bear false witness.

6)Thou shalt not copy or use proprietary software for which you have not paid.

7)Thou shalt not use other people's computer resources without authorization or proper

compensation.

8)Thou shalt not appropriate other people's intellectual output.

9)Thou shalt think about the social consequences of the program you are writing or the system

you are designing.

10)Thou shalt always use a computer in ways that ensure consideration and respect for your fellow

humans.

Figure 9.3   The ten commandments of computer ethics.

The *Ten Commandments of Computer Ethics* was proposed in 1992 by the Computer Ethics Institute (see Figure 9.3).

The University of Southern California statement on Internet Ethics identifies six types of unethical behavior on the Internet (see Figure 9.4):

9.4 The Future Studies on Cyberethics

By analyzing the characteristics of cyberethics, cyberethics will develop in the following directions.

9.4.1 Based on the New Information Technologies

When mentioning new information technology, artificial intelligence (AI) is one of the most significant ones. AI will reshape productivity, relations of production and modes of production, and reconstruct social relations and lifestyles. The discrimination created by AI algorithms is subtle and far-reaching.

1)Intentional disruption of network traffic or unauthorized entry into a network and its associated systems;

2)Commercial or deceptive use of university computer resources;

3)Stealing data, equipment, or intellectual property;

4)Access to other people's documents without permission;

5)Engage in disruptive or disruptive behavior in a public user setting;

6)Forging email messages.

Figure 9.4   The University of Southern California.

The asymmetry and opacity of information as well as the inevitable knowledge and technology threshold of information technology will objectively lead to and aggravate the phenomenon and trend that violates the principles of social equity, such as the information barrier and the digital divide. How to narrow the digital divide to improve the overall welfare of human beings and ensure social equity is a problem of ethical value with worldwide significance.

According to Miroslav Vacura [16], new information technologies, such as new electrical sensors, virtual currencies, and advanced AI, will challenge cyberspace and its users.

9.4.2 Based on Legislations and Globalization

Shrearer suggests that the goal is to develop a minimal Cyber Ethic concept that can be accepted by all the people, and the immediate strategy for an ethical Internet community is to realize an optimal Internet infrastructure and to provide leadership in the global internet to coordinate policy-making processes. Legislation about issues such as Cryptography, copyright censorship, software patents, privacy universal access, and content provision should be acted [16].

Spinello views online legislation as a struggle between governments and the Internet. The center of the struggle is the code of cyberspace. Compared with laws, regulations, or markets, network legislation is a more effective constraint. One can envision many possibilities on both sides when using that code to gain control. For example, the Internet's architectures currently facilitate electronic anonymity, but governments could respond by requiring people to mandate digital identity before one can even enter cyberspace [14].

9.4.3 Based on Intercultural Communications

In his keynote speech "Cross-Cultural Information Ethics", Rafael Capurro [17] pointed out that if we try to establish a real dialog on moral values in cyberspace, we cannot just confine ourselves to our cultural traditions. For example, the reasons for the

Chinese and Indians studying ethics to solve their ethical dilemmas may be the same or different from that in Western society. For proper cross-cultural information ethics, we must take both multiple cultures in the world and their historical traditions seriously.

By summarizing the history of studies on cyberethics, we make it more transparent in mind what cyberethics is about and how it will develop. Cyberethics is essential because we human beings are the only link between cyberspace and the physical world. Using cyberspace correctly and avoiding unethical behaviors are the best ways to keep the Internet safe.

References

1. G. E. Gorman, Readings in cyberethics, *Online Information Review*, Vol. 28; No. 2, pp. 165–166, 2004.
2. N. Wiener, *The Human use of Human Beings: Cyberethics and Society*, Da Capo Press, United States, 1988.
3. R. O. Mason, Four ethical issues of the information age, *MIS Quarterly*, Vol. 10, No. 1, pp. 5–12, 1986.
4. D. G. Johnson, Ethics online, *Communications of the ACM*, Vol. 40; No. 1, pp. 60–65, 1997.
5. J. H. Moor, Reason, relativity, and responsibility in computer ethics, *ACM SIGCAS Computers and Society*, Vol. 28; No. 1, pp. 14–21, 1998.
6. B. Philip, Disclosive computer ethics, *ACM SIGCAS Computers and Society*, Vol. 30; No. 4, pp. 10–16, 2000.
7. A. Alison, Computer ethics in a different voice, *Information and Organization*, Vol. 11; No. 4, pp. 235–261, 2001.
8. A. Adam, *Gender, Ethics and Information Technology*, Palgrave Macmillan, UK, 2005.
9. D. G. Johnson, Computer ethics, In: *The Blackwell Guide to the Philosophy of Computing and Information*, John Wiley & Sons, USA, pp. 65–75, 2004.
10. J. J. Baum, Cyberethics: The new frontier, *TechTrends*, Vol. 49; No. 6, pp. 54, 2005.
11. J. Q. Michael, On teaching computer ethics within a computer science department, *Science and Engineering Ethics*, Vol. 12; No. 2, pp. 335–343, 2006.
12. M. Maslin, I. Zuraini, Computer security and computer ethics awareness: A component of management information system, *2008 International Symposium on Information Technology, IEEE*, Kuala Lumpur, Malaysia, Vol. 3; pp. 1–20, 2008.
13. A. Kuzu, Problems related to computer ethics: Origins of the problems and suggested solutions, *Turkish Online Journal of Educational Technology*, Vol. 8; No. 2, pp. 1–20, 2009.
14. R. Spinello, *Cyberethics: Morality and Law in Cyberspace*, Jones & Bartlett Learning, Burlington, Massachusetts, 2010.
15. P. Pusey and W. A. Sadera, Cyberethics, cybersafety, and cybersecurity: Preservice teacher knowledge, preparedness, and the need for teacher education to make a difference, *Journal of Digital Learning in Teacher Education*, Vol. 28; No. 2, pp. 82–85, 2011.
16. J. A. Shearer, *Cyber Ethics: Communications Principles and Policies of the Internet*, PhD Dissertation, University of Auckland, 1999.
17. T. Froehlich, *A Brief History of Information Ethics*, Bid Textos Universitaris De Biblioteconomia I Documentació, Kent State Univeristy, Vol. 13; No. 12, pp. 11–25, 2004.

Chapter 10

Cyber-Religion: Past, Present, and Future

10.1 Introduction

The transmission, freedom, real-time, exchange, sharing, openness, and other characteristics of the Internet have formed a unique virtual space, which is intertwined with the real space, affecting and changing the entire social economic phenomenon and operating mechanism.

The Internet has promoted the emergence of new religious expressions – cyber-religion. To meet the needs of cyberspace reality, many traditional forms of religion have established online religious communities represented by online mosques, online ceremonies (e.g., electronic prayers and virtual pilgrimages), and online Muslims. And the new religious space produced under the "Internet Plus Initiative" has had an important influence on religion, religious organizations, believers, and society. The research of cyber-religion has become the focus of scholars.

According to the literatures published in the recent 20 years about cyber-religion, this chapter gives a comprehensive overview of the course, hot issues, and methods, and expounds the history and research track of cyber-religion via literature analysis and inductive analysis.

DOI: 10.1201/9781003257387-10

10.2 Cyber-Religion and its History, Research Trajectory, and Perspectives

10.2.1 History of Cyber-Religion

The Internet emerged in the 1980s, which has been used as a space for spiritual ceremonies and discussion of traditional religious beliefs. Rheingold's studies showed that the original religion-oriented online activities took place in the BBS called CommuniTree in the mid-1980s. According to the Rhineland expedition, soon religious sections spread to BBS, such as, Orthodox Christian BBS, Corpus Christi BBS, and so on. During this period, people began to use the Internet as a new tool for expressing religious opinions.

In the 1990s, many church, such as Catholicism, Christianity, Judaism, Islam, Hinduism, and Buddhism, began to use the Internet as a media tool to preach and organize its congregation, and set up their websites, as shown in Table 10.1.

10.2.2 Research Trajectory

Since the mid-1990s, cyber-religion has attracted the attention of theoretical researchers and religious practitioners, and has formed different research topics and methods. Pioneering studies, such as O'Leary and Brasher (1996), explored how religion began to be affected in the cyber environment and the specific manifestations of cyber-religion [1]. Later, some researchers began to focus on describing the general phenomenon of cyber-religion, analyzing the relationship

Table 10.1 Websites or Electronic Resources Created by Sects in the 1990s

Year	Website Content/ Meaning	Website	Name of Website/Alias
1992	Virtual Christian association	www.godweb.org	Cyberspace first church
1993	Judaism	www.h-net.org/ judaic/	H-Judaic
1996	First monastery website	www.christ-desert. org	Christian abbey in the desert
	First Islamic electronic journal	www.renaissance. com. Pk	Revival: Monthly Islamic journal
	The first online temple in Zoroaster	www.zarathushtra. com	Journal
	Salute people and pets	www.catless.ncl.ac. Uk/vmg/	Virtual memorial park

between cyber-religion and ethics, the combination of technical level and spiritual belief, and the transplantation of traditional religious practice on the Internet [2–4]. With the deepening of the research, scholars began to study the attitude of cyber-religion. Some scholars have strongly criticized cyber-religion, while others have advocated the Internet as a religious tool, which emphasizing the benefits of the Internet and the weaknesses of traditional religious communities reflectively. Based on the combination of the two views, some scholars have emphasized that the advantages and disadvantages of the development of cyber-religion coexist [5].

At the beginning of the 21st century, scholars paid more attention to cyber-religion, and it was increasingly regarded as a serious issue. These researches mainly focused on the change and development of self-identity, community, and rituals on the Internet to help scholars carry out more in-depth research on cyber-religion, which is divided into five categories: observation and analysis, online religious influence survey, theoretical development, online culture, and community survey. This research framework provides an important theoretical basis for future research and points out the future development direction.

Moreover, Hojsgaard and Warburg [6] proposed three waves of cyber-religion. The first wave focused on how the Internet created possibilities for religion and online practice, and how computers changed traditional religion and cultures. The second wave focused on a more realistic perspective on online religious expression and online identity and community issues. The third wave focused on "in front of the eyes" and described "the state of the field" to support the sustainable development of cyber-religion and met the actual needs of current believers.

Based on the three waves, some scholars used the evolution of cyber-religion to describe how different research problems and the four waves appeared, and the new research focused areas.

The first wave was the descriptive age, as scholars tried to explain what was happening to religious practice on the Internet.

The second wave was the age of categorization – scholars tried to provide specific types and identify trends emerging in religious Internet practices, such as "online religion", which some scholars cite as distinct from traditional forms of religion.

In the third wave (the theoretical turn) – scholars focused on identifying methods and theoretical frameworks to help analyze offline religious communities' strategies related to new media usage, such as scholars who explored how transcriptional Jewish users could rhetorically justify their Internet participation to incorporate it into the community's religion.

The fourth wave of researchers had focused primarily on the interaction between online and offline religion and how this affected the broader understanding of religion in contemporary society. For example, scholars had discussed how the Internet could both consolidate and weaken traditional forms of online religious authority, while forcing religious leaders to evaluate the uneven benefits that social media bring to authorities [7].

10.2.3 Perspectives on Cyber-Religion Studies

The current research on cyber-religion is mainly based on the following research perspectives:

- **Technical application**: Description of the phenomenon of religious organizations and individuals using the Internet for religious activities.
- **Theological aspects**: The reflection and reinterpretation of the significance of new phenomena in various religions in the new era.
- **Sociological aspects**: The study of the influence of Internet on religion.
- **Political science and international political science**: The professional study of the impact of the networking of religious extremist and terrorist organizations on international security.

10.3 Web-Based Religious Studies

10.3.1 The Concept of Cyber-Religion

Cyber-religion, also called e-religion, digital religion, internet religion, online religion, first exists through communication technology and is shaped by communication technology: creed forums, believer blogs, newsletters lists, tweets from major religious figures, including the pope, and various services (virtual blessings) provided through connected applications on smartphones and laptops, are some of the interfaces that cyber-religion produces through mediation practices, whether it is worship, learning, meditation, prayer (online prayer), or repentance [8]. Cyber-religion is understood as a new type of religious activity carried out in cyberspace by religious organizations (sites) or believers who spread religion by using the Internet.

Heidi Campbell defined religion as a system of symbols that help people build strong, universal, and lasting emotions and motivations through concepts and symbols of the general order of existence, with a sense of reality that makes emotions and motivations seem unique realities. It shows that religion involves a system of cultural practices based on a unique model of reality and the ability to change people's daily perceptions [9,10].

Some scholars believed that cyber-religion had broad sense and narrow sense. In a broad sense, it refers to all religious phenomena on the Internet, while in a narrow sense, it refers to the spread of religion on the Internet. The concept of cyber-religion does not form a consistent connotation. Their emphases are different, and scholars have different understandings on the characteristics of cyber-religion. Some scholars focused on the "network" basis of cyber-religion, and understood the connotation of cyber-religion from the aspects of the development of cyber-religion behavior, the virtual nature of cyber-religion behavior, the arbitrariness of cyber-religion behavior, the equality of participants, and the interaction of cyber-religion.

Some scholars paid attention to the connotation of "religion" of cyber-religion, and thought that the space-time ambiguity between individuals and groups of cyber-religion, the deterrence of institutions and websites (network temples or network churches), the dematerialization of religious organizations and commitment modes (network communities), the symbolization of religious authority and the flattening of organizational hierarchy, and the sanctification of technology itself become the common characteristics of cyber-religion.

10.3.2 The Web-Based Religious Functional System

Religious social media applications are applications that embed religious ideas, beliefs, and information and support social media interaction with such platforms. The design of network platform function system is the core content of religious social media application design, and it is also an important factor affecting the experiences of religious people. Research and identification of religious online platform design and use trend have become the focus of scholars.

AbromsL put forward an application research model in the process of APP function research of iPhone, and designed four basic functions: input, calculation, execution, and output [11]. In the process of studying the functions of religious website, WebSphere points out that the functions should include history, background, belief, religious service, program, map, location, accessibility, photo library, podcast, webcast, audio-visual, and online forum. The most common iTunes application categories of religion are lifestyle, reference, education, books, utilities, entertainment, games, and music [12]. It was noted in the study that websites serving religions should include functions such as community, religion, spirituality, morality and culture, inspiration, family and life events, charity and service, news, and columnists. These achievements are mainly classified from a practical or utilitarian perspective and cannot accurately describe the purpose or function of religious online platforms.

It is very important for online religious platforms to adapt to the religious needs of religious people and communities and conform to their practice and habits. Wagner proposed the basic functions of the religious application platforms outside the iTunes category by focusing on religious experiences and identity formation, focusing on six types of religious application functions in the iTunes: dissemination of doctrines, organization of religious seminars, donations, religious health applications, self-expression applications, and focus/meditation applications [13]. The dissemination of religious teaching is based on the sharing of the content of religious classics through the Internet in the form of words, pictures, audio and video, the publication of relevant news reports, and the answering of questions for the congregation in order to expand the number of believers and religious influences. The organization of religious seminars is mainly through the invitation of religious people to give lectures, organizing online lectures, or online and offline group discussion and learning, to enhance the religious concept and cohesion of the religious people. Religious donations are mainly carried out through traditional offline activities such as online chanting of scriptures, releasing animals and offering lanterns, etc. In the name of online donations, believers can directly remit funds to online accounts as economic source. The promotion of religious health preservation mainly utilizes modern people's psychological pursuit of health preservation and releases relevant guidance content to attract development followers. For example, Taoism and Buddhism have rich health-keeping and mind-nourishing skills and other related contents, which are easily reprinted and read by netizens on the Internet, causing concern. When some major disasters occur, religious associations launch online blessing relief activities at the first time, surpassing the dead, soothing the soul, and spread their doctrines to expand their followers.

On the above basis, Campbell made a more detailed elaboration and identified and defined seven new and unique categories, which centered on the application of religious practice and the application of embedded religious content. Eleven functional types of religious-oriented applications have been formed – prayer, concentration/meditation, ritual, sacred text participation, pious worship, religious utility, religious social media, religious games, religious wisdom and leaders, religious media channels, and children's religious applications [14] (As shown in Table 10.2).

10.3.3 The Expression of Cyber-Religion

The multimodal (e.g., visual and auditory forms, functional text, and visual data, etc.) and diversified means (e.g., hyperlinks, interactive functions, etc.) of cyber-religion presentation directly affect the effect of communication.

Churches with large-scale and high participation are mostly characterized by audiovisual culture, which simulates real and imaginary space through video editing, worship, preaching audiovisual materials, architectural visualization, and religious space interpretation, thus attracting the attention of believers, evoking believer's association with things in cyberspace, and leaving a deep impression on believers. As the research progresses, geographers emphasize the importance of social situational expression in online communication [15]. The visualization of active geospatial spaces in reality and virtual environment becomes the research focus. The multiscale GIS environment is used to describe different space presented by real and virtual space, so as to construct visual situational space.

Functional texts play an important role in the communication of cyber-religion. Cyber-religion is mostly a combination of visual data and functional texts that reflects diverse situations such as online religious information, church worship, worship/reform (e.g., electronic prayer and virtual pilgrimage), missionary activities and religious communities [16]. What visual data and functional texts relate to each other is of great significance for the construction of religious context and the creation of goods.

Table 10.2   Function System of Network Platform

Function	Specific Content
Pray for prayer	Prayer is framed as communication with a higher being. Mainly by reading text on the device, listening to audio prayers, joining prayer requests, and building private, personal prayers.
Focus/ meditation	Meditation and focus are defined as a personal practice that includes contemplation of higher existence and spiritual thoughts to improve self.
ceremony	Providing users with instructions, guidance, and visual props that reproduce religious artifacts in real life.
Holy text	Associated with classical texts in particular religious traditions such as the Bible, the Koran, Torah and the Bhagavad Gita.
Worship	Promoting spiritual practice and encouragement by using this information, not only provide text for research, but also to include comments and inspiring references and pictures.
Religious utility	Mainly referring to functional applications that provide information to help users conduct specific religious practices, such as remembering when to pray and finding churches and temples.
Religious social media	Communicating with each other through sharing texts, prayers, and comments for like-minded people, and allow them to meet new friends and expand their religious social resources.
Religious games	Teaching users the rules of tradition, history, text, ritual, and specific religious traditions through games.
Religious wisdom and leadership	Religious wisdom is associated with major religious leaders who provide books, lectures, and proverbs to provide insights into religious life. Religious leaders are defined as key authority figures from specific religious traditions, both historical and contemporary.
Religious media outlets	Referring to media products specially developed by religious organizations, institutions and other media channels that provide religious content. Applications may include connections to websites, news sources, and other promotional and informational sites.
Religious application of children	Referring to the teaching and information application for children. Many applications in this category include religious stories with animated and cartoon characters.

Some scholars have proposed that the organization of visual data and functional text of online religion, the classification of content, the style presented on the online platform, and the creation of atmosphere are all important factors to attract the attention of believers. Artistry, timeliness, theatricality, vividness, fast pace, personalization, and celebrity effect are interpreted as the core criteria of cyber-religion [17]. Religion entering online religious platforms should emphasize the all-round presentation of visual materials in order to pave the way for special situations, dramas, and conflicts; it should meet the emotional needs of believers and stimulate their imagination space in the form of sympathetic and inflammatory expressions.

Some scholars believe that on the basis of interaction, believers provide their own real information and narration on online platform to reflect their perception of the daily activities relating to church, which can transcend the control of religious organizations and create a new space for social communication.

10.3.4 The Impact of Cyber-Religions on Communities

The core idea of cyber-religion is to study the social field formed in the network interaction of religious practice. The key to the study of cyber-religion is to investigate the emergence of online religious groups/institutions. Researchers have made great efforts on how online religious communities negotiate and create public meanings, special identities, online communication modes and its impact on traditional religious practices, use online communities to build individual religious identities, and create virtual religious groups [18,19].

These studies not only emphasize the practical role and value of the construction of online religious groups but also emphasize how the Internet can change and reshape the communities in the digital environment. Researchers have shifted their focus from the discussion on whether online communities can be portrayed as religious communities to the research on the motivation of members to join religious communities, and on how online religious communities affect offline religious ones.

Online religious community used to be regarded as "assemblies separated from entities", with relatively loose and flat organizational structures and strict boundaries with offline religious community. With the deepening of research, some scholars believed that although religious practice entered the online platform, its community ritual and practice need to be adjusted in some form, but the online religious community was not without contact with the offline community. Online religious communities could not fully meet the needs of believers. The online community is not a substitute for the offline church but maintains and establishes interaction with the offline religious community through the cyberspace platform, which has an important impact on the operation of the offline community and the whole religious organization. Meanwhile, offline community also reacts with online religious community, so whether it is online or offline community, it is no longer a single static religious community, but a highly personalized religious community. Online community and offline community interact with each other and integrate into an important part of social network.

10.3.5 The Impact of Cyber-Religion on Identity

Baym (1998) believed that social identity is that individuals obtain information resources from various kinds of communication through dramatic means to create and perform a given role [20]. With the deepening of research, some scholars have realized that identity is no longer fixed, simple acceptance or rejection of behavioral patterns, but a highly plastic one. Individuals choose, integrate, and use various resources in social space to present self-consciousness, thus shaping individual identities. The Internet challenges the role of traditional religion in the process of socialization. Religious identity is not acquired through the Internet, nor is it purely introduced from the offline environment. Religious identity is not simply constructed and implemented. There are many resources in online platforms. Through the selection and combination of them, a vague description is constructed, thus giving the individual the meaning and responsibility of existence. Multiple resource choices and combinations make identity presenting the characteristics of complexity [21].

Researchers have great interest in how the Internet empowers religious Internet users to create and perform religious identity online. Research shows that online religious practice can create opportunities for belief self-expressions and religious lifestyle practices compared with traditional religious environment. Traditionally, religious studies have focused on the control of religious identity by groups/institutions. However, because cyberspace technology can regulate social relations, the construction of identity can often bypass the influence of institutions. This undoubtedly provides new ways and possibilities for the construction of religious identity, especially for those who lack such opportunities in the local or offline environments [22].

In addition, some scholars pointed out that the anonymity and transience of online interactions may also bring about unexpected consequences, such as identity division, leading to increased insecurity in the process of studying the negative effects of religious network. In some cases, it may lead to conflicts between the true claims of cyber-religion leaders or groups and their offline counterparts.

In fact, people's online identities are often close to their real identities. People tend to maintain the continuity of identity online and offline. The complete reconstruction of self and identity is a misreading of the Internet. Like the relationship between online religious experiences and real religious ones, online religious identity is inseparable from real religious identity. The Internet is indeed a new place to shape religious self, but individual self-identity is more based on traditional religious roles rather than online fragmented identity, which proves once again that cyber-religion is an extension of and supplement to real religion [23].

10.3.6 The Impact of Cyber-Religion on Authority

Due to the emergence of online religious communities and the plasticity of identity, online authority has attracted the attention of researchers. Some researchers have found that webmasters or bloggers who are not religious leaders or even technicians are given new leadership and act as new authority agents. Some scholars began to explore how the online religious platforms challenge and create online religious authority.

Barker [24] studied the influence of new media on authority structure based on the theory of structure and function construction of natural resource management system. The new media means and the functional content of the online religious platform can promote the adjustment and reorganization of the hierarchical organizational structure, and have the ability to create religious power position outside the traditional structure. New media can threaten the authority of an inherent organization, and can also be used to maintain the original organization and its authority [24].

Some scholars believed that the Internet can be used to consolidate rather than challenge religious authority. Religious communities can "cultivate" a technology that preserves rather than subverts the unique culture of the group. They emphasized how to use the Internet to influence the four basic characteristics (e.g., hierarchy, patriarchy, discipline, and segregation) of religious communities to uphold religious authority.

According to Cukier and Middleton, the Internet is not only regarded as a threat to certain established roles and hierarchies but also as a tool to empower certain people. The Internet has become an area of competition and power transfer [17].

On this basis, some scholars have also studied the influence of the emergence of new online authority on offline authority. Online leadership roles may affect the status of individuals in offline religious groups. The Internet provides the ability to change the hierarchy of offline religious power by introducing new forms of governance authority [25]. There are also some scholars who have explained the reasons for the emergency of the new authority. Online groups interpret religious beliefs and policies in a way different from official positions and views [26]. This has become a new source of religious authority. Some scholars believed that the mobility and transience of online environment affect the traditional authority structure and role. In addition, the Internet is a source of religious information and knowledge, and religious network gurus, forum moderators, and professional bloggers provide recognition of online knowledge, making the Internet a recognized authority.

10.3.7 The Behavior of Cyber-Religion Participants

■ **Influencing factors of participation in online religious activities**

Whether to participate in online religious activities is related to many factors. The cognitive attitude toward new media is an important factor affecting the participation in online religious activities. Attitude is a positive or negative evaluation of an action or consequence. People tend to form a positive attitude toward favorable consequences, while negative attitudes toward adverse consequences [27]. Under the same conditions, people with positive attitude to new media are more likely to engage in religious activities in new media than those who have a negative attitude.

Meanwhile, some scholars also studied the influence of subjective norms on the participation of online religious activities. Subjective norms are social pressures that individuals feel when they act in a particular way. Individuals will, to some extent, follow the same group as they believe in when deciding whether to participate in online religious activities. Joining religious groups helps to build stronger social bonds and influence individual participation behavior and motivation. In addition, families also influence individuals' participation in online religious activities. Research shows that not only in childhood but also in adulthood, the religious beliefs of children and their parents are interrelated, and the subjective norms from the family are positively related to their participation in online religious activities [28].

Based on the theory of planned behavior, some scholars put forward the factors that affect the participation of Muslim Internet users in online religious activities in Singapore from three aspects: personal attitude, subjective norms, and self-efficacy. These three factors jointly determine the formation of behavior intention. The more favorable the attitude is, the greater the perceived social pressure and perceived behavior control ability are, and the stronger the desire of the individual to carry out behavior is.

Whether or not to participate in online religious activities is also affected by individuals' religious piety and demographic attributes. Religious belief is positively related to participation in online religious activities. The more devout a person is, the more likely he is to use new communication technologies to promote the progress of knowledge. These people are more willingly to use online tools to enrich their belief knowledge and participate in religious practice. Women, middle-aged people, college-educated people, and relatively wealthy people are more likely to use the Internet for religious or spiritual purposes.

■ **Online religious experience**

Online religious experiences refer to the feelings of believers participating in online religious activities. There are two extremes in the study of attitude towards online religious experiences. Some scholars believe that the practice of traditional religion cannot be completely restored on the online platform, and the development of cyber-religion can only weaken the social activities and organization of traditional religion; the characteristics of open, tolerant, and decentralized online media are just contrary to the tradition of religious emphasis on authority and hierarchical order. The development of cyber-religion will lead to the "out of control" of information and the spread of a large number of knowledge contrary to the orthodox church doctrine, which will lead to the elimination of religious authority and sanctity and the rise of heresy; some scholars believed that the construction of surrealism through online religious platforms can give believers a new religious experience and promote the sustainable development of traditional religion [29].

The content of online religious experiences involves pilgrimage, worship, online prayers, online ritual, and so on. The experience effect also varies greatly due to individual differences. Some scholars argue that cyber-religion, with its unique characteristics, transcends the limitation of time and space, and may lead to individualism. Through the online platform, individuals bypass traditional barriers and resource constraints, and realize online Individualism [30]. The connection of people-to-people replaces the connections of place-to-place. Individuals can maintain multiple identities simultaneously in different social contexts, especially in the era of mobile Internet, when the personal restriction of identity is gradually broken. Individuals have super-autonomy, and have greater control over resources, knowledge, and connected objects. Individual super-autonomy emphasizes contemporary religious life that pays attention to experience and belief, and despises creed and doctrines. Under the influence of individual super-autonomy, different individuals have various experiences of cyber-religion [31].

In addition, some scholars studied some details relating to belief and induced religious experiences from people's daily life and special religious experiences in specific occasions. The studies found that love, hate, death, games, humor, hope, and curses in daily life all contain religious traits [32]. Cyber-religion brings new experience to believers. Some believers consider that they are involved in online religious activities and feel the existence of God; some feel that they are being concerned by God; and others experience the excitement and pleasure of communicating with God.

Some scholars have compared online religious experiences with offline religious experiences. Some believers image that the virtual scene in cyberspace and the mobility of believers' virtual identity have changed the original relationship between God and man. This has fundamentally changed the believer's emotional experiences of religious organizations. Some believers consider that cyber-religion cannot be compared with traditional offline religion, and offline religious activities can have a deeper understanding of religious doctrines and form a closer social network through face-to-face communication [33].

10.4 The Development Trend of Cyber-Religion

According to the number of published literatures on cyber-religion, cyber-religion has great development potential in the future. This chapter mainly elaborates the concept and functional system of cyber-religion, the influence of cyber-religion on religious community, identity, and authority, and the behavioral law of the subject of cyber-religion participation. In the future, it can be further extended on the basis of the current research.

■ **Perfecting the theoretical system of research**

Since O 'Leary and Brasher [1] initiated the study of cyber-religion, the research on the connotation and extension of the concept of cyber-religion began. So far, the characteristics of cyber-religion can be summarized as follows: (1) It is based on the Internet, information communication, new media, and other platforms; (2) it is a dynamic and profound process of creating religious culture; (3) it has the functions of giving gifts, repentance, thanks, pleading, praying, and preaching. However, the concept and overall characteristics are not unified. Therefore, the future research should strengthen the definition and interpretation of the concept of cyber-religion based on existing research, and clarify its connotation and extension, so as to provide support for theoretical research and empirical analysis.

In the future, the theoretical framework of cyber-religion should be strengthened on the basis of conceptual research. Cyber-religion belongs to the sacred knowledge and belief, but its construction depends on information resources, the needs of believers, the mode of dissemination, and the mechanism of dissemination, which is different from the general sense of the construction of knowledge and culture. In the future, on the basis of summarizing the commonalities, cyber-religion will explore their own characteristics and construct a theoretical system.

■ **Strengthening the research on the behavioral rules of online religious believers**

The research on the behavioral law of online religious believers is helpful to understand the social identity, authority, and formation mechanism of online religious communities, accurately grasps the development direction of cyber-religion, and develops an online platform to meet the needs of online religious believers. At present, the research on cyber-religion behavior mainly focuses on the nature and quality of believers' experiences. In the future, cyber-religion can be combined with the different social and demographic attributes of online believers to carry out research on cyber-religion experiences, offline behavioral experiences and online behavioral experiences. In terms of research methods, cyber-religion can obtain quantitative data by means of market research, text analysis, comparative analysis, empirical analysis, and normative analysis in management, economics, and sociology, and put forward research paradigms in this aspect. In the study of the behavior of religious believers, in addition to individual experiences, scholars should strengthen the research on the motivation and emotions of cyber-religion participation.

■ **Strengthening the study of the influence of cyber-religion on religion**

The new spatial form and social structure formed by the development of cyber-religion have multiple effects on religion. In the future, scholars should study cyber-religion from a larger perspective and link it to the whole study of the Internet. Some important topics in network research, such as feminism, public domain, knowledge production, language rhetoric, and so on, are closely related to religion, but they have not been explored yet. At the same time, it should also be linked to the broader study of religion, which currently only studies the impact of online and offline religion. Although some scholars have studied the relationship between the concepts of online religious community and offline community, few scholars have paid attention to the research on the interaction between cyber-religion and offline religion, and the influence of their relationship on the sustainable development of religion. In the future, cyber-religion can strengthen the research on religious authority, how online activities reshape our identity, and the interaction mechanism between online and offline religion.

■ **Promoting Innovative Research Methods**

For the research of cyber-religion, qualitative analysis methods (e.g., single case analysis, literature analysis, descriptive analysis, etc.) are used to carry out descriptive research. In the future, cyber-religion can integrate research techniques, methods, approaches, concepts, and languages. Meanwhile, there is a lack of frontier research methods for the combination of religion and Internet of Things, big data, and artificial intelligence (AI). In terms of the Internet of Things (IoT), it is necessary to explore the relationship between the Internet of Everything and the animality of all things, the experiences of believers brought by the Internet of Things technology, and how to reshape the religious world of the network by IoT. How to use big data and cloud computing to achieve the aggregation and precise push of religious information, and how to use big data and cloud computing to achieve the governance of religious information. In the aspect of artificial intelligence, we need to answer the question of how to integrate and develop AI with religion, the relationship between artificial intelligence and religious ethics, and the relationship between AI and people's spiritual experiences.

References

1. S. O'Leary and B. Brasher, *Philosophical Perspectives on Computer-Mediated Communication*, SUNY Press, New York, 1996.
2. B. Brasher, *Give me that Online Religion*, JosseyBass, San Francisco, 2001.
3. G. Houston, *Virtual Morality: Christian Ethics in the Computer Age*, Leicester, Apollos, New York, United States, 1998.
4. J. C. Cybergrace, *The Search for God in the Digital World*, Crown Publishers, New York, 1998.
5. J. Casanova, Religion, the new millennium and globalization, *Sociology of Religion*, Vol. 62; No. 4, pp. 415–441, 2001.

6. M. Hojsgaard and M. Warburg, *Religion and Cyberspace*, Routledge, London, 2005.
7. H. A. Campbell, Surveying theoretical approaches within digital religion studies. *New Media & Society*, Vol. 19; No. 1, p pp. 15–24, 2017.
8. I. Chiluwa, Religious vehicle stickers in Nigeria: A discourse of identity, faith and social vision, *Discourse and Communication*, Vol. 2; No. 4, pp. 371–387, 2008.
9. H. Campbell, Spiritualising the internet: Uncovering discourses and narratives of religious internet use, *Online-Heidelberg Journal of Religion on the Internet*, Vol. 1; No. 1, pp. 23–42, 2005.
10. H. Campbell and P. Calderon, The question of Christian community online: The case of the'artist world network, *Studies in World Christianity*, Vol. 13; No. 3, pp. 261–277, 2007.
11. L. Abroms, N. Padmanabhan, and L. Thaweethai, iPhone apps for smoking cessation, *American Journal of Preventive Medicine*, Vol. 40; No. 3, pp. 279–285, 2011.
12. H. Campbell, *Digital Religion: Understanding Religious Practices in New Media Worlds*, Routledge, UK, 2013.
13. R. Wagner, *You are What You Install: Religious Authenticity and Identity in Mobile Apps*, Routledge, Oxfordshire, UK, 2013.
14. H. A. Campbell, There s a religious app for that! A framework for studying religious mobile applications, *Mobile Media & Communication*, Vol. 2; No. 2, pp. 154–172, 2014.
15. M. P. Kwan, Cyberspatial cognition and individual access to information: The behavioral foundation of cybergeography, *Environment and Planning B*, Vol. 28; No. 1, pp. 21–37, 2001.
16. A. Roosvall, Religion, globalization and commodification in online world news slideshows: The dis/connection of images and texts, *Social Semiotics*, Vol. 26; No. 1, pp. 76–93, 2016.
17. W. Cukier and C. A. Middleton, voluntary sector organizations on the internet: The Canadian experience, *IT and Society*, Vol. 1; No. 3, pp. 102–130, 2003.
18. J. Fernback, *Internet Ritual: A Case of the Construction of Computer-Mediated Neopagan Religious Meaning*, Columbia University Press, New York, United States, 2002.
19. G. Bunt, *Virtually Islamic: Computer-Mediated Communication and Cyber Islamic Environments*, University of Wales Press, Cardiff, UK, 2000.
20. N. K. Baym, *The Emergence of On-Line Community*. Sage Publications, California, United States, 1998.
21. B. Brukhalter, *Reading Race On-line: Discovering Racial Identity*, Routledge, UK, 1999.
22. L. Kendall, *Hanging Out in the Virtual Pub: Masculinities and Relationships Online*, University of California Press, Oakland, California, 2002.
23. N. Elias and D. Lemish, Spinning the web of identity: The roles of the Internet in the lives of immigrant adolescents, *New Media & Society*, Vol. 11; pp. 533–551, 2009.
24. E. Barker, *Crossing the Boundary: New Challenges to Religious Authority and Control as a Consequence of Access to the Internet Religion and Cyberspace*, Routledge, UK, 2005.
25. S. Thumma, *Religion and the Internet*, Hartford Institute for Religion Research, 2000.
26. D. Piff and W. Margit, *Seeking for Truth: Plausibility on a Baha'iEmail List*, Routledge, London, UK, 2005.
27. J. W. Andersen, New media, new publics: Reconfiguring the public sphere of Islam, *Social Research*, Vol. 70; No. 3, pp. 887–906, 2003.
28. S. M. Myers, An interactive model of religiosity Inheritance: The importance of family context, *American Sociological Review*, Vol. 61; No. 5, pp. 58–66, 1996.

29. K. Randolph and H. C. Pauline, Technological modernization, the internet, and religion in Singapore, *Journal of Computer-Mediated Communication*, Vol. 12; pp. 1122–1142, 2007.
30. O. Kruger, The Internet as a mirror and distributor of religious and ritual knowledge, *Asian Journal of Social Science*, Vol. 32; pp. 183–197, 2004.
31. R. Lee and B. Wellman, *Networked: The New Social Operating System*, MIT press, Cambridge, 2014.
32. G. G. Armfield and R. L. Holbert, The relationship between religiosity and Internet use, *Journal of Media and Religion*, Vol. 2; pp. 129–144, 2009.
33. J. K. Hadden and D. E. Cowan, Religion on the internet: Research prospects and promises, *Sociology of Religion*, Vol. 8; pp. 25–54, 2002.

Chapter 11

Cyberspace Culture and Art Research History

11.1 Introduction

Culture refers to all human spiritual activities and products relating to economy and politics. Broadly speaking, culture represents the way of life of a nation, and it includes language, skills, knowledge, customs, and art. Cyberspace is a new development space for mankind. It integrates nature, mankind, and society, allowing different groups, different cultures, and arts to communicate with and influence each other. Mankind has entered an era of digital survival with numbers as the basic unit. The emergence and development of cyberspace has changed people's real-life conditions. Cyberspace not only affects and changes the way people live, socialize, and work, but also affects and reshapes people's aesthetic experience. Emerging media, close connections between smart terminals and subjects, multidimensional links of information and data, etc., have exerted profound influences on culture and art.

This chapter introduces the development and evolution of cyberspace culture and art. It also introduces the mutual influence of culture and cyberspace. Then it introduces the different forms of culture and art in cyberspace. Finally, it summarizes and discusses this chapter.

11.2 Development and Evolution

11.2.1 Information Digitization

The evolution of media and communication media has promoted the development of human culture and art. Every change in culture and art is related to the

DOI: 10.1201/9781003257387-11

development of certain media carriers and communication technologies. Before the advent of electronic technology, human culture has gone through two stages: "oral culture" and "written culture", and the digitization of information is an important sign that human culture has entered a new era.

During the development of the entire human culture, before the emergence of cyberspace, most information and materials were disseminated through traditional media; after the emergence and development of cyberspace, all information and materials were used by emerging media digital symbol dissemination, and this dissemination method greatly surpassed the traditional information dissemination method. Meanwhile, computers and networks have had a huge and profound impact on human social activities and ways of thinking.

The emergence of the Internet has brought culture and art into cyberspace. Meanwhile, a brand-new culture and art have developed in cyberspace, which has become a new force that cannot be ignored.

11.2.2 Development Timeline

According to the characteristics of the propagation and evolution of culture and art in cyberspace in different periods, its development can be divided into the following three stages:

Stage 1: Cyberspace will only broaden the channels for cultural and artistic communication.

In the initial stage, the culture and art of cyberspace still possess the characteristics of traditional human social culture and art. During this period, the Internet, as a carrier of culture and information, spreads culture and art outside the cyberspace, that is, traditional culture and art. The Internet has not yet created new culture and art. Culture and art in cyberspace were just the reproduction and dissemination of culture and art outside cyberspace in the form of digital information. Networks mainly solve the technical problems of traditional cultural and artistic exchanges.

Stage 2: Cyberspace culture and art exist independently.

The condition for the development and evolution of culture and art in cyberspace is the progress of network technology, which has produced new ways of thinking and network aesthetics, and provided new tools and methods. With the development of network society, culture and art in cyberspace exist as an independent culture and art. Cyberspace broadens people's horizons, prompts the collision and fusion of ideas, and enables people to invent a series of new expressions in cyberspace that are completely different from before. Meanwhile, computers and networks provide people with more new creative methods and tools, resulting in more diverse cultural and artistic models. At this time, culture and art in cyberspace are obviously different from the traditional culture and art. They exist independently and have a huge and far-reaching impact on human society.

The culture and art in cyberspace can be divided into three categories:

■ The existing cultural and artistic works are digitized and spread to the cyberspace.
■ Cultural and artistic works are published through cyberspace.
■ Cultural and artistic works are created by computer software and published in cyberspace.

Stage 3: Cyberspace culture and art are gradually industrializing.
As the cultural and artistic development of cyberspace gradually matures, it is showing a trend of industrialization. A typical representative is online game, which can clearly show the industrialization trajectory of cyberspace culture and art. The online culture and art industry represented by online games has revolutionized the traditional way of cultural and art communication. Online games have created a new online entertainment lifestyle, greatly promoted the production, dissemination and consumption of cultural and artistic works, and further developed the aesthetic concept in cyberspace. Nowadays, new ideas of network culture and art have gradually penetrated into people's minds, contributing to the popularization of culture and art, and at the same time creating a new era of network space culture and art.

11.3 Cyberspace and Traditional Culture

The development of cyberspace and culture is interdependent and mutually restricted. Culture and art in cyberspace are completely different from all the previous culture and art in content and form, and have a huge impact on traditional culture and art. The two usually contradict and fuse.

The way of communication and interaction in cyberspace has characteristics similar to primitive culture. In primitive culture, signs and actions are used to express it and symbolize it. Symbols can represent abstract things, and their meanings are diverse. The communication characteristics of primitive culture are similar to the communication in cyberspace. Symbolism and diversity also play an important role in electronic interfaces in cyberspace such as icons and hypertext links. In cyberspace, a good audio-visual interface can effectively attract users and reduce users' understanding and cognitive burden [1].

Individuals need to learn how to use the Internet and how to adapt to cyberspace. At a deeper level, the entire culture should also adapt to cyberspace [2].

11.3.1 The Influence of Traditional Culture and Art on Cyberspace

First, the term cyberspace originated from cultural and artistic works. The term cyberspace comes from the work of Canadian science fiction writer William Gibson. It was originally proposed in the short story "Burning Chrome" and was promoted in the later work "Neuromancer".

Second, the development of culture and art has promoted the expansion of cyberspace. Before cyberspace penetrated into our daily lives, many literary and artistic works of science fiction have conceived cyberspace. In recent years, cultural and artistic works with the theme of cyberspace have emerged continuously. Cultural and artistic works not only deepen people's understanding of cyberspace but also promote the widespread use of cyberspace.

Third, the ethics and values conveyed by culture and art have influenced cyberspace's development trend and explored cyberspace's potential. The exploration and imagination of various functions of cyberspace in cultural and artistic works have greatly improved the social values and functions contained in cyberspace. The values conveyed by cultural and artistic works are also continuously affecting people's thinking and judgment on cyberspace.

11.3.2 The Influence of Cyberspace on Traditional Culture and Art

First, through cyberspace, people can more easily find, collect, save, and understand various cultural and artistic information. In cyberspace, culture and art are digitized. As an information resource, cultural and artistic works can be shared, spread, and used by people. In this process, various cultures can influence each other. Cyberspace has greatly accelerated the dissemination of culture and art.

Second, cyberspace provides a supporting platform for cultural globalization. Spreading information and displaying culture and art in cyberspace are effective ways for national culture to break through the barriers of knowledge and language [3].

Third, as a spiritual product, culture is a dynamic reflection of the relationship between man and nature, between man and society, and between man and man. Cyberspace broadened the channels for people to exchange ideas, broke geographical and historical restrictions in reality, and greatly promoted the diversified development of culture and art. In cyberspace, various cultures and arts can break through the limitations of time and geography and be completely exposed to global platforms. The globalization of culture and art in cyberspace means that all kinds of culture and art no longer develop in isolation [3].

Fourth, as a platform for cultural and artistic dissemination and exchange, cyberspace affects the unity and integrity of traditional culture with its uniqueness and diversity. People can conduct online activities anytime, anywhere through any networked computer. Compared with real life, people are less restricted by economy, politics, and culture. On the Internet, people can express their thoughts, feelings, and emotions at will. This personalized approach has spawned the collision and exchange of ideas among people, and to a certain extent promoted the diversity of online culture. Traditional culture is a collection of humanistic spirit, values, folklore, language system, etc., formed and developed in a country's long-term productive, social, and aesthetic practices. The individual and diversified characteristics of cyberspace culture and art will inevitably affect traditional culture.

11.3.3 *Cyberspace and National Cultural Industry*

Cyberspace should be a creative extension of human beings, a new structure, and spatial paradigm. But as a virtual world, cyberspace should not be seen as a simple imitation and copy of the real world. It should be regarded as a new dimension to broaden the expression and dissemination of literature and art. Cyberspace lacks substantial freedom from physical conditions, so it can get rid of the shackles of traditional definitions and has great imagination and creativity. Mankind can use cyberspace to transcend the boundaries of reality and display cultural heritage in it. Through multimedia and other technologies, cyberspace can provide good interactions. By simplifying easy-to-understand audiovisual information, it helps users achieve a better perception and understanding of cultural content [4].

National cultural industry refers to an industrial form that utilizes national cultural resources to provide products and services with distinctive regional and national characteristics. The national cultural industry is an important driving force for promoting regional economic development. In the past, consumers of ethnic cultural products and services mainly came from economically developed regions. Nowadays, with the emergence and development of cyberspace, how to increase the influence and market value of the national cultural industry through the Internet has become the key to its development. The use of cyberspace to increase the influence of the national cultural industry has also become an important strategy for the development of cultural industries in countries around the world. In cyberspace, the widespread application of e-commerce, social media, and various online service platforms provides new opportunities for the development and promotion of the national cultural industry to cyberspace. In this process, issues such as cross-cultural cognition, industrial chain reconstruction, and evolutionary models need to be systematically considered. Cyberspace can provide a low-cost, optimized, and integrated network industry cluster model to help promote the rapid development of the national cultural industry. The process of promoting the national cultural industry to the cyberspace is essentially the process of cultural industry rebuilding its ecological chain and community in the Internet environment. It will be influenced by factors such as concepts, infrastructure, laws and regulations, cross-cultural awareness, and professional training [5].

11.4 Culture and Art in Cyberspace

The development of the Internet has created new living space for mankind. The existence and development of the Internet are profoundly affecting and changing people's lifestyles and values. While it changes human culture, it also changes the aesthetic concept of art. The fast transmission speed, strong interactivity, and large capacity of the Internet pose severe challenges to traditional media.

Network culture and art are produced through computer networks. It uses computers and auxiliary equipment as the material carrier, the Internet as the main body, virtual space as the main communication field, and digitization as the basic technical means to create the human world. It has produced a new way of life, activity, and thinking. Network culture is a special culture in the information age and a product of the development of human society. From the perspective of the network, network culture and art are a new cultural and artistic style, which is a cultural exchange revolution of traditional cultural and artistic paradigms formed by technological changes. From the perspective of culture and art, the content of culture and art has provided better ways for innovation, and the representation of culture and art has been changed.

Cyberspace provides new tools for cultural and artistic creation (e.g., websites, blogs, video media, and themes and activities widely spread through the Internet.). With its own distinctive characteristics, Internet culture has had a huge impact on cultural communication methods, language expression methods, knowledge storage methods, and audience psychology. Network culture combines the main characteristics of traditional culture and art, and at the same time expresses the characteristics of contemporary aesthetic culture.

In cyberspace, culture is open to everyone, everyone has the right to spread and exchange culture, and everyone can express their thoughts and various cultural concepts relatively freely. Therefore, the culture in cyberspace is a true mass culture. It makes people begin to regard themselves as the main body of speech and express their culture freely and independently.

11.4.1 Cyberliterature

Cyberliterature, that is, literature created on a computer and presented on the Internet; it has the following characteristics: multithreading, use of hyperlinks to link different text content, integration with multimedia, interactivity, and so on. The emergence of cyberliterature represents the change of literary concepts and the expansion of literary forms. The popularization of computer technology has brought about the need to modify and redefine humanities. With the innovation of technology and the emergence of cyberspace, new forms have emerged in the field of literature, and computer technology and literature can be interconnected. As a conceptual term, online literature includes the following parts:

- All available literary publications on the Internet, including digitized publications, texts of works provided on the author's homepage, etc.
- Nonprofessional texts circulated on the Internet, including texts of works published on the homepages of amateur writers, blogs describing life, etc.
- Hypertext literature and multimedia network text, which are typical representatives of the combination of multimedia technology and literature.

Cyberliterature has changed not only in the form of creation but also in writing style and writing habits. For example, in hypertext network literature, link is created by the original author, but readers can choose the link and read it actively. This way of active reading is called "interactive reading", and readers are considered to be able to become authors in this way.

Cyberliterature provides an opportunity for independent online publishing and solves the problems caused by the limitations of print media. In the cyberspace, literary concepts have also been expanded on the previous basis, such as the characteristics of postmodernist writing reflected in online literature. Cyberliterature appears in the form of multimedia, combining elements such as literature, vision, and music. Computer technology has played the following roles: first, computers can present complex nonlinear text structures and create new forms of literary expression; second, in the cyberspace, elite literature is gradually replaced by ordinary popular literature [6].

11.4.2 Simulate Reality

Cyberspace brings an overall change to the expression, communication, and delivery strategy of culture and art. For example, computer graphics (CG) technology and three-digit digital scenes have been widely used in digital image processing and production. With the help of virtual reality technology, people's imagination and creativity can be greatly brought into full play. Virtual reality technology has further expanded people's perception and experience in cyberspace. Using computer technology, it can create multidimensional dynamic simulation effects and simulation environments for users themselves to immerse in and experience them such as popular virtual classrooms, buildings, and tours.

11.4.3 Streaming Media

Streaming media occupies a core position in the global digital economy industry. The U.S. Digital Content Industry Analysis Platform AppAnnie's report shows that among the top ten nongaming paid apps in 2019, streaming media platforms occupy five seats, namely, Netflix, Tencent Video, iQIYI, You Tube, and Youku, with streaming media platforms in the U.S. and China as the main forces [7].

The current U.S. streaming media industry has two main categories: one is self-produced and self-broadcast platforms represented by Netflix and HBO; the other is self-produced and self-produced by You Tube as a typical example. Platform for authoring and uploading is referred to as UGC. The former is often referred to as OTT streaming (Over-The-Top TV), the latter is called instant streaming media.

OTT streaming media platforms refer to streaming media services that provide audiences with audiovisual works based on the Internet. Users can directly watch movies, dramas, variety shows, and other audiovisual works online without downloading. Audiovisual works can be put on fixed devices such as TVs and projectors, and mobile terminals such as laptops, tablets, and mobile phones can also be used.

The digital economy of the streaming media industry has brought brand-new profit methods and economic models, and the new media of streaming media has also launched competition against the traditional film industry. It has changed the ecology of the current film industry, brought challenges to traditional cinema movies, and greatly threatened the interests of the traditional cinema market. Meanwhile, streaming media platforms also bring opportunities for small- and medium-cost movies [8].

Meanwhile, algorithm strategies represented by recommendation algorithms have begun to permeate streaming media platforms, such as using big data statistics to count and predict audience preferences for plot trends, and create audiovisual works based on this. This will have a great impact on the independence of audiovisual creation in the film and television industry and the aesthetic perception of the audience.

11.4.4 Social Network

Social network is an extension of real life. In cyberspace, the number of people socializing through the Internet is increasing, and social networks are developing rapidly, bringing great convenience to people's lives, and new social culture and social methods have emerged. Social interaction is a form of interpersonal communication based on the Internet, using various social platforms as the media, and using text, audio, video, and pictures as expression methods.

Social network has the characteristics of strong timeliness. Users do not need to have a high level of electronic information technology to quickly operate through a simple and easy-to-understand interface, using web pages, clients, and other methods to receive and publish messages. Traditional media, such as newspapers and television, is usually limited by time and location, and cannot provide timely feedback and lack certain timeliness. In cyberspace, the release and reception of information are carried out almost simultaneously, which greatly improves the timeliness of information dissemination. Social network also has the characteristics of strong interaction. As a freer and more open social platform, users can interact and communicate in real time in the cyberspace, and there are many ways to interact and communicate.

11.4.5 Cyberpunk

Cyberpunk is a multilevel dynamic concept, which originated from literary creation and then spread to other fields of artistic expression. So far, it has developed into a subcultural form with strong vitality, especially an important rhetorical method for visual digital media. Etymologically speaking, cyberpunk is a combination of cybernetics and punk, and refers to sci-fi works with cyberspace and virtual world as the story context [9].

In literary works, cyberpunk writers have thought and explored the future society, deliberately forming a strong contrast between the highly developed human civilization and the real life of the people living at the bottom of society, who were full of dystopia and pessimism. Common elements in cyberpunk literature are: hackers, virtual reality, artificial intelligence (AI), etc.

With the development of society, part of cyberpunk's early ideas became reality, which made it no longer just exist on the surface of the text but gradually penetrated into modern life.

In modern society, the relationship between man and machine, virtual, and reality is closer and more real. It has been widely used in visual digital media; it not only conforms to the development trend of times but also establishes a realistic relationship with the audience.

Therefore, cyberpunk is no longer just a literary creation mode, but a cultural concept, which is explored and applied by innovators in various fields, spread to various forms of media, and has gradually formed a subculture. Nowadays, the influence of cyberpunk in the fields of film, television, cartoon, music, and design has far exceeded the original field of literature, and will further spread with the development of the times [10].

Cyberpunk's worldview is usually based on predictions of future and technological development, and reflects the characteristics of multiracial cultural integration in the social structure. Cyberpunk is essentially the product of mankind's fantasy of the future, and its creative concept has guiding significance for future design. Cyberpunk-style works convey cultural needs such as dystopia, counter-mainstream discourse, and the promotion of independent thinking. With the development of people's multidimensional cognition of technology, culture, and aesthetics, cyberpunk will be further applied and developed in a broader field.

11.5 Conclusion and Discussion

Meanwhile, cyberspace poses a threat to culture and art.

First, the virtual content in cyberspace has entered our lives on a large scale, and the virtual consumption scene in cyberspace is too attractive to some groups and has a negative impact; second, nowadays, the creation of culture and art is increasingly dependent on cyberspace and information technology, and some traditional methods of creation (especially the culture and art that are difficult to be compatible with cyberspace) are gradually disappearing; third, the creation and dissemination of art forms in cyberspace has an increasing influence, further squeezing the position of traditional culture.

Culture is often regarded as something of the past. Computer technology has brought the new living space for mankind. In cyberspace, the future and the past are integrated in a unique way. Technology will change the way people interact with people and the environment, and it will also greatly affect the development of culture and art. It is necessary for people to realize, understand, and accept this situation, and adapt to these new and different forms of life [11].

References

1. P. Search, Ancient voices and cyberspace: Exploring the past to reshape the future, IPCC 99. Communication Jazz: Improvising the new international communication culture. *Proceedings 1999 IEEE International Professional Communication Conference* (Cat. No.99CH37023), New Orleans, LA, United States, pp. 225–230, 1999.
2. E. A. Philip, Cyberspace as American culture, *Science as Culture*, Vol. 11; No. 2, pp. 171–189, 2002.
3. C. Wang and M. He, National culture and visual culture communication under the dual background of globalization and networking, *International Joint Conference on Information, Media and Engineering*, Osaka, Japan, pp. 46–48, 2018.
4. E. M. Elgewely, W. M. Sheta, and M. M. Metwalli, Virtual cultural gates: Exploring cyberspace potentials for a creative cultural heritage: An experimental design approach for the on-line 3D virtual environments, *2013 Digital Heritage International Congress (DigitalHeritage)*, Marseille, pp. 443–443, 2014.
5. X. Zhou, W. Dai, D. Xu, and C. Ye-Sho, The evolution of ethnic cultural industry towards a cyberspace: A perspective of generalized ecosystem, *2016 IEEE International Conference on Systems, Man, and Cybernetics (SMC)*, Budapest, pp. 004756–004761, 2016.
6. Literature in Cyberspace. https://elib.ustb.edu.cn/https/77726476706e69737468656 265737421e7e056d2283164597c468aa395/paper/2051905.
7. W. Wang, Research on industrial transition of American audio-visual streaming, Cyber Economic and Algorithmic Distribution, *Contemporary Cinema*, Vol. 5; pp. 112–117, 2020. [in Chinese]

8. Y. Chen, Challenge from cyberspace: Global development and status quo of streaming films in nowadays, *Contemporary Cinema*, Vol. 5; pp. 103–111, 2020. [in Chinese]
9. H. Zhang and M. Zhang, Research on cyberpunk images in the visual digital media, *2020 International Conference on Computer Vision, Image and Deep Learning (CVIDL)*, Chongqing, China, pp. 39–43, 2020.
10. G. Hu, Postmodern crisis: A review of cyberpunk science fiction by William Gibson. *Time literature (Theory Academic edition)*, Vol. 3; pp. 119–120, 2007.
11. G. Mantovani and A. Spagnolli, Imagination and culture: What is it like being in the cyberspace? *Mind Culture & Activity*, Vol. 7; No. 3, pp. 217–226, 2000.

Chapter 12

Cyberspace Sovereignty Development and Research History

12.1 Introduction

National sovereignty is the essence of a country. As cyberspace has gradually become a new living space, cyberspace sovereignty has become an international issue. Is cyberspace a place of freedom? Cyberspace should be managed by the government? The international community, experts, and scholars have different opinions about it, so there are many branches of governance and research on cyberspace. In this chapter, the development, governance, and research will be discussed in detail around cyberspace sovereignty.

12.2 Background, Definition, and Sovereign Governance

12.2.1 Background

The Treaty of Westphalia[1] signed in 1648 marked the beginning of a modern international system based on the concept of Westphalian sovereignty. Based on the concept of the coexistence of sovereign states, a new political system was formed in central Europe. Among them, the concept of state sovereignty has gradually

---

[1] https://www.britannica.com/event/Peace-of-Westphalia

DOI: 10.1201/9781003257387-12

become popular as the central principle of international law and world order [1]. In the new system of international relations formed around the United Nations after World War II, sovereignty signifies the autonomy of a country's internal affairs and diplomacy in addition to its ability to assume international rights and obligations independently. Nowadays, sovereignty has extended from territorial land to territorial waters and airspace, from politics to culture and economy, constantly enriching new connotations. The Internet has become a new space for human life and naturally expanded new areas of national governance. Following the land, sea, air, and sky, cyberspace has become the fifth frontier of human production and life [2]. Sovereignty is a hot issue that has been studied internationally. The basic principles of international law established in the *Charter of the United Nations*[2] have not been changed due to the rapid development and the unbounded nature of cyberspace. Respect for national sovereignty is still a basic principle of international law, which naturally applies to cyberspace. The term *Cyberspace Sovereignty* used in the 1997 *"Cyberspace Sovereignty – The Internet and the International* System" article [3] and the following two decades have witnessed the transformation process from resistance to conditional acceptance in Western theoretical circles.

12.2.2 Definition

The definition of cyberspace sovereignty has always been a vague concept. Different countries have various definitions, but they are all based on their own national interests. For example, the U.S. Department of Defense (DoD) introduced a new cyberspace strategy in 2015 divided into three aspects to elaborate on the U.S.' attitude toward cyberspace security and pledge its sovereignty. China passed the *National Security Act of the People's Republic of China* in 2015, clarifying the concept of cyberspace sovereignty for the first time and safeguarding national cyberspace sovereignty, security, and development interests. The definitions of cyberspace sovereignty in other countries have their own descriptions, which are not universal in the world.

On June 24, 2013, the sixth United Nations General Assembly issued document *A/68/98*,[3] which passed the U.N. *"Group of Governmental Experts on Developments in the Field of Information and Telecommunications in the Context of International Security"* resolution. The content of 20 resolution is *"State sovereignty and international norms and principles that flow from sovereignty apply to State conduct of ICT-related activities, and to their jurisdiction over ICT infrastructure within their territory"*. In 2015, document *A/70 /174*[4] pointed out that *"the principle of national sovereignty is the foundation for enhancing the security of the country's use of information and communication technology"*. It can be seen that the U.N. organization's

---

[2] https://www.un.org/en/charter-united-nations/index.html
[3] https://undocs.org/A/68/98
[4] https://undocs.org/A/70/174

expression of "cyberspace sovereignty" relies on state sovereignty, which means that national sovereignty extends to cyberspace.

Cyberspace sovereignty is the natural extension and manifestation of a country's national sovereignty to a platform based on information and communication technology. Internally, cyberspace sovereignty refers to the country's independent development, supervision, and management of its own Internet affairs; externally, cyberspace sovereignty refers to prevent the country's Internet from external intrusions and attacks [4].

12.2.3 Sovereign Governance

The *Charter of the United Nations*,[5] signed at the San Francisco Conference on June 26, 1945, contains discourses on states and national sovereignty, as well as the *International Law*[6] (International law refers to the application of legal rules between state sovereign and other entities with international personality) summed up traditional national sovereignty. As cyberspace has become a new living space, the principle of equality of national sovereignty is also applicable to cyberspace. According to the content of the "*United Nations Charter*" and "*International Law*", the four basic rights of national sovereignty can be summarized: equality, independence, jurisdiction, and self-defense. These four powers have similar expressions in different countries' official documents, such as the *U.S. Department of Defense's statement on cyberspace strategy*,[7] and *China's cyberspace security Act*.[8] Based on these four points, this section summarizes traditional national sovereignty, explains its connotation, and gives new connotations that extend to cyberspace, as shown in Table 12.1.

This section discusses the governance of cyberspace sovereignty. During these decades of development, there have been two major factions of struggle, cyberspace liberalism and cyberspace sovereignism. The *Declaration of independence for cyberspace* [5] published by Barlow in 1996 is an extreme expression of cyberspace liberalism. It calls on the government to leave cyberspace, believing that cyberspace has no sovereignty and cyberspace does not exist within the borders of any country. Besides, the government's control of the Internet is futile. Barlow eagerly hopes that cyberspace can become an "independent territory" and "extra-legal pure land", severing all ties to the traditional real society in terms of governance. The *Declaration of independence for cyberspace* not only depicts the fantasy of this utopian world but also expresses optimistic expectations for the realization of network autonomy. In

---

[5] https://www.un.org/en/about-us/un-charter

[6] https://www.un.org/en/global-issues/international-law-and-justice

[7] https://www.itu.int/net/wsis/docs2/tunis/off/6rev1.html; https://www.defense.gov/Newsroom/Speeches/Speech/Article/744066/

[8] http://www.cac.gov.cn/2017-08/07/c_1121443864.htm; http://www.cac.gov.cn/2017-08/07/c_1121443864.htm

Table 12.1   The Extension of Traditional National Sovereignty to Cyberspace

Category of Sovereignty	Traditional Meaning	Cyberspace Meaning
Equal	All countries enjoy equal qualifications and identities to participate in international relations.	Sovereign countries have an equal status in network interconnection and network operation, and have an equal right to speak and participate in international cyberspace governance.
Independence	The right of each country to deal with its own internal and external affairs according to its own will, without any external control and interference.	The network of each country can operate independently, not to stop services due to interference from other countries and to independently formulate its own Internet policy.
Jurisdiction	The power of a state to exercise jurisdiction over all people and things in its territory and its own people outside the territory.	The right of a sovereign state to exercise jurisdiction over the cyberspace on its own territory.
Self-Defense	When a country is under armed attack, the right to resist the attack alone or with other countries.	Sovereign countries have the power to take self-defense measures in the event of any external cyberspace attacks and threats.

the eyes of cyberspace liberalists, the emergence of cyberspace will bring about an era of de-authorization and de-government [6]. At the domestic political level, the existence of cyberspace will individualize and socialize power, and the authority of the state will give way to individuals and civil society organizations in cyberspace; at the international political level, the transnationality and decentralization of the network will. The borders of national sovereignty are becoming increasingly blurred, posing a challenge to the traditional state-centered international mechanism. Brenner believes that various forms of "threat" in cyberspace have broken away from the "regional" characteristics of the traditional era, and the governance paradigm based on sovereignty cannot be extended [7]. The *"National Security Strategy Report"* issued by the U.S. in 2010 used the concept of *"global commons"*.

In the U.S. strategic concept, the *"global commons"* is not dominated by any single country. But it is closely related to the security and prosperity of all countries. The *"global commons theory"* of the U.S. in cyberspace is based on liberalism. This view holds that cyberspace is shared by all mankind without sovereignty. The private sector and global civil society should play an important role in cyberspace governance. In this way, liberal thinking dominates people's early understanding of the effects of network politics [8].

However, cyberspace is a reflection of the real world, and unconstrained space is bound to be chaotic and disorderly. The concealment and openness of the Internet facilitate the spread of Internet rumors and seriously interfere with social order. Faced with the chaos brought to the real world by the disorder of cyberspace, all countries have unanimously chosen to strengthen cyberspace governance. There is a trend of *"the resurgence of national sovereignty"* in cyberspace: cyberspace liberalism has declined, and cyberspace realism has returned strongly. *The resurgence of national sovereignty* in cyberspace is mainly manifested in two aspects. On the one hand, the national authority clarifies the jurisdiction and method of sovereignty in cyberspace by establishing and improving the legal and institutional system of cyberspace supervision and will. The social behaviors and actors of the country are re-incorporated into the internality of sovereignty; on the other hand, state actors establish their status as the main body in cybersecurity through external development of cyberspace offenses and defenses, and formulation of cybersecurity strategies [9].

12.3 The History of Governance

As mentioned in the previous section, there have been controversies about "cyberspace reality". One view is that the concept of cyberspace is a libertarian fantasy that does not describe real things. Another point of view is that cyberspace is a truly international space. Therefore, any disputes related to cyberspace activities should be governed. However, regardless of any viewpoint, there is governance on a global scale in cyberspace. Global governance does not refer to the creation of a global government but to countries, international organizations, and nonstate actors to meet common challenges that transcend national boundaries [10].

After World War II, there were international armed information conflicts (e.g., the information war between Israel and Egypt, India and Pakistan, the U.K. and Argentina, or Iraq and Iran), but there was no sovereignty in cyberspace. The focus of attention between countries is still traditional national sovereignty. Since the 1990s, cyberspace sovereignty has been valued by some countries. Since 1995, South Korea has strengthened the government's unshakable position in cyberspace governance by revising old laws such as the *Telecom Business Act* and passing new laws such as the *National Informatization Basic Act* and *Network Security Management Regulations* [11].

The Telecommunications Act of 1996,[9] which was promulgated in 1996, was the first to govern the Internet, and its provisions granted the U.S. government authority to govern the Internet. Japan proposed the idea of establishing a "cyberspace police" in 1998, which embodies the early idea of establishing the authority of the government in cyberspace through systems. In 2005, the *Cabinet's Official Information Security Center* was established, and it rose to the central level. In 2003, the U.S. published "*The National Strategy to Secure Cyberspace*".[10] After Obama took office, he inherited the cyberspace security strategy of his predecessor and published "*International Strategy for Cyberspace*"[11] in 2011. In 2005, the "*Strategy for Homeland Defense and Civil Support*"[12] issued by the U.S. DoD stated: "Global commons include international waters, air space, outer space, and cyberspace". That is, for the first time, the U.S. classified cyberspace as global commons. Developed countries hope that cyberspace would refuse to inherit the concept of sovereignty. Besides, they strongly advocate the concept of "*global networked commons*"[13] to maximize the advantages of network technology without being criticized and obstructed by other countries. For example, secretary of state Hillary Clinton mentioned in 2010 "*global networked commons*" in his speech on Internet freedom and used this to accuse other countries of the implementation of network management policies. However, there is also opposition to the "*global commons*" claim within the U.S. Kanuck [12], the drafter of the *White House Internet Policy Commentary*, believed that the theory of global commons lacks the theoretical support of *International Law* and political economy. Franzese [13], an official of the *U.S. Strategic Command*, analyzed the five major characteristics of the global commons, which are not available in cyberspace.

After the publication of "*Declaration of independence for cyberspace*", a wave of freedom has been set off, but the changes in the practice of various countries in the past two decades have fully proved that the Internet is not a place outside the law. Also, national sovereignty is necessary and capable of intervening and managing cyberspace. With the frequent occurrence of network intrusions, cyberspace attacks, and cybercrime since the 1990s, sovereign countries have realized the seriousness of cybersecurity threats and have gradually participated in cyberspace governance. After *September 11 attacks*, the U.S. successively promulgated the "*USA Patriot Act*",[14] "*Homeland Security Act of 2002*", and "*Protect America Act of 2007*" to impose strict controls in cyberspace. The "*Comprehensive National Cybersecurity Initiative*" adopted in 2008 advocates the defense of cyberspace security, and this proposition carries an "ilitarized" deterrent.

---

9   https://www.britannica.com/topic/Telecommunications-Act

10 https://georgewbush-whitehouse.archives.gov/pcipb/

11 https://obamawhitehouse.archives.gov/sites/default/files/rss_viewer/international_strategy_for_cyberspace.pdf

12 https://fas.org/irp/agency/dod/homeland.pdf

13 https://2009-2017.state.gov/secretary/20092013clinton/rm/2010/01/135519.htm

14 https://www.fincen.gov/resources/statutes-regulations/usa-patriot-act

Since 1999, the U.N. has held various conferences on Internet governance issues, such as *World Summit on the Information Society (WSIS)* and *Internet Governance Forum (IGF)*. Issues surrounding cyberspace security are one of the main topics discussed. On December 12, 2003, the *"Declaration of Principles"* published on WSIS clearly stated that the decision-making power of Internet-related public policy issues is the sovereignty of each country. With regard to international public policy issues related to the Internet, countries have rights and responsibilities. The *"unis Agenda for the Information society"*[15] passed at the second phase of the 2005 meeting stated that "Internet sovereignty has become a true and objective practice of the international community". At this meeting, the participating countries unilaterally emphasized their sovereign rights in formulating relevant Internet policies and chose to maximize their power, which in turn led to competition in cyberspace. In 2011, China, Russia, Tajikistan, and Uzbekistan jointly drafted the *"International Code of Conduct for Information Security"* and called on all countries to initiate further discussions on this within the framework of the U.N. to regulate the international norms and regulations of their behavior in information and cyberspace as soon as possible [14]. In 2012, the guidelines were formally submitted to the *66th United Nations General Assembly,* and the concept of cyberspace sovereignty was proposed. It pointed out that cyberspace governance should respect human rights and fundamental freedoms, as well as the diversity of the history, culture, and social systems of various countries. It was strongly resisted by western countries. In December 2012, in the *World Conference on International Telecommunications (WCIT-12)*, 89 developing countries and 55 developed countries agreed on the clause that "member countries have the right to access international telecommunications services and the country's right to manage information content". Disagreements appeared and challenged the Internet Multistakeholderism governance model supported by the U.S. As a result, the U.S. strongly opposed and refused to sign the *International Telecommunication Regulations* (ITRs)[16] after the conference passed. WCIT-12 has actually become a battlefield for the West against all other countries [15].

In 2013, The *NATO Cooperative Cyber Defence Centre of Excellence* released the *"Tallinn Manual on the International Law Applicable to Cyber Warfare"*.[17] The first chapter discusses the relationship between state sovereignty and cyberspace, and stipulates that a country has the right to control the network infrastructure and network activities within its territory. It is clarified that without prejudice to assume relevant international responsibilities, a country has jurisdiction: (a) personnel performing cyberspace operations in its territory; (b) network infrastructure located in its territory; (c) extraterritorial jurisdiction in compliance with *International*

---

[15] https://www.itu.int/net/wsis/docs2/tunis/off/6rev1.html

[16] https://www.itu.int/en/wcit-12/Pages/itrs.aspx

[17] https://www.cambridge.org/core/books/tallinn-manual-on-the-international-law-applicable-to-cyber-warfare/50C5BFF166A7FED75B4EA643AC677DAE

Law. In 2017, the *"Tallinn Manual 2.0 on the International Law Applicable to Cyber Warfare"*[18] published by the organization provided more direct provisions on cyberspace sovereignty in corresponding provisions. Its first article stipulates: the principle of national sovereignty applies to cyberspace. Article 2 explains the state sovereignty: without prejudice to the performance of international legal obligations, the state has sovereignty over the network infrastructure, people, and network activities on its territory.

In recent years, vicious incidents in cyberspace have occurred from time to time. On June 6, 2013, The Washington Post and The Guardian disclosed the existence of *Planning Tool for Resource Integration, Synchronization, and Management (PRISM).* PRISM is a "data tool" designed to collect and process "foreign intelligence" that passes through American servers.[19] Edward Snowden, a 29-year-old National Security Agency (NSA) contractor who leaked the details and fled the U.S. to seek international political asylum. PRISM directly enters the central server of the U.S. Internet company to mine data and collect information. Nine international Internet giants (e.g., Microsoft, Yahoo, Google, Apple, etc.) are all participating in it.

Internet Corporation for Assigned Names and Numbers (ICANN) is responsible for the space allocation of Internet protocol addresses, the management of top-level domain name systems and regions, and the management of root service systems. Countries and organizations, including China, Russia, and the E.U., have been calling for the internationalization of ICANN supervision. After Edward Snowden exposed PRISM, the international community fell into a panic. Germany proposed a plan to build a European-wide Internet to avoid U.S. surveillance. In September 2015, Russia authorized the Internet Service Provider (ISP) to host Russian citizens' data servers, thereby protecting these data from intrusive global surveillance by the NSA (and allowing Federal'nayasluzhba bezopasnosti Rossiyskoy Federatsii (FSB) to monitor Russia political opinions). In October 2015, the European Court of Justice rejected the Safe Harbor Agreement.[20] Before this, the agreement allowed U.S. companies to transfer data from European users outside the E.U. [16]. In 2015, China stipulated that foreign companies must disclose the source code of their software and firmware to export to the mainland. After the promulgation of this regulation, companies such as IBM and Microsoft have installed software backdoors in the Chinese market. Under tremendous pressure from the international community, the U.S. was forced to announce in 2016 that it was conditionally abandoning ICANN supervision. However, it still set the basic prerequisite to hand over management to a private organization that follows the multi-stakeholder principle and opposes handing over to multilateral organizations led by sovereign

---

[18] https://www.cambridge.org/core/books/tallinn-manual-20-on-the-international-law-applicable-to-cyber-operations/E4FFD83EA790D7C4C3C28FC9CA2FB6C9

[19] https://www.cnet.com/news/what-is-the-nsas-prism-program-faq/

[20] https://www.enisa.europa.eu/topics/threat-risk-management/risk-management/current-risk/laws-regulation/data-protection-privacy/safe-harbor-privacy-principles

governments. Since the ICANN organization is located in the U.S. and is subject to U.S. laws, the U.S. can still control and manage global Internet resources indirectly.

Although there are different definitions and opinions on sovereignty in cyberspace, the international recognition of "cyberspace sovereignty" is gradually strengthening. A series of rules and laws issued by the international community are also measured to protect sovereignty in cyberspace.

12.4 The History of Research

12.4.1 Governance Rules

There are many kinds of research on cyberspace governance rules, which can be divided into three governance models: distributed governance, Multilateral Governance, and multi-stakeholder [17]. With the publication of the declaration of independence for cyberspace, the liberalism proposed by Barlow has been widely publicized. However, this kind of liberalism thought is not completely without governance. In the early development of the Internet, people advocated the freedom of information, and the governance in cyberspace is unorganized and restricted. Therefore, this governance model can be described as a distributed system [18]. Its mode reflects a small-scale, homogeneous, and self-regulated network era, which is also the early era of the Internet. In the 1990s, the number of Internet users was less than 1 million. Nowadays, it has exceeded billions. Cyberspace has become an integral part of modern society, and it needs to be regulated. Obviously, this kind of distributed governance cannot afford such a huge scale of cyberspace governance.

The second kind of governance rule is multilateral governance. The people who put forward this kind of governance rule think that cyberspace is a chaotic field, i.e., the actions in cyberspace cannot be guaranteed, and the country should be the one to make cyberspace policy. Such governance rules require the establishment of an agency in the U.N. responsible for the governance of cyberspace, and each country has the right to formulate its cyberspace policy. Multilateral Governance is supported by Russia, China, and India. This kind of governance rule has been studied by many scholars, such as Goldsmith and others. In view of the fact that the hardware and software of the Internet are located in the territory of a country, the sovereignty based on the territory legitimizes the state's regulation of its network users [19]. Brian et al. [20] proposed a new network governance paradigm to recognize the complexity of regulatory power center, using new policy tools such as technology standardization to achieve regulatory objectives, endowing the network with semi-sovereign entity status, and shifting the role of the state to create an incentive structure for network self-regulation. Cattaruzza et al. [16] studied the fragmentation of the network and called for the supervision of cyberspace to be realized through the Multilateral Governance model that can strengthen collective security.

It also lists the major differences in Internet governance at the international level. On the one hand, the U.S. and other countries believe that multi-stakeholder governance will be the only way to more democratic cyberspace. On the other hand, the concept of multilateral governance is based on sovereignty represented by Russia or China. The middle way is inclusive multilateral Governance or national democratization promoted by the E.U.

The third kind of governance rule is the multi-stakeholder model. Advocates believe that government-related organizations cannot successfully regulate cyberspace, and cyberspace norms will only be accepted by Internet users if they participate in the design, which will enhance the legitimacy and authority of institutions, organizations, and commercial companies in cyberspace. On the one hand, its core principle is inclusiveness and representativeness. All relevant actors can participate equally and express their opinions. In an ideal situation, stakeholders should not only formulate norms and set their own standards but also define the possible consequences or penalties of noncompliance. On the other hand, because many enterprises can participate in this governance model, massive data can flow into their hands, and the privacy of users cannot be protected. Especially after the Snowden incident, the legitimacy and credibility of this governance model have been weakened. Aiming at the problems of the governance model, Almeida et al. [21] gave three suggestions: (a) Improving the communication between state and non-state actors to bring together the most diverse and relevant actors in the field of cyber warfare and cybersecurity. (b) Promoting the discussion of cyber norms and making appropriate norms for behaviors in cyberspace. (c) Using network security practices to properly protect and maintain systems and devices connected to the Internet.

12.4.2 Governance Technology

In terms of governance, there are a variety of governance rules, which have their own characteristics, advantages, and disadvantages. Most of the research on rules is theoretical and institutional. In the field of governance, there is also research and development at the technical level. Chu et al. [22] established a digital network authentication system to solve international conflicts in cyberspace. This system provides Internet users with the opportunity to authenticate their nationality. Using information technology to provide nationality recognition in cyberspace not only lays the cornerstone for resolving national sovereignty but also contributes to the development of International Law in cyberspace. Besides, it provides feasible solutions for international arbitration to resolve international cyberspace conflicts. Maurer et al. [23] provided a comprehensive mapping and impact assessment of these proposals, ranging from technical ones, such as new undersea cables, encryption, and localized data storage, to nontechnical ones, such as domestic industry support, international codes of conduct, and data protection laws.

12.5 Future Governance

A new form of cyberspace sovereignty may emerge. Certain groups of nonsovereign state units actually have the willingness and ability to demarcate boundaries in cyberspace to a certain degree, using interests, values, or behavior patterns as criteria to identify and build communities. Once the external cyberspace can maintain a certain standard of universal security through a certain method or mechanism, these groups are likely to become a new power of promoting the "Balkanization" of cyberspace.

As countries strengthen the construction of network infrastructure, cyberspace's future governance is full of uncertainty. No one dares to say whether a new governance model will be born or whether a new governance conflict will break out. However, the concept of cyberspace sovereignty has spread all over the world, and the international community is strengthening cooperation to safeguard global cyberspace. More and more regulations have confirmed that cyberspace sovereignty is an extension of traditional national sovereignty. To maintain the existing cyberspace order, respect and cooperation between countries may be an effective way to govern cyberspace sovereignty, but also provide experience for future governance.

References

1. T. Britannica, Editors of Encyclopaedia, Peace of Westphalia, Encyclopedia Britannica, https://www.britannica.com/event/Peace-of-Westphalia [Accessed 8 May 2021].
2. L. F. Zhi. Network sovereignty is rooted in modern jurisprudence, Guangming Daily, 2015. [in Chinese]
3. S. W. Timothy, Cyberspace sovereignty--The internet and the international system, *Harvard Journal of Law & Technology*, Vol. 10; No. 3, pp. 647–665, 1997.
4. B. Fang, *Cyberspace Sovereignty, Cyberspace Sovereignty: Reflections on Building a Community of Common Future in Cyberspace*, Springer, Singapore, 2018.
5. J. P. Barlow, A Declaration of Independence of Cyberspace, *Humanist*, Vol. 18; No. 1, pp. 5–7, 1996.
6. K. E. Eichensehr, The cyber-law of nations, *The Georgetown Law Journal*, Vol. 103; No. 2, pp. 317–380, 2014.
7. S. W. Brenner, *Cyberthreats: The Emerging Fault Lines of the Nation State*, Oxford University Press, United States, 2009.
8. M. Wang, The future of global cyberspace Governance: Sovereignty, competition and consensus, *Frontiers*, Vol. 4; pp. 15–23, 2016.
9. Y. Liu and Y. Yang, "Re sovereignty" of cyberspace and the future of international network governance, International Forum, 2013. [in Chinese]
10. S. Patrick, The unruled world. The case for good enough global governance, *Foreign Affairs*, Vol. 93; No. 1, pp. 58–73, 2014.
11. D. Ronald, J. Palfrey, R. Rohozinski, and J. Zittrain, *Access Contested*, The MIT Press, United States, 2011.
12. S. Kanuck, Sovereign discourse on cyber conflict under international law, *Texas Law Review*, Vol. 88; pp. 1571–1597, 2010.

13. P. W. Franzese, Sovereignty in cyberspace: Can it exist? *Air Force Law Review*, Vol. 64; pp. 1–42, 2009.
14. U. G. Assembly, International code of conduct for information security, Developments in the field of information and telecommunications in the context of international security of the General Assembly, 2011.
15. WCIT-12: The shadow at evening rising – by Alexander Klimburg, https://cyberdialogue. ca/2013/03/wcit-12-the-shadow-at-evening-rising-by-alexander-klimburg/ [Accessed January 23, 2021].
16. A. Cattaruzza, D. Danet, S. Taillat and A. Laudrain, Sovereignty in cyberspace: Balkanization or democratization, *2016 International Conference on Cyber Conflict (CyCon U.S.)*, Washington, DC, USA, pp. 1–9, 2016.
17. S. M. West, *Globalizing Internet Governance: Negotiating Cyberspace Agreements in the Post-Snowden Era*, TPRC Conference Paper, 2014, available at SSRN: https://ssrn. com/abstract=2418762 or http://dx.doi.org/10.2139/ssrn.2418762.
18. R. Deibert, and M. Crete-Nishihata, Global governance and the spread of cyberspace controls. *Global Governance*, Vol. 18; No. 3, pp. 339–361, 2012.
19. J. Goldsmith, The Internet and the abiding significance of territorial sovereignty, *Indiana Journal of Global Legal Studies*, Vol. 5; No. 2, pp. 475–491, 1998.
20. K. Brian and N. Charles, *Governing Networks and Rule-Making in Cyberspace*, MIT Press, USA, 1997.
21. V. A. F. Almeida, D. Doneda, and S. A. Jacqueline, Cyberwarfare and digital governance, *IEEE Internet Computing*, Vol. 21; No. 2, pp. 68–71, 2017.
22. C. Chih-Ping, L. Te-Chao, and H. Ku-Chen, International security competition and debates on state sovereignty in the cyberspace and suggest plausible means, *2018 IEEE International Conference on Applied System Invention (ICASI)*, Chiba, Japan, pp. 1334–1337, 2018.
23. T. Maurer, I. Skierka, R. Morgus, and M. Hohmann, Technological sovereignty: Missing the point? *2015 7th International Conference on Cyber Conflict: Architectures in Cyberspace*, Tallinn, pp. 53–68, 2015.

Chapter 13

Cyberspace Governance Coordination Mechanism

13.1 Introduction

The coordination and governance of cyberspace are born and developed together with cyberspace. There are different governance and coordination mechanisms for cyberspace in different periods. These mechanisms regulate the activities of cyberspace, restrict behaviors that violate the power of others, and protect the harmonious development of cyberspace. In this chapter, starting from the definition, the development of the definition of cyberspace coordination and governance and the change of governance objects are described, and then the scope and development history of cyberspace coordination and governance are discussed. Finally, a specific example of coordinated governance among countries in recent years is given to prove the necessity and advantages of coordinated governance.

13.2 Cyberspace Coordination Governance and Governance Objects

In the early days of its founding, cyberspace was considered a pure land without government. However, with the popularization of the Internet, various new types of problems were frequently occurring in cyberspace. In order to better develop the Internet, various international and national organizations had begun to try to formulate a series of policies and laws to take over cyberspace.

DOI: 10.1201/9781003257387-13   **139**

13.2.1 Cyberspace Coordination Governance

As a traditional definition, the "government" often is synonymous with governance and coordination. The government adopts a certain method to carry out macrocontrol on the country to promote the development of the country. Kooiman described it as "a method through which we can search for a specific social and/or political (subsystem) system operation mode, as well as social forces play a role in it" [1]. Cyberspace is different from traditional coordination and governance due to its virtual characteristics. In the 1970s, when the Internet was in its infancy, the awareness of governance and coordination of cyberspace needed to be strengthened urgently. Besides, people mainly focused on technological development and popularization. At this time, the main role of cyberspace governance was the U.S. government. The U.S. set the tone for equality, freedom, development, and sharing for the Internet. U.S. government believed that cyberspace should not be excessively interfered by the government, and should be allowed to develop freely and build a kind of freedom an equal platform. The governance and coordination of the U.S. government also focus on technologies such as Transmission Control Protocol/Internet Protocol (TCP/IP)[1] and Network Control Program (NCP).[2]

In the 1980s, the major Internet organizations formed in the early stages also had antigovernment and antipolitical ideas. This kind of equality, liberalization, and various institutions' technical specifications had stimulated the innovation and popularization of the Internet. People were actively participating in this free space and had made outstanding contributions to the ecology of the Internet. At this time, the meaning of network governance and coordination was based on the premise of freedom and equality, and the potential rules established by the self-consciousness of the Internet masses under the guidance of the U.S. government.

In the 1990s, the Internet was rapidly spreading around the world. The Internet was no longer a small space independent of reality and embedded in many aspects of people's lives and national governance. Many scholars had gradually noticed the complexity of cyberspace governance and coordination, and had conducted extensive research on this. For example, Powell et al. and Larson et al. studied Network forms of organization and gave their own definitions [2,3]. Candace Jones et al. proposed a theory on cyberspace governance. However, in the 20th century, international organizations and officials still had not given a formal definition [4].

After entering the 21st century, international organizations began to notice the importance of cyberspace governance and coordination. In 2003, the World Summit on the Information Society (WSIS) was held in Geneva. This meeting brought together more than 40 members from the government and the private sector to discuss various issues of Internet coordination and governance. This meeting established the Working Group on Internet Governance (WGIG) and the

---

[1] https://tools.ietf.org/html/rfc1180
[2] http://mercury.lcs.mit.edu/~jnc/tech/arpaprot.html

Internet Governance Forum (IGF). In the WSIS-II/PC-3/DOC/5-C work report,[3] the Internet governance was defined as "Internet governance was the development and application by governments, private sector and civil society, in their respective roles, of shared principles, norms, rules, decision-making procedures, and programs that shape the evolution and use of the Internet".[3] At the same time, it was clear that the coordination and governance of the Internet should not only include the name and address of the Internet but should also include some public policy issues. Meanwhile, it should be responsible for the role and responsibilities of the government, the private sector, civil society, and detailed division. This conference marked that the main body of the Internet had shifted from academia to society, and the Internet was no longer just a platform for academic exchanges but had become a popular platform.

In the 2010s, with the intensification of networking, the role of cyberspace had been further enhanced. The following new types of crimes and wars also began to develop on the Internet. In August 2008, during the Russian-Georgian conflict,[4] Russia seized Georgia's Internet before the war began, and the Georgian government website was paralyzed for 24 hours. In 2010, the world's first worm aimed at destroying industrial infrastructure in the real world, the "Stuxnet"[5] virus attacked uranium enrichment infrastructure in Iran and Siemens industrial control systems, causing a lot of economic losses. In 2013, former Central Intelligence Agency (CIA) employee Edward Snowden disclosed a large number of incidents such as the PRISM,[6] which accelerated the government's attention to cyberspace. Major governments had begun to strengthen the management and restraint of cyberspace. In order to strengthen international cooperation, a series of organizations such as the Asia-Pacific Economic Cooperation (APEC), Forum of Incident Response and Security Teams (FIRST), and the Group of Eight (G8) had also been established. They announced that national organizations had begun to station in cyberspace to regulate and organize a series of activities in cyberspace. Various countries and organizations had begun to formulate laws and norms regarding cyberspace conduct. As the Internet's influence on the world continues to increase, it had become a trend for national organizations to take over cyberspace.

13.2.2 Governance Objects

In the 20th century, cyberspace governance and coordination agencies had not yet formed a management system for cyberspace participants. The main object of

---

[3] http://www.wgig.org/docs/WGIGREPORT.pdf
[4] https://web.archive.org/web/20090416225801/http://www.mdb.cast.ru/mdb/3-2008/item3/article1/
[5] https://www.wired.com/images_blogs/threatlevel/2010/11/w32_stuxnet_dossier.pdf
[6] https://www.washingtonpost.com/investigations/us-intelligence-mining-data-from-nine-us-internet-companies-in-broad-secret-program/2013/06/06/3a0c0da8-cebf-11e2-8845-d970ccb04497_story.html

governance was the basic computer architecture and protocol specifications. Vinton Cerf and Kahn used the TCP/IP protocol to solve the problem that NCP could not connect to heterogeneous networks, laying the foundation for information transmission in cyberspace. The International Organization for Standardization (ISO) took the lead in formulating the Open System Interconnection Model (OSI),[7] which became the underlying transmission protocol in cyberspace. Because most of the members of cyberspace at that time were scholars and government officials, the almost-open space stimulated creativity and vitality, and the normative agreements formed in innovation laid the foundation for the popularization of the Internet.

After entering the 21st century, the popularization of the Internet has injected new vitality into the cyberspace, and at the same time brought problems such as information loss and data explosion. In order to solve these problems, the governance and coordination objects in cyberspace have been extended to data and users. The data included various data, software, and works uploaded by users. In order to ensure the vitality of innovation, intellectual property protection was provided for original authors. Simultaneously, a series of regulations had been formulated to ensure the orderliness of Internet participants, and a series of constraints had been formulated for users. Besides, punitive measures had been formulated for those who harm interests.

With the deeper development of cyberspace, various international organizations and countries had begun to take the initiative to formulate detailed strategies and laws to restrict objects in cyberspace. Most countries and organizations divided cyberspace into three layers, namely the physical layer, the logical layer, and the content layer. At the physical layer, further adaptive formulation of the underlying architecture and specifications was carried out, and a series of regional standards were formulated under international standards. Regulating information in cyberspace at the logical level affirms the value of innovation and protects the interests of creators. At the content level, countries and institutions have established codes of conduct, and online communities ethically restrict individual corporate behavior. At this time, the objects of governance were transformed into organizations and individuals.

13.3 The Scope of Coordinated Governance in Cyberspace

Different institutions have different binding forces and directions for different countries, organizations, enterprises, and individuals. The binding of international and national organizations is essentially the regulation of activities through treaties and laws. In this section, the scope of coordinated governance of cyberspace progressively is discussed from five directions.

---

[7] https://www.iso.org/standard/20269.html

13.3.1 *International Governance*

The coordination and governance of international cyberspace organizations are mainly aimed at the member states of the organization. A global organization recruit's member from all countries in the world and participates in discussions together. International organizations had made great contributions to the standardization and harmonious development of cyberspace, and departments and agencies hold some substantive powers in cyberspace. For example, Internet Corporation for Assigned Names and Numbers (ICANN) had the power to manage the allocation of IP address space and the management of domain names. The control of these powers in nonprofit organizations makes cyberspace truly fair. Regional organizations provide a platform for fair exchanges and cooperative development among members of the region. Compared with global organizations, regional organizations were closer to the actual development of each region, formulated corresponding measures from the perspective of their own development, and had more practical cooperation due to geographical factors, such as network infrastructure transactions, cyberspace criminal investigation, etc.

13.3.2 *Country Governance*

The country's governance of cyberspace was realized only by international recognition based on sovereignty. Each country's research on its own cyberspace was based on its own national conditions, giving full play to its own advantages, increasing the coverage of cyberspace and the degree of integration with tradition. Furthermore, the importance of various countries on cyberspace governance had increased over time. The emphasis on cyber sovereignty was also increasing year by year. With the deepening of the integration of government and cyberspace, areas related to national core interests such as national defense, medical care, and social governance had gradually become networked. Therefore, many people in the world believe that cyberspace security issues had become a part of national strength. The 2010 war between Russia and Georgia revealed that if the security of cyberspace cannot be guaranteed, the country will face great danger. Therefore, many countries had elevated the protection of cyber sovereignty and cyberspace to the military aspect, and invested talents and large amounts of funds on issues of cyber sovereignty and cyberspace security. There were also some differences in the actual process of different international governance concepts for cyberspace. This chapter lists the governance directions and representative laws of five influential countries in the world for cyberspace governance, as shown in Table 13.1.

13.3.3 *Society Governance*

After the popularization of the Internet, the network society represents an extension of the real society. The difference from real society is that the network society

Table 13.1 Comparison of Five Countries' Governance Methods in Cyberspace

Country	Governance Way	Fundamental Laws
U.S.	Internal defense, external expansion and cooperation	"Strengthening the Cybersecurity of Federal Networks and Critical Infrastructure"[59]
Japan	Led by large enterprises, with policy support from the state	"The Basic Act on Cybersecurity"[60]
Germany	Manufacturing-based, Focus on small businesses	"German High-Tech Strategy"[61]
Russia	Government-led, big companies hold power	"The Strategy of Scientific and Technological Development of the Russian Federation"[62]
China	Government support, integration, and innovation	"Cyber Security Law"[63]

[59] https://www.energy.gov/sites/prod/files/2018/05/f51/EO13800%20electricity%20subsector%20report.pdf

[60] http://www.japaneselawtranslation.go.jp/law/detail/?id=2760&vm=04&re=02

[61] https://www.research-in-germany.org/dam/jcr:8d61ee98-26bd-4606-a21d-1b97b17ca611/HTS_Broschuere_eng

[62] https://www.hse.ru/en/edu/vkr/206731724

[63] http://lyj.jiujiang.gov.cn/zwgk_185/jc/zcfg/202008/P020200805619989405641.pdf

has the characteristics of virtualization, and the governance of the network society involves cyberspace public opinion, public environment, culture and art, and daily life. This requires society to have a certain self-direction mechanism and a certain ability to maintain the public environment. Countries have formulated corresponding laws for their own network society to maintain the health of the public environment. For example, Germany has enacted a series of laws that stipulate the rules of online speaking. However, the high circulation of online social information makes it more difficult to influence and govern public opinion after the occurrence of public opinion than in real society. Even if relevant organizations use a lot of human resources to dispel rumors, rumors will have a big impact. For example, the New Mexico Central Community College (CNM) announced the death of Jackie Chan, which caused widespread condolences. As a result, Jackie Chan himself confirmed that this was fake news, which aroused even greater condemnation from CNM. Cyberspace society is also the dissemination and carrier of art and culture in the new era. Many cultural works use the Internet as a carrier of dissemination, so good works are no longer affected by spatial location and can be appreciated by people all over the world in a short time. The creation of the

Network Art Museum has also enriched people's spiritual world. It can be seen that cyberspace redefines people's daily life and provides more choices.

13.3.4 Enterprise Governance

Enterprises are an important part of cyberspace. The diversity of enterprises brings more prosperity and creativity to cyberspace and promotes the development of cyberspace. However, with the diversification and enrichment of network enterprises, enterprises had also paid attention to the maintenance of their own development. First of all, companies attach great importance to the maintenance and dissemination of their own public image and corporate culture. For example, Facebook had established a fair, open, and protected privacy by promulgating a series of codes of conduct, corporate regulations, and advertising regulations.[8] Google also put forward the "10 things"[9] that define the corporate culture. Through a lot of publicity, the "Code of Conduct" also provides a lot of traffic for enterprises. However, when the company gets a lot of traffic, the company will also bear the impact of emergencies on the company. In order to cope with emergencies, companies had strengthened their investment in crisis public relations while restraining themselves.

In addition to maintaining their own image and crisis public relations, international companies had also made great efforts in their own data security. Nowadays, many criminals on the Internet steal targets and put them in the databases of large enterprises, and obtain illegal benefits by stealing a large number of core user information. Such behavior will cause a devastating blow to the company's reputation. Therefore, most enterprises had established their own network security departments to protect the data security of users and enterprises. Some cloud computing providers, such as Amazon and Alibaba Cloud, combine the network fluctuations of cloud computing in network security to further strengthen the network security of enterprises.

13.3.5 Person Governance

Cyberspace behavior refers to all activities that an individual does in cyber. The governance and coordination of individual behavior in cyberspace are divided into autonomy and heteronomy. Autonomy refers to an ethical norm formed during the development of cyberspace, requiring that individuals' actions in cyberspace should be true, logical, civilized, and polite, protect their own data security, and refrain from leaking state secrets and harming national interests. These customary ethics restrict individual's behavior in cyberspace. Heterogeneous governance was an individual's self-management and restraint in accordance with laws and regulations in

---

[8] https://www.facebook.com/communitystandards/
[9] https://www.google.com/about/philosophy.html?hl=zh_EG

cyberspace, such as the German Freedom of Information Act.[10] Unlike autonomy, heteronomy is the minimum of individual behavior in cyberspace. Individual violations of the established treaty will result in punishment.

13.4 Cyberspace Coordination Governance History

The history of cyberspace governance and coordination had witnessed the various historical nodes of the Internet from its creation to its popularization. This section reviews the development history of cyberspace governance and coordination from four perspectives.

13.4.1 International Coordination Governance

In the early development of the Internet in the 1970s, the coordination and governance of the network did not attract attention. At this time, most organizations that formed and participated in cyberspace were devoted to standardization. At the first International Conference on Information Processing in 1959, Christopher Strachey et al. proposed the original idea of the Internet [5]. Based on this conference, the International Federation for Information Processing (IFIP) was formally established in 1960 under the auspices of UNESCO. The organization was committed to promoting standardization and information sharing in cyberspace. In 1972, because the interconnection protocol of cyberspace at that time was only provided interconnection services for homogeneous networks, it was impossible to interconnect heterogeneous networks. In order to realize the development of cyberspace and promote the standardization of cyberspace, the International Network Working Group (INWG) was formally established based on the ARPANET "Network Working Group"[11] created by Steve Crocker, and this organization was an informal group mainly used to study collaborative communication problems in heterogeneous networks. The group provided many directions for the realization of heterogeneous networks. These new ideas led to the proposal of Protocol for Packet Network Intercommunication, but the group only existed for a short time [6]. It was accepted by International Federation for Information Processing (IFIP) as a subordinate group. In 1979, Advanced Research Project Agency (ARPA) established the Internet Configuration Control Board (ICCB) to supervise the development of international cyberspace technology. In 1982, under the impetus of the U.S. Department of Defense (DoD), the TCP/IP protocol became the standard specification for cyberspace information transmission. In 1983, ARPANET also announced that ARPANET replaced NCP with TCP/IP. In the same year,

---

[10] http://www.gesetze-im-internet.de/englisch_ifg/englisch_ifg.pdf

[11] https://www.princeton.edu/news/2014/03/18/internet-founders-say-flexible-framework-was-key-explosive-growth

the Internet Action Committee (IAC) replaced ICCB in monitoring technologi-cal development. In 1984, ISO and the International Telecommunication Union (ITU) jointly issued the famous ISO/IEC 7498 standard, which was based on the Open System Interconnection Reference Model (OSI) draft proposed by Hubert Zimmermann in 1980 and incorporated the ideas of both parties [7]. Finally, a standardized OSI model was formed, which promoted the standardization of cyberspace interconnection. In 1985, the standardization organization The Internet Engineering Task Force (IETF) was established to promote the development of cyberspace from a technical perspective.

After entering the 1990s, as the standardization process of the underlying issues in cyberspace came to an end, and the rapid development of the Internet brought many new problems, some of the first international organizations began to merge and transfer. The newly established institutions were gradually transi-tioning to solving new problems in cyberspace. At the same time, major regional institutions had also begun to appear in the arena of cyberspace governance and played an important role in regional cyberspace governance. In 1990, The Forum of Incident Response and Security Teams (FIRST) was established, focusing on promoting cooperation between computer security incident response teams. In the same year, the Asia-Pacific Economic Cooperation (APEC) established the Asia-Pacific Economic Cooperation Telecommunications and Information Working Group, a platform for the liberalization of cyberspace trade and the exchange of cyberspace policies in the Asia-Pacific region. In 1992, the Internet Society (ISOC) was established, and the IAC organization was renamed the Internet Architecture Board (IAB). Besides, the IETF organization announced its integration into the Internet Association. The ISOC played an important role in promoting the global-ization of the Internet, accelerating network interconnection technology, develop-ing application software, and increasing Internet penetration.[12] The establishment of ISOC also marked that the Internet was no longer limited to the academic world but the business world too. The Organization for Economic Cooperation and Development (OECD) also established the Working Party on Information Security and Privacy (WPISP) to improve the level of national privacy protec-tion and security. In 1994, ISOC and the Institute of Electrical and Electronics Engineers (IEEE) jointly established the Internet Technology Committee (ITC), dedicated to interdisciplinary technical exchanges and the application of the most advanced communications and related technologies in Internet infrastructure and services.[13] In 1998, ICANN was established to take over the coordination and issuance functions of IANA for network addresses and domain names, marking the first time that the Internet became independent.

After entering the 21st century, with the widespread development of the Internet, many new types of problems such as cybercrime, public opinion, and other incidents

[12] https://www.internetsociety.org/
[13] https://en.wikipedia.org/wiki/Internet_Technical_Committee

frequently occur. Promoted by the United Nations, The Working Group on Internet Governance (WGIG) and Internet Governance Forum (IGF) established in 2005, expanding the scope of governance and coordination of cyberspace, and began to use some methods of real government to restrict users and data. At this time, major traditional organizations also began to participate in the governance of cyberspace. In 2001, the Council of Europe adopted the first international convention against cybercrime, the Cybercrime Convention,[14] and a batch of Internet space behaviors were defined as criminal behaviors. Besides, countries in the organization were called on to define these behaviors as criminal behaviors and enact corresponding laws. It was worth noting that the U.S. also signed this convention in 2006. In 2003, the European Union established the European Network and Information Security Agency (ENISA) to build a network security communication platform. However, this agency did not have law enforcement powers. In 2004, the Subcommittee on High-tech Crime of the Group of Eight (G8) also formulated guidelines for cybersecurity, providing Ten Principles[15] in the combat against computer crime. In the same year, the Organization of American States (OAS) also adopted a comprehensive strategy for cybersecurity in the U.S.[16] In 2005, the Meridian Conference provided a platform for exchanges on cyberspace security issues. The OECD established the WPISP to address the issue of privacy protection in cyberspace. ISO organizations had also begun to work on cyberspace information security and standardization. The North Atlantic Treaty Organization (NATO) adopted a cyber defense policy in 2008 and established the Cyber Defense Administration to defend cyberspace warfare. The Association of Southeast Asian Nations (ASEAN) also called on Southeast Asian countries to improve their information infrastructure and promote a Roadmap for an "ASEAN community 2009–2015".[17] The International Criminal Police Organization (INTERPOL) plays the role of the collector in the coordination and governance of cyberspace, helping the country to collect and obtain evidence of cybercrime. It holds the first conference on cybersecurity in 2010.[18]

In the 2010s, the influence of cyberspace on daily life was increasing. Organizations had gradually changed from isolation to cooperation. With the deep participation of the government, the exchanges between international organizations and the government were also increasing. In 2011, with the support of the British government, the International Cyber Security Protection Alliance (ICSPA) was established. Its members include many well-known companies around the world. The goal was to combat cybercrimes effectively. In 2013, at the BRICS Senior Advisors Meeting

---

[14] https://www.onacademic.com/detail/journal_1000036327328410_e0f3.html

[15] https://www.cybercrimelaw.net/G8.html

[16] https://www.oas.org/juridico/english/cyb_pry_strategy.pdf

[17] https://www.asean.org/wp-content/uploads/images/ASEAN_RTK_2014/2_Roadmap_for_ ASEAN_Community_20092015.pdf

[18] https://www.customs.gov.hk/en/publication_press/press/index_id_757.html

on Security Affairs, the BRICS countries established a BRICS Cyber Security Working Group to collect new updates about cybersecurity issues and promote information exchange. In 2016, the European Parliament promulgated the General Data Protection Regulation (GDPR),[19] strengthening citizens' right to information and standardized international business. This regulation was known as the most stringent data protection regulation in history, and it had a profound impact on countries all over the world. In 2019, the European Union proposed a cybersecurity bill to further organize cybersecurity issues while giving WPSIP certain ruling powers. In 2020, FIRST and ICANN signed the Memorandum of Understanding (MoU),[20] dedicated to enhancing information security in cyberspace. It could be seen that in the future, various organizations will continue to deepen cooperation and jointly deal with various risks in cyberspace.

13.4.2 *National Coordination Governance*

Any national plans and laws in cyberspace were based on the country's sovereignty over cyberspace. In the 1970s, the U.S., as the founding country, enjoyed absolute jurisdiction over cyberspace. Internet founding institutions and scholars had also tried to form a special field of cyberspace independent of national sovereignty. Every country except the U.S. had no clear understanding of the importance of cyberspace. As the country of origin of the Internet, the U.S. government attaches great importance to cyberspace. Before the first network ARPANET was proposed in 1969, Willis H. Ware realized that there might be security problems in cyberspace,[21] but that did not get the government's attention. ARPANET only proposes NCP to regulate interconnection communication. What is interesting was that Ronald Reagan, who became later the President of the U.S. in 1983, after watching the movie *War Games* aroused his attention to cyberspace security issues. Fifteen months later, he signed the "Electronic Communication and Automation Information System Security" – National Security Decision-Making Guidance Program *NSDD-145*.[22] This policy was too forward-looking and caused widespread controversy in academia for a time. At that time, the Internet was in a period of rapid rise, and the policy did not distinguish between civilian and military, so it did not have much effect. In 1987, the U.S. Congress promulgated the *Computer Security Act of 1987*,[23] which established a new level of security in a forward-looking manner: "sensitive". It required uniform methods to protect sensitive materials.

In the 1990s, the widespread use of the Internet brought various cyberspace security and privacy issues, and cyberspace governance and coordination were truly

---

[19] https://eur-lex.europa.eu/legal-content/EN/TXT/?uri=celex%3A32016R0679
[20] https://www.icann.org/en/system/files/files/mou-first-icann-07may20-en.pdf
[21] https://www.rand.org/pubs/papers/P3544.html
[22] https://fas.org/irp/offdocs/nsdd145.htm
[23] https://www.congress.gov/bill/100th-congress/house-bill/145

valued. On September 15, 1995, the Clinton administration promulgated the *National Information Infrastructure: Agenda for Action*,[24] proposed to build more network infrastructure to promote network reliability and allow more people to use the network. In 2000, the Japanese government promulgated the *Basic Law of the Advanced Information and Telecommunications Network Association (IT Basic Law)*,[25] creating a precedent for Japanese cyberspace legislation. China promulgated the first law on cyberspace in 1994, The *Regulations of the People's Republic of China for Safety Protection of Computer Information Systems*,[26] to protect the privacy and network security.

After entering the 21st century, various countries had a deeper understanding of cyberspace. Under the guidance of international organizations and targeting their own national conditions, plans, laws, and regulations had been issued to regulate and promote the development of cyberspace. In 2000, China put forward the *Decision of the Standing Committee of the National People's Congress on Preserving Computer Network Security*,[27] defined cyberspace crime, and linked it with real world crimes. In 2001, Japan proposed the e-Japan[28] to vigorously develop cyberspace infrastructure and promote cyberspace coverage and talent training. In the U.S., the 2002 Federal Information Security Management Act[29] replaced the Computer Security Act of 1987 and made a more detailed approach to cybersecurity. In 2003, the U.S. government proposed the *National Strategy to Secure Cyberspace*,[30] which proposed cybersecurity as a national strategy. It marked that the country's strategic position in cybersecurity had been confirmed. In 2004, the UK proposed the *Science & innovation investment framework 2004–2014*[31] to announce the enhancement of funding for cyberspace. In 2005, Japan introduced the i-Japan plan[32] on the basis of e-Japan to promote the construction of information society and strengthen independent innovation. China issued the *Provisions for the Administration of Internet News Information Services*[33] to regulate news services. 2006 was an important year to promote cyberspace governance. The same for Germany, which released the new government's first technology policy, *German High-Tech Strategy*[34] and continued to increase funding

---

[24] https://clintonwhitehouse6.archives.gov/1993/09/1993-09-15-the-national-information-infrastructure-agenda-for-action.html
[25] https://www.kantei.go.jp/jp/singi/it2/hourei/honbun.html
[26] http://www.gov.cn/gongbao/content/2011/content_1860849.htm
[27] http://www.npc.gov.cn/wxzl/gongbao/2001-03/05/content_5131101.htm
[28] https://www.kantei.go.jp/jp/it/network/dai5/5siryou2.html
[29] https://csrc.nist.gov/topics/laws-and-regulations/laws/fisma
[30] https://www.cisa.gov/national-strategy-secure-cyberspace
[31] http://news.bbc.co.uk/nol/shared/bsp/hi/pdfs/science_innovation_120704.pdf
[32] http://www.kogures.com/hitoshi/webtext/shakai-ijapan/index.html
[33] http://www.gov.cn/flfg/2005-09/29/content_73270.htm
[34] https://www.research-in-germany.org/dam/jcr:8d61ee98-26bd-4606-a21d-1b97b17ca611/HTS_Broschuere_eng

for technology. The U.S. issued *the American Competitiveness Initiative*[35] to promote capital investment in scientific and technological development. At the same time, the National Aeronautics and Space Administration (NASA) proposed a *back to the moon* program,[36] which stimulated the development of cyberspace in the aerospace field. Russia proposed the *Implementation of Russia's Innovative Development Strategy* in 2015–2016[37] to promote the innovative development of Russian cyberspace. In 2010, Germany launched the *Digital Germany 2015*,[38] which promoted the innovative development of small- and medium-sized technology companies and strengthened investment in cutting-edge technologies. In 2014, Germany adopted the *Digital Agenda (2014–2017)*,[39] which clarified development goals and investment directions. China had launched the *Interim Provisions on the Administration of the Development of Public Information Services Provided through Instant Messaging Tools*,[40] which emphasizes citizens' right to privacy. In 2016, Germany launched the *Digital Strategy 2025*,[41] focusing on strengthening Germany's cyberspace coverage.

In 2017, the Trump administration promulgated the *National Security Strategy Report*,[42] which put forward six key areas: national security, energy and power, banking and finance, health and safety, communications, and transportation. It was effective for foreign evidence collection and judicial enforcement. Russia had published *Digital Economy Development in Russia*,[43] which clarifies the five major directions of management, talent, research and development, infrastructure, and cyberspace security.

13.4.3 Social Coordination Governance

Cyberspace society and corporate behavior originated relatively late. In the early stage of development, most companies in cyberspace were founding companies. They were committed to network standardization and popularization activities,

---

[35] http://www.casted.org.cn/upload/news/Attach-20080805111202.pdf
[36] https://www.nasa.gov/specials/apollo50th/back.html
[37] http://government.ru/en/docs/17169/
[38] https://www.gtai.de/gtai-en/invest/industries/life-sciences/initiatives-programs-digital-germany-2015--105348.pdf
[39] https://www.bmi.bund.de/SharedDocs/downloads/EN/publikationen/2014/digital-agenda.pdf?__blob=publicationFile
[40] http://politics.people.com.cn/n/2014/0807/c1001-25423647.html
[41] https://www.de.digital/DIGITAL/Redaktion/EN/Publikation/digital-strategy-2025.pdf?__blob=publicationFile&v=9
[42] http://www.realinstitutoelcano.org/wps/wcm/connect/25d788de-9e45-4c6d-acb6-d4e98f89845c/WP14-2018-GarciaEncina-Trump-Administration-National-Security-Strategy.pdf?MOD=AJPERES&CACHEID=25d788de-9e45-4c6d-acb6-d4e98f89845c
[43] https://openknowledge.worldbank.org/bitstream/handle/10986/30584/AUS0000158-WP-REVISED-P160805-PUBLIC-Disclosed-10-15-2018.pdf?sequence=1&isAllowed=y

and they did not regulate companies and social behavior in cyberspace. Companies also regulate the interconnection technology and the underlying architecture. Companies entering the network need to adapt to it.

After entering the 21st century, more companies began to settle in cyberspace. With the frequent occurrence of various incidents in cyberspace, cybercrimes, privacy leaks, and other incidents had affected normal life. Therefore, the management of society and enterprises was gradually put on the agenda, and it was mainly divided into autonomy and heterogeneous governance. Autonomy was a self-governing group formed by various enterprises and organizations in society due to certain problems. It was used to standardize interorganizational behavior and promote trade simplification. Heterogeneity was mainly the national and international norms of corporate behavior. Autonomy and heterogeneity complement each other to promote the governance and coordination of social and corporate cyberspace. In 2000, Google issued the *Google Code of Ethics*,[44] which stipulated its own behavior and formed a corporate culture. Simultaneously, it stipulates user codes, supplier codes, etc., which were used to restrain cooperative enterprises and users.

In the 2010s, the Internet had deepened into society and enterprises, and many enterprises place entities in cyberspace. Moreover, various new types of cybercrime and privacy emerge in an endless stream. Enterprises and society had also paid great attention to the governance of their own data centers and their own image. In addition, the people's requirements for privacy had gradually increased, and various social groups and enterprises had also formulated targeted policies. ISOC issued the *Internet Society Statement of Privacy*[45] in 2011, which elaborated on its own policies on public privacy and database protection. ISOC also issued a Code of conduct for participating members.[46] After receiving more and more requests from the public, Facebook had restricted its advertising behavior,[47] emphasizing that advertising behavior would not infringe on public privacy. Google subsequently issued similar regulations,[48] restricting the content, proportion, and types of advertisements. In 2016, Alibaba Cloud, as a representative cloud computing provider in China,[49] made detailed textual specifications for its own behavior. It first gave out the specifications for virus prevention and the management of security incidents and passwords. The maintenance and cleaning of logs and security equipment were given later, including vulnerability scanning and port management.

---

[44] https://sites.google.com/a/email.vccs.edu/bus100mawan/google-code-of-ethics
[45] https://www.internetsociety.org/privacy-policy-2011/
[46] https://www.internetsociety.org/become-a-member/code-of-conduct/
[47] https://investor.fb.com/corporate-governance/code-of-conduct/default.aspx
[48] https://support.google.com/adspolicy/answer/6008942?hl=en-GB
[49] https://developer.aliyun.com/article/719700

13.4.4 Personal Coordination Governance

Cyberspace was composed of a group of individuals, and the regulation of individual behavior was the foothold of any laws and agreements. In the early days of network formation, the constraints on individuals were still dominated by technology. Since various institutions had not formed a systematic standard for cyberspace, different networks cannot communicate with each other, which had a great impact on the popularization of cyberspace. For example, ARPANET adopts the NCP protocol and can only communicate with the homogeneous network but cannot communicate with other networks the birth of the TCP/IP protocol solved this problem, allowing heterogeneous networks to communicate with each other. At this time, the major organizations led by the U.S. began to formulate consistency plans, such as the OSI agreement. Many solutions had been passed down to this day.

With the popularity of the Internet, the governance of personal behavior had gradually become an important aspect of network governance. Various countries and organizations had begun to formulate corresponding rules and legislation on the issue of personal norms in cyberspace. V Shea-Educom published a creative network etiquette code in 1994 [8]. This code was aimed at citizens who flooded into the Internet during the rapid development of cyberspace. Starting from some real-life examples, it describes the cyberspace code and points out many wrong examples. This had also become the memory of some people first entering the Internet.

In 2016, the European Commission jointly issued the *CODE OF CONDUCT ON COUNTERING ILLEGAL HATE SPEECH ONLINE*[50] with Facebook, Twitter, YouTube, etc., to combat online hate speech.

13.5 A Case: Transnational Crime Coordination in Cyberspace

Due to national policies and economic development in Southeast Asia, large-scale crimes frequently occur. After the Internet became popular in the world in the 21st century, criminal groups began to focus on telecom fraud and network fraud. The main characteristics of Southeast Asian fraud groups were internationalization, multideaminization, and systemization. In order to ensure security, fraudulent groups often set up their servers in other countries, using high-paying methods to coax young people who were not deeply involved in the world to apply for jobs overseas, and then put them under house arrest as a tool for making money.[51] Each fraud organization had a systematic fraud process, covering all steps from training to transfer of funds. Compared with other crimes, it was more flexible,

---

[50] https://ec.europa.eu/info/sites/info/files/code_of_conduct_on_countering_illegal_hate_speech_online_en.pdf
[51] https://www.sohu.com/a/323209995_649781

which increased the difficulty of detection. In order to solve the long-standing fraud problem, Asian countries had signed a series of treaties to solve transnational cybercrimes through cooperation. In 2002, China and ASEAN signed the *China-ASEAN Joint Declaration on Cooperation in Non-traditional Security Fields*,[52] and in 2004 signed the *Memorandum of Understanding on Cooperation in Non-traditional Security Fields between the Government of the People's Republic of China and the Governments of the Association of Southeast Asian Nations*.[53] This memorandum joins the content of joint law enforcement. In 2011, China, Laos, Thailand, and Myanmar established a law enforcement and security cooperation mechanism in the Mekong River Basin.[54] In 2015, the 4th ASEAN and China (10+1) and the 7th ASEAN and China, Japan, and South Korea (10+3) Ministerial Conference on Combating Transnational Crime were held in Kuala Lumpur.[55] The meeting issued the *Joint Statement of The Fourth ASEAN Plus China Ministerial Meeting on Transnational Crime (4TH AMMTC+ CHINA) Consultation*.[56] In 2017, the Lancang-Mekong Comprehensive Law Enforcement and Security Cooperation Center was officially launched.

It was precisely based on this mechanism of international cyberspace coordination and governance that the crackdown on cybercrimes in Southeast Asia was getting stronger and stronger. In 2011, the "3.10" extraordinarily large cross-border telecom fraud case[57] was successfully solved with the efforts of the Chinese police. The cause of this case was a number of large-scale telecom fraud cases in many provinces of China since December 2010. The scammer called himself a government employee and used various reasons to trick the party into transferring funds to a "secure account". Therefore, on March 10, the Chinese police closely cooperated with local police in Cambodia, Indonesia, and other countries to conduct a secret investigation and successfully closed the Internet on June 9, arresting 598 suspects.

After entering the 2010s, criminal groups have updated their criminal methods. They no longer use false identities to trick victims into transferring to a secure account but use more covert and authentic methods to commit fraud. More famous is the "killing pig pan". Killing pig pan is a way for criminals to make friends through the Internet, pretend to be girls or successful people, establish relationships with victims, love online, and recommend stocks and other forms to obtain money. This method was more concealed and more difficult to detect. However, in 2019, the Chinese police successfully cracked down on a "killing pig pan" incident

[52] http://www.scio.gov.cn/ztk/xwfb/2014/31239/xgzc31249/Document/1375883/1375883.htm
[53] 13878731_2.htm
[54] http://www.gov.cn/gzdt/2011-10/31/content_1982676.htm
[55] http://www.gov.cn/govweb/jrzg/2009-11/18/content_1468044.htm
[56] https://asean.org/joint-statement-of-the-fourth-asean-plus-china-ministerial-meeting-on-transnational-crime-4th-ammtc-china-consultation/
[57] http://www.gov.cn/jrzg/2013-02/03/content_2326112.htm

in Southeast Asia.[58] This case successfully destroyed a criminal gang composed of Chinese in Cambodia and protected people's property.

13.6 Conclusion

The governance and coordination of cyberspace are accompanied by the development and popularization of cyberspace. With the development of cyberspace technology and the increase of people, the mechanism of governance and coordination is constantly updated. This chapter started from the definition of cyberspace governance and coordination, explored the scope and development history of cyberspace coordination and governance, and finally added a common case to study how the country treats cyberspace security and harmony in specific areas. It can be seen that the governance and coordination of cyberspace is a key means to protect the harmony of cyberspace. As the Internet continues to deepen life, coordination and governance mechanisms must also continue to develop, strengthening the protection of national and personal interests to ensure that cyberspace becomes a trustworthy space.

References

1. J. Kooiman, *Modern Governance: New Government-Society Interactions*, Sage, United States, 1993.
2. W. Powell, Neither Market nor Hierarchy: Network forms of organization, *Research in Organizational Behavior*, Vol. 12; No. 2, pp. 295–336, 1990.
3. A. Larson, Network dyads in entrepreneurial settings: A study of the governance of exchange relationships, *Administrative Science Quarterly*, Vol. 37; No. 1, pp. 76–104. 1992.
4. J. Candace, H. William, and P. B. Stephen, A general theory of network governance: Exchange conditions and social mechanisms, *Academy of Management Review*, Vol. 22; No. 4, pp. 911–945, 1997.
5. C. Strachey, Time sharing in large fast computers, *Communications of the ACM*, 1515 Broadway, New York, NY 10036L ASSOC COMPUTING MACHINERY, Vol. 2; No. 7, pp. 12–13, 1959.
6. V. Cerf and R. Kahn, A protocol for packet network intercommunication, *IEEE Transactions on Communications*, Vol. 22; No. 5, pp. 637–648, 1974.
7. A. L. Russell, The internet that wasn't, *IEEE Spectrum*, Vol. 50; No. 8, pp. 39–43, 2013.
8. V. Shea, Core Rules of netiquette, *Educom Review*, Vol. 29; No. 5, pp. 58–62, 1994.

---

[58] https://www.sohu.com/a/375677512_175528

Chapter 14

Cybercrime and Research History

14.1 Introduction

With the emergence of cyberspace, various forms of cybercrime come into being. Almost all the crimes that can be committed in the real world have been newly developed and realized in cyberspace. Since cybercrime came into being, it has been in the process of continuous development and change, and many new forms of crime have appeared in cyberspace. As the harm of cybercrime is recognized all over the world, plenty of research has been conducted and new legislation has been introduced.

14.2 The Definition of Cybercrime

With the development of computer technology, people's work and life are more and more closely related to cyberspace, and cybercrime is becoming more and more diverse. With the development of the technical means of cybercrime, the term used to refer to this kind of crime has experienced a process from computer crime to cybercrime, and its definition has also changed. The definitions from different sources are listed in chronological order in Table 14.1.

14.3 A Brief History of Cybercrime

With different criminal motives, there are various forms of cybercrimes. Cybercrimes are divided into two categories in this chapter, because some of them are brand new and are usually committed entirely in cyberspace while others are usually

DOI: 10.1201/9781003257387-14

Table 14.1 Definition of Cybercrime and its Related Terms

Year	Source	Definition
1979	National Institute of Justice (the U.S.)	Computer crime: One definition is that it is a form of white-collar crime committed inside a computer system; another definition is that it is the use of a computer as the instrument of a business crime [1].
1979	National Institute of Justice (the U.S.)	Computer-related crime: Any kind of illegal act based on an understanding of computer technology can be a computer-related crime [1].
1995	The United Nations Manual on the Prevention and Control of Computer Related Crime	Cybercrime includes fraud, forgery, and unauthorized access [2].
2000	The 10th United Nations Congress on the Prevention of Crime and the Treatment of Offenders	Cybercrime in a narrow sense (computer crime) covers any illegal behavior directed by means of electronic operations that target the security of computer systems and the data processed by them [3]. Cybercrime in a broader sense (computer-related crimes) covers any illegal behavior committed by means of, or in relation to, a computer system or network, including such crimes as illegal possession and offering or distributing information by means of a computer system or network [3].
2005	The Council of Europe's Cybercrime Treaty	Cybercrime includes offences ranging from criminal activity against data to content and copyright infringement [2].
2008	Government of Goa	Cybercrime shall mean and include all offences under the Information Technology Act, 2000 (Central Act No. 21 of 2000), and any other offences committed by use of electronic devices. Such as, computers, credit cards, internet, ATM, etc.[20]

(Continued)

Table 14.1 (*Continued*) **Definition of Cybercrime and its Related Terms**

Year	Source	Definition
2021	Wikipedia	Cybercrime, or computer-oriented crime, is a crime that involves a computer and a network. The computer may have been used in the commission of a crime, or it may be the target. Cybercrime may threaten a person, company or a nation's security and financial health.[21]

[20] http://goaprintingpress.gov.in/downloads/0809/0809-23-SI-OG.pdf
[21] https://en.wikipedia.org/wiki/Cybercrime

traditional ones that are changed or improved in cyberspace. Having brought a lot of new problems in response and governance, the former kind of crimes is called crimes in cyberspace; the latter one is called cyber-enabled crimes which can be governed by traditional methods.

14.3.1 Crimes in Cyberspace

With the development of new technology and new way of life in cyberspace, some new forms of crime have emerged. Not like traditional ones, these new crimes often take place in cyberspace. In addition, the criminals often have excellent computer skills and they always commit crimes by invading or attacking other people's information systems. These new crimes are called crimes in cyberspace.

According to the impact on the system, crimes in cyberspace can be divided into four types. In the first type, the crime does no harm to the system; in the second type, the system does not crash, but outputs wrong results; in the third type, the resources of the system are stolen; in the fourth type, the system is broken down and the user cannot use the system. The features and typical cases of these four types are shown in Table 14.2.

According to the above definition and classification, the first crime in cyberspace occurred in 1971. John Thomas Draper, an American computer programmer, tricked the American Telephone & Telegraph Company (AT&T) telephone network into giving free telephone calls by using toy whistles found in Cap'n Crunch cereal boxes.[1]

In 1981, Ian Murphy, also known as Captain Zap, became the first person convicted of a cybercrime for what he had committed 11 months ago. He hacked into AT&T network and changed its internal clocks that metered billing rates. Because of making people get late-night discount in the afternoon, he got 1000 hours of community service and two and a half years' probation.[2]

---

[1] https://en.wikipedia.org/wiki/John_Draper
[2] https://hackstory.net/Captain_Zap

Table 14.2 Types of Crimes in Cyberspace

Types	Features	Typical Cases
The crime is harmless to the system.	Although the system is attacked or invaded, its operation logic and resources are safe.	Cyber prank
The system fails to output correct results.	The system is maliciously modified, resulting in incorrect results even if the users think they are using the system correctly.	The modification of the system's input, the system's internal logic, or the system's output
Resources of the system are stolen.	The system is maliciously invaded and the access to particular resources of the system is gained by the unauthorized attacker.	The theft of confidential documents, confidential data, confidential codes, computing resources, etc.
The system is broken down.	The system is maliciously attacked leading to its users are unable to use the system.	Software breakdown or hardware breakdown

In 1982, the first computer virus was created as a prank by Elk Cloner, a 15-year-old high school student. Being named after its author, the virus Elk Cloner spread through floppy disks and made the computers infected show a poem about the virus every 50th time they were started. As a cyber prank, this virus did nothing else except showing this poem: "Elk Cloner: The program with a personality It will get on all your disks It will infiltrate your chips Yes it's Cloner! It will stick to you like glue It will modify ram too Send in the Cloner!".[3]

In 1989, one of the first large-scale cases of ransomware occurred. Spreading via floppy disk, the malicious software called AIDS, also known as Aids Info Disk or PC Cyborg Trojan, was distributed to up to 20,000 attendees of the World Health Organization's Acquired Immune Deficiency Syndrome (AIDS) conference. Files in computer would be encrypted after the computer was rebooted 90 times once the ransomware was installed. And the owner of the computer was asked to send a $189 "licensing fee" to the PC Cyborg Corporation in exchange for a decryption key to get his or her computer unlocked. Identified as the author of this virus, evolutionary biologist Dr. Joseph Popp, he was eventually discovered by the British antivirus industry, named on a New Scotland Yard arrest warrant and eventually detained in Brixton Prison.[4]

---

[3] https://en.wikipedia.org/wiki/Elk_Cloner
[4] https://en.wikipedia.org/wiki/AIDS_(Trojan_horse)

In 1995, the first Macro-viruses called Concept appeared. Macro-viruses are viruses that are written in a macro language: a programming language which is embedded inside a software application.[5,6] As for the Concept virus, in the first half year of 1996, the Concept only accounted for less than 20% of all virus infections, but it had infected over 35,000 computers by the end of February 1997.[7] As the company of the main target, Word, of this virus, Microsoft uploaded a scanning and repairing tool on its website to combat the virus.

In 1999, the first mass-emailing virus – the Melissa virus – invaded more than a million e-mail accounts worldwide and caused an estimated loss of $80 million. The virus creator, New Jersey computer programmer David L. Smith, served 20 months in federal prison and was fined $5,000. It is regarded as the first successful mass-emailing virus.[8]

In 2003, SQL Slammer became the fastest spreading worm in history. It infected SQL servers and created a denial-of-service attack which affected the speed of the Internet for quite some time. In terms of infection speed, it spread across nearly 75,000 machines in less than 10 minutes.[9]

And recently in 2017, WannaCry, a global ransomware attack, halted computer systems in more than 150 countries and affected more than 300,000 people.[10]

14.3.2 Cyber-Enabled Crimes

With the development of computer and related technology, some traditional crimes have also been developed. These developed crimes are named as cyber-enabled crimes. The stronger concealment, larger scale, and easier cross-region of cyber-crime lead to the reduction of crime cost, the complexity of crime subject, and the great increase of crime frequency. And with the great impact on physical space, social space, and thinking space, cyber-enabled crimes have also brought more challenges to crime governance.

Cyber-enabled crimes have made great impact on physical space. Traditional crimes in physical space always require direct contact with the victim. But they have been developed in cyberspace. For example, when the system is invaded and controlled, the offenders can order the system to overload, so that the damage to the devices of the system can be completed through a remote operation. At the same time, many traditional economic crimes like fraud, embezzlement, etc., are much more easy to commit in cyberspace. With the increasing time people spend in cyberspace, more and more traditional crimes will develop into cyber-enabled crimes and have an impact on physical space.

---

[5] https://www.kaspersky.com/resource-center/definitions/macro-virus

[6] https://en.wikipedia.org/wiki/Macro_virus

[7] http://virus.wikidot.com/concept

[8] https://en.wikipedia.org/wiki/Melissa_(computer_virus)

[9] https://en.wikipedia.org/wiki/SQL_Slammer

[10] https://en.wikipedia.org/wiki/WannaCry_ransomware_attack

Cyber-enabled crimes have made great impact on social space. The sharing and transmission of information play an important part in social space, and the information technology represented by the Internet has greatly promoted the flow of information, and its transmission speed and scope are incomparable to the traditional information dissemination channels. A small rumor or false information can be instantly sent to millions or even tens of millions of users through the Internet, and its influence is multiplied due to retweets and comments. For instance, lawbreakers use Internet platforms to spread false information and rumors, thus causing social chaos. Online rumors include defamation of individuals and fabrication of public events. They will damage personal reputation, cause significant mental harm to the victims, affect people's lives, and then have a serious impact on human relations. Meanwhile, Internet rumors and false information will destroy the public trust in the government, society, and political system, cause serious ideological confusion, and affect people's confidence in the stability of social development.

Cyber-enabled crimes have made great impact on thinking space. In thinking space, intellectual property is intangible and unique, so the infringement of intellectual property is not about the products with physical shape, but about the economic and personal rights contained in these products. Today, people's lives have become Internet-based, and they can search the resources they want to know through the Internet. Compared with the traditional text resources, network resources have their own unique characteristics. First, the basic characteristics of network information resources are digitalization and networking. Second, there is a large amount of information and a wide variety of browser views every day. Third, the information update cycle is short, the network information saves printing, transportation, and other links, and the data can be uploaded in time. At the same time, the network information resources are enormous and open, and information resources are not subject to geographical restrictions. Any networked computer can upload and download information. Finally, the organization is decentralized and there is no unified management mechanism and organization.

With the rapid development of information technology in the Internet era, a large number of artistic works have changed from their traditional form to the online form and spread rapidly in cyberspace. In this process, cybercrime will pose a threat to intellectual property rights. For individuals, cybercrime infringes their copyright and intellectual achievements, shaking people's enthusiasm in scientific research and literary and artistic creation. They are not willing to share knowledge on the Internet, and ideas cannot be exchanged with each other. As a result, people's thinking is greatly limited, and talents cannot be developed, so it is difficult to innovate. For an enterprise, cybercrime steals and infringes the intangible property of technology, brand, and patent of the enterprise, which will lead to unfair competition in the market and seriously reduce the economic profits of the enterprise. The enterprise has no motivation to innovate. For a country, people's motivation for innovation, an important role in intellectual property rights and a driving force of national development, is weakened because of cybercrime.

Here are some representative cyber-enabled crime cases. The world's first computer-related crime occurred in Silicon Valley in 1958, but it was not discovered until October 1966. In October 1966, when Don B. Parker was investigating computer-related accidents and crimes at the Stanford Institute in the U.S., he found that a computer engineer had tampered with the bank balance by tampering with the program [4]. In 1973, a teller at a local New York bank used a computer to embezzle more than 1.5 million dollars.[11] In 2010, the Stuxnet computer virus, which is widely believed to have been developed by the U.S. and Israel, was discovered after it was used to attack the Natanz facility in Iran.[12] In 2018, 144 universities based in the U.S. and 176 universities in 21 foreign countries were attacked by Iranian hackers. The 3-year campaign resulted in $3 billion in intellectual property loss, with 31 terabytes of information being stolen. Many of the attacks used sophisticated spear-phishing techniques that targeted more than 10,000 professors. 47 private sector companies were also attacked.[13]

14.4 Cybercrime Research Institutions

Cybercrime not only poses great threat to public and private property, intellectual property and personal privacy, but also directly endangers politics, economy, culture, and other aspects of the country, even national sovereignty and national security. As the Internet and the purpose of using it evolve every day, the criminal techniques, tools, and even purposes of cyber criminals are constantly changing. As a result, the necessity of doing research on cybercrime is very high.

Many companies, universities, and research institutions have added new departments or projects on cybercrime, and many institutions specializing in cybercrime have been set up. Their research results on cybercrime have greatly helped people to understand and deal with cybercrime, and some of them have been directly transformed into cybercrime laws. The information of some cybercrime research institutions is listed in Table 14.3.

14.5 A Summary of Cybercrime Legislation

Because of a lack of consideration on cybercrimes in online society in traditional laws, it is not adequate to vaguely interpret traditional laws to protect information and communication in cyberspace. In order to better prevent cybercrimes and make sure that perpetrators are convicted for the crime explicitly done, most countries and some international organizations have legislated against cybercrime.

Early In 1979, *Computer Crime: Criminal Justice Resource Manual*, the first basic federal manual for law enforcement in the U.S. was published, and Donn B. Parker,

---

[11] https://www.nytimes.com/1973/03/23/archives/chief-teller-is-accused-of-theft-of-15million-at-a-bank-here-teller.html

[12] https://en.wikipedia.org/wiki/Stuxnet

[13] https://www.floridatechonline.com/blog/information-technology/a-brief-history-of-cyber-crime/

Table 14.3   Cybercrime Research Institutions

Name	Belong to	Location	Website
International Cybercrime Research Centre	Simon Fraser University	Canada	https://www.sfu.ca/iccrc.html
Crime and Security Research Institute	Cardiff University	England	https://www.cardiff.ac.uk/crime-security-research-institute
Research center on security and crime (RISSC)	Nonprofit nongovernmental	Italy	https://www.rissc.it/
Computer Crime Research Center	Nonprofit nongovernmental	Ukraine	https://www.crime-research.org/about/
Australian High Tech Crime Centre	Australia government	Australia	Ahtcc.gov.au
U.S. Department of Justice Criminal Division Computer Crime and Intellectual Property Section	U.S. government	USA	www.cybercrime.gov
The CERT Division	Carnegie Mellon University	USA	https://www.sei.cmu.edu/about/divisions/cert/index.cfm
Asian school of cyber laws	Nongovernmental profit-making	India	https://www.asianlaws.org/
UCD Centre for Cybersecurity and Cybercrime Investigation	University College Dublin	Ireland	https://www.ucd.ie/cci/
Data Protection and Cybercrime Division	Council of Europe	Europe	http://www.coe.int/cybercrime

(Continued)

Table 14.3 (*Continued*) Cybercrime Research Institutions

Name	Belong to	Location	Website
Cyber Security and Crime Research Center	Chinese government	China	Unknown
Center for Cybercrime Studies	John Jay College of Criminal Justice	USA	https://www.jjay. cuny.edu/ center-cybercrime-studies
European Cybercrime Centre	Europol	Netherlands	https://www.europol. europa.eu/ about-europol/ european-cybercrime-centre-ec3
Microsoft Digital Crimes Unit	Microsoft	USA	Unknown
Computer Crime and Intellectual Property Section	U.S. government	USA	https://www.justice. gov/criminal-ccips

who is known as the father of the knowledge of computer crime, was the main author of this manual. And this manual became soon an encyclopedia also for law enforcement outside the U.S. [5]. The first federal computer crime statute was the *Computer Fraud and Abuse Act of 1984*.[14] After this, a series of laws have been introduced in the U.S. to govern computer fraud and abuse, electronic communications, stored communications, wiretap, digital copyright, etc. And as another important participant in international cyberspace, China has also issued a series of laws against cybercrime. For example, in its *Criminal Law* of 1997, China stipulated clear punishment standards for the criminals who destroy computer systems, hack into computer systems, use computers to commit financial fraud, theft, embezzlement, misappropriation of public funds, theft of state secrets or other crimes, or use computers to commit crimes of infringement.[15] According to the United Nations Conference on Trade and Development (UNCTAD), 154 countries (79%) have enacted cybercrime legislation by February 4, 2020.[16]

In 2001, the first international treaty on crimes committed via the Internet and other computer networks, the Budapest Convention on Cybercrime, was drawn up

---

[14] https://en.wikipedia.org/wiki/International_cybercrime
[15] https://www.spp.gov.cn/spp/fl/201802/t20180206_364975.shtml
[16] https://unctad.org/page/cybercrime-legislation-worldwide

by the Council of Europe in Strasbourg, France. Aiming at providing a basis of an effective legal framework for fighting cybercrime, the observer states of the Council of Europe's, Canada, Japan, Philippines, South Africa, and the U.S. have made great contributions to the drafting of the convention.[17] In 2002, the Asia-Pacific Economic Cooperation (APEC) issued its Cybersecurity Strategy in the *Shanghai Declaration* to increase cooperation in specific areas, including legal development.[18] In 2004, aiming to get a worldwide cooperation on international spam enforcement cooperation, *London Action Plan* was issued with the efforts of Economic Cooperation and Development (OECD) and the OECD Spam Task Force, the International Telecommunications Union (ITU), the European Union (EU), the International Consumer Protection Enforcement Network (ICPEN), and the APEC.[19]

14.6 Conclusion

The development of technology in cyberspace brings convenience to people, but it also provides ideal breeding ground for cybercrime. With the increasing proportion of network life in people's life, the forms of cybercrime are becoming more and more diverse, and the impact of cybercrime on people is becoming greater. Therefore, it is necessary to explore the history of cybercrime.

The definition of cybercrime, the brief history of cybercrime, the research institutions of cybercrime and the legislation of cybercrime are introduced in this chapter, in the hope of being helpful to those who are interested. It would be better if it could arouse more relevant thinking.

References

1. D. B. Parker, *Computer Crime: Criminal Justice Resource Manual*, Department of Justice, Washington, DC. National Inst. of Justice; Abt Associates, Inc., Cambridge, MA, 1989.
2. G. Sarah and F. Richard, On the definition and classification of cybercrime, *Journal in Computer Virology*, Vol. 2; No. 1, pp. 13–20, 2006.
3. M. Gercke, *Understanding Cybercrimes: Phenomena, Challenges and Legal Response*, International Telecommunication Union, Geneva, 2012.
4. X. L. Johannes, Cybercrime and legal countermeasures: A historical analysis, *International Journal of Criminal Justice Sciences*, Vol. 12; No. 2, pp. 196–207, 2017.
5. S. Schjolberg, The history of global harmonization on cybercrime legislation–The road to Geneva, *Journal of International Commercial Law and Technology*, Vol. 1; No. 12, pp. 1–19, 2008.

---

[17] https://en.wikipedia.org/wiki/Convention_on_Cybercrime
[18] https://en.wikipedia.org/wiki/International_cybercrime#Regional_responses
[19] https://www.ucenet.org/history/

Chapter 15

A Brief History of Cyberspace Legislations

15.1 Introduction

Cyberspace has gradually become another space of human life, greatly changing and influencing people's social activities and lifestyle. With the influence of cyberspace, the security, governance, and norms of cyberspace became a growing concern. At this time, legislation is needed to regulate and restrict social behaviors and social relationships in cyberspace. This chapter presents a brief history of cyberspace law in North America, Europe, and Asia from national, social, and individual perspectives.

This chapter first introduces the origin of cyberspace law. Second, it mainly describes the legislative history of cyberspace in North America, Europe, and Asia from national, social, and individual perspectives to improve the security of cyberspace. Among them, North America is represented by the U.S. Then it presents the electronic forensics technology derived from cyberspace laws, and finally, it puts forward the legislative trend of cyberspace in the future.

15.2 The Birth of Cyberspace Law

To maintain the security of cyberspace and create a harmonious living cyberspace environment, it is necessary to use the law to regulate people's behaviors in cyberspace. Law can regulate social behaviors, social relations, and maintain social order. It is a social phenomenon only when human society develops to a certain historical stage. Without the development of human evolution, there will be no birth, development, and perfection of the law. As far as our current scope of

DOI: 10.1201/9781003257387-15

knowledge is concerned, although there are various communication tools in the animal world outside human society, researchers have not found any adjustment tool like human law in the living space of any animal.[1]

Facing the virtual, global, and real-time cyberspace, the traditional law was unable to effectively solve a series of problems, so a novel legal system – cyberspace law – came into being. Cyberspace law is the general term of legal norms to adjust various social relations related to the networks [1]. David R. Johnson and David G. Post pointed out in their paper that it was necessary for the Internet to conduct self-management rather than obeying the laws of specific countries/regions, and netizens would abide by the laws of electronic entities such as service providers [2].

Every space must have a certain order. As the most specialized, effective, and coercive tool, the law is of great significance to maintaining order. Cyberspace law has the general attribute of law, and its pursuit of order is no exception. In addition, it determines the boundaries of power and obligation, solves the inevitable disputes by legal means, protects the basic rights of cyber-man, and makes cyberspace develop in the direction of humanization and harmony.

15.3 The Development History of Cyberspace Law

The legal system of cyberspace is gradually established in various countries and regions of the world, and theoretical research of cyberspace law is also booming. Early cyberspace laws and regulations focused on the protection of critical information infrastructure, including not only the security of physical entities (i.e., to prevent the operation interruption of infrastructure systems caused by natural disasters, accidents, or man-made destruction) but also the logical security of infrastructure (i.e., to ensure the availability, reliability, integrity, and confidentiality of information resources and information technology supporting the operation of infrastructure).[2] With the development of the Internet, while strengthening the protection of information infrastructure, the legislation of various countries also emphasizes information security in cyberspace and supports the fight against cybercrime. Due to different national conditions and historical traditions, the legal norms of cyberspace content and behaviors in different countries are also different. The following part describes cyberspace legislation in major countries in North America, Europe, and Asia.

15.3.1 Northern American

The U.S. has the most comprehensive cyberspace security legislation in the world. The U.S., as the birthplace of the world's information industry, has been at the forefront of

---

[1] https://wenku.baidu.com/view/3573d12dc9d376eeaeaad1f34693daef5ff71347.html
[2] http://www.npc.gov.cn/npc/c16115/201211/a4fa87828d0444d7904a3372b1ad800e.shtml

the world in terms of its information development. In the mid-1980s, due to the development and catch-up of Japan, South Korea, Western Europe, and other countries, the leading position of the U.S. in the information industry was greatly impacted and challenged. In addition, the development of the network itself brought various problems. Under the internal and external troubles, the U.S. government accelerated cyberspace construction and formulated a set of rules and policies to coordinate with the Internet to protect and promote the development advantages of its information security. The high popularity of the Internet made the U.S. always attach importance to the security of cyberspace. Whether in network management or information technology, the U.S. is one of the most experienced counties in the world. The cyberspace security law of the U.S. can be divided into the following three periods.

Embryonic Stage

Before the 1980s, cyberspace security legislation in the U.S. was in its infancy. During this period, the *Atomic Energy Act of 1946*[3] and the *National Security Act of 1947* [3] promulgated by the U.S. under Reagan and George W. Bush could be regarded as the sign of the germination of American network information security policy, which also represented the awakening of cyberspace security awareness in the U.S. In 1966, the case of bank computer system intrusion was the first to occur in the U.S., which caused widespread concern. To regulate the behavior in cyberspace and ensure the security of computer systems, the U.S. has issued a series of laws and regulations since then. As shown in Table 15.1, the laws issued before the 1980s are summarized.

The Computer Security Act of 1987 was the local laws and regulations enacted by the states of the U.S. It was the fundamental law on cyberspace security in the U.S., which opened the door to the legal construction of cyberspace security. Since the 1990s, cyberspace security legislation has sprung up.

Forming Stage

In the 1990s, Internet gradually developed and matured. The development of the Internet provided the foundation for the information of cyberspace from the aspects of infrastructure, widely interconnected network, data storage, communication, and sharing. The U.S. gradually realized that pure passive legislation cannot effectively protect cyberspace security, so it began to pay attention to deeper security issues. At this stage, the U.S. was under the leadership of President Clinton. The connotation of its cyberspace security expanded from the original confidentiality and security to the protection of the confidentiality, integrity, availability, and controllability of cyberspace content. Meanwhile, cyberspace security strategy became an independent part of national security strategy. During this period, relevant laws and regulations were also issued, as shown in Table 15.2.

---

[3] https://www.energy.gov/management/august-1-1946-atomic-energy-act

Table 15.1 The Important Laws Established in the U.S. in the Embryonic Stage

Year	Law/Regulation	Important Features
1966	Freedom of Information Act[8]	The foundation and scope of network information protection are defined.
1974	Privacy Act[9]	It focuses on protecting the privacy of citizens from infringement and balances the contradiction between public interests and private interests.
1978	Federal Computer System Protection Act[10]	It is the first time that this law has incorporated computer systems into the law. People noticed that the law could protect the social relations caused by a computer system.
1978	Florida Computer Crime Act[11]	It convicts and metes out punishment for infringing computer users, infringing intellectual property rights, infringing computer devices, and equipment in the network society.
1984	Comprehensive Crime Control Act [4]	It includes some provisions for the inclusion of computer activity in modern crimes.
1984	Computer Crime Prevention Act[12]	It governs governments, financial institutions, and intercontinental computers, guided by fraud, sabotage, and unauthorized use.
1985	Computer Pornography and Child Exploitation Prevention Act[13]	Purohits transmission of lewd or obscene material via computer, especially child pornography.
1986	Computer Fraud and Abuse Act[14]	It stipulates that abusing confidential information, deceiving others with the help of a computer, and refusing to use computer service are the three most serious criminal circumstances.
1986	Electronic Communications Privacy Act[15]	It focuses on the protection of information generated in the field of electronic communication.

(Continued)

Table 15.1 (*Continued*)   The Important Laws Established in the U.S. in the Embryonic Stage

Year	Law/Regulation	Important Features
1987	Computer Security Act [5]	It improves the confidentiality and security of the federal government's computer system, and formulate feasible legal norms in the field of information security.

Notes: The year of the law in the table is the time of the first law promulgation, and the year of the subsequent law revision is not listed.

[8] The Freedom of Information Act of 1966: https://www.archives.gov/about/laws/foia.html
[9] The Privacy Act of 1974: https://www.archives.gov/about/laws/privacy-act-1974.html
[10] The Federal Computer System Protection Act of 1978: https://www.gao.gov/products/106293
[11] The Florida Computer Crime Act of 1978: https://fortune.com/2014/08/28/digital-forensics/
[12] The Computer Crime Prevention Act: http://www.princeton.edu/~ota/disk2/1986/8611/861107.PDF
[13] The Computer Pornography and Child Exploitation Prevention Act of 1985: http://www.princeton.edu/~ota/disk2/1986/8611/861107.PDF
[14] The Computer Fraud and Abuse Act of 1986: https://freejeremy.net/the-case/cfaa/
[15] Kosseff, J. (2017). Text of the Electronic Communications Privacy Act. In Cybersecurity Law, J. Kosseff (Ed.). https://doi.org/10.1002/9781119231899.app5

Table 15.2   The Important Laws Established in the U.S. During the Forming Stage

Year	Bill	Important Features
1995	Paperwork Reduction Act[16]	The White House Office of management and budget is given the responsibility to formulate and promulgate national cybersecurity policies.
1996	Information Technology Management Reform Act[17]	It requires government department heads to be responsible for formulating their information security policies and procedures and to set up "chief information officers" in various government departments.

(Continued)

Table 15.2 (*Continued*)   The Important Laws Established in the U.S. During the Forming Stage

Year	Bill	Important Features
1996	National Information Infrastructure Protection Act[18]	Linking the interests of the private sector with the security of critical infrastructure, while safeguarding national security, respecting individual privacy, the will, and interests of the private sector.
1997	Computer Security Enhancement Act[19]	The key infrastructure, strengthening electronic signature management, protecting Federal computers, and network security are proposed.
1998	Children's Online Privacy Protection Act[20]	This Act protects children's privacy by giving parents tools to control what information is collected from their children online.
1999	Cyberspace Electronic Security Act [6]	It provides that the federal government law enforcement agencies can obtain encryption keys and encryption methods, and makes detailed provisions on the protection of confidential information, information interception, and other issues.
2000	Government Information Security Reform Act [6]	It stipulates that measures should be taken to strengthen the protection of government information, and determines the responsibilities of various government departments in the protection of government information.

Notes: The year of the law in the table is the time of the first law promulgation, and the year of the subsequent law revision is not listed

[16] Paperwork Reduction Act of 1995: https://www.energy.gov/sites/prod/files/cioprod/documents/Information_Collection_Program_Training.pdf

[17] National Information Technology Management Reform Act of 1996: http://govinfo.library.unt.edu/npr/library/misc/itref.html

[18] Information Infrastructure Protection Act of 1996: https://www.epic.org/security/1996_computer_law.html

[19] Computer Security Enhancement Actof 1997: https://www.congress.gov/bill/105th-congress/house-bill/1903

[20] Children's Online Privacy Protection Act of 1998: https://wenku.baidu.com/view/2323f481e53a580216fcfe3a.html

In 2000, the National Security Strategy Report formally included "network information security" in the framework of national security strategy. The report took information security as an official part of the U.S. security strategy and made it independent.

Developing Period

During this period, the U.S. emphasized the overall layout, formulated comprehensive cyberspace security laws and regulations, improved, and supplemented the original laws and regulations. At this stage, the bill mainly laid in the improvement of the legislative level, and the social relations contained in the law were also qualitatively expanded. The U.S. is undergoing a developing period at present. The laws introduced at this stage are divided into three levels: national security, social security, and personal security. The specific laws are shown in Table 15.3.

15.3.2 *Europe*

■ European Union

Since its establishment, the European Union has issued resolutions, directives, suggestions, and regulations on the legal regulation of cyberspace security covering many aspects of Cybersecurity, such as digital network integration services, network access system, and information protection, to guide the Internet management practice of member states. So far, a legal framework with rich content and a complete system has been formed, and it is at the forefront of the world. The formulation and continuous improvement of the EU cybersecurity framework effectively ensure the network security of the whole EU and provides a legal blueprint for the security legislation of other countries. The current laws are shown in Table 15.4.

In November 2001, the EU adopted the first international multilateral agreement on computer systems, networks, or data crimes, the *Convention on Cybercrime*, which defined the types and contents of cybercrime. It required its member states to take legislative and other necessary measures to recognize these acts in their domestic laws, to establish corresponding law enforcement organs and procedures, and stipulate specific reconnaissance measures and jurisdiction. It strengthened international cooperation among member states to investigate computer and data crimes (including electronic evidence collection) and take joint actions to extradite criminals to protect personal data and privacy. According to the unified directive and the actual situation of the EU, EU member states issued their information security laws and regulations.

■ Germany

As one of the most developed countries in Europe, Germany's network development has always been at the forefront of the world. Germany is one of the first countries in the world to formulate laws to regulate the use of the

Internet. It maintains the information security of the Internet through legislation, popularizes the rule of law to the network society, and realizes the harmony and stability of the whole society. As one of the member states of the EU, Germany's legal system also has its particularity. In addition to its domestic laws, it also includes the laws and regulations uniformly applied by the EU. Domestic laws and EU laws are equally applicable, forming a two-tier

Table 15.3   The Important Laws Established in the U.S. During the Developing Stage

Level	Year	Law
National security	2001	Critical Infrastructure Protection in the Information Age [7]
	2001	Patriot Act[21]
	2002	Homeland Security Act [8]
	2002	Federal Information Security Management Act [9]
	2002	Cyber Security Enhancement Act[22]
	2003	National Cyberspace Security Strategy[23]
	2014	National Cybersecurity Protection Act[24]
	2015	National Cybersecurity Protection Advancement Act[25]
	2019	National Security and Personal Data Protection Act (Proposal)
Social security	2002	E-government Act[26]
	2007	America Competes Act[27]
	2010	Cybersecurity Act[28]
	2013	Cyber Intelligence Sharing and Protection Act[29]
	2014	Cybersecurity Enhancement Act[30]
	2015	Cybersecurity Information Sharing Act[31]
Personal security	2019	National Security and Personal Data Protection Act (Proposal)

Notes: The year of the law in the table is the time of the first law promulgation, and the year of the subsequent law revision is not listed

[21] Patriot Act of 2001: https://www.govinfo.gov/content/pkg/PLAW-107publ56/html/PLAW-107publ56.htm
[22] Cyber Security Enhancement Act: https://www.congress.gov/bill/107th-congress/
[23] National Cyberspace Security Strategy: https://www.senki.org/operators-security-toolkit/sp-security/uss-national-strategy-to-secure-cyberspace-2003/

(Continued)

Table 15.3 (*Continued*)   The Important Laws Established in the U.S. During the Developing Stage

Level	Year	Law

[24] National Cybersecurity Protection Act: https://www.congress.gov/bill/113th-congress/senate-bill/2519

[25] National Cybersecurity Protection Advancement Act: https://www.cbo.gov/publication/50116

[26] E-government Act: https://www.archives.gov/about/laws/egov-act-section-207.html

[27] America Competes Act: https://www.govinfo.gov/content/pkg/PLAW-110publ69/pdf/PLAW-110publ69.pdf

[28] Cybersecurity Act: https://www.congress.gov/bill/111th-congress/senate-bill/773/text

[29] Cyber Intelligence Sharing and Protection Act: https://www.cbo.gov/publication/44084

[30] Cybersecurity Enhancement Act: https://www.congress.gov/bill/113th-congress/senate-bill/1353/text

[31] Cybersecurity Information Sharing Act: https://www.cbo.gov/publication/50113

Table 15.4   EU Cybersecurity Laws and Regulations

Year	Bill	Description
1992	Directive on the Legal Protection of Databases [10]	It adjusts the application of copyright to the database and protects the databases accessed by EU countries through the network.
1992	Security of information systems [11]	It provides effective and practical security protection for each department to store electronic information.
1995	The lawful interception of telecommunications [11]	It puts forward the topic of public power exercise and human rights protection under the network environment.
1995	Data Protection Directive 95/46/EC[32]	It was established to provide a regulatory framework to guarantee a secure and free movement of personal data across the national borders of the EU member countries.
1999	Adopt a multiannual community action plan on promoting safer use of the Internet by combating illegal and harmful content on global networks [11]	It emphasizes the safe use of the Internet and provides a legal basis for the EU to intervene in Internet control and eliminate illegal and harmful information such as racial discrimination and separatism.

(Continued)

Table 15.4 (*Continued*)   EU Cybersecurity Laws and Regulations

Year	Bill	Description
1999	Agreement on Computer Crime (1999/364/JHA)[33]	It stipulates the obligations of member states in investigating transnational computer crimes (the agreement was solicited and signed in 2001).
1999	EU Directive on a Community Framework for Electronic Signatures[34]	It guides and coordinates the legislation of electronic signature in EU member states.
2001	Convention on Cybercrime[35]	It is necessary to determine the types and crimes of cybercrime and increase the ability of corporate bodies for cybercrime.
2016	Network and Information Security Directive (NIS)[36]	It strengthens and improves the resilience of networks and information systems in Europe.
2018	General Data Protection Regulation	Any organization that collects, transmits, retains, or processes personal information involving all Member States of the EU is bound by the regulation.
2019	Cybersecurity Act[37]	The EU network and information security agency is designated as a permanent EU security function.

[32] Data Protection Directive 95/46/EC: https://link.springer.com/chapter/10.1007/978-1-4471-5586-7_2

[33] Agreement on Computer Crime (1999/364/JHA): http://www.e-gov.org.cn/article-57091.html

[34] EU Directive on a Community Framework for Electronic Signatures: https://op.europa.eu/en/publication-detail/-/publication/5456910f-06ec-46dc-80e6-545a5f5ecc9b/language-en

[35] Convention on Cybercrime: http://www.itu.int/osg/spu/cybersecurity/presentations/session14_esposito.pdf

[36] Network and Information Security Directive (NIS): https://www.linkedin.com/pulse/network-information-security-directive-nis-beverley-flynn

[37] Cybersecurity Act: https://www.doc88.com/p-61273120476392.html

system. Particularly speaking, Germany not only promotes cybersecurity legislation in its own country but also in the whole EU, that is, when a certain law cannot be passed in Germany, it can be passed in the EU first, and then the EU law can be transformed into German law according to the stipulation that "all member states are obliged to abide by the EU law". The current cyberspace security legislation is shown in Table 15.5.

Table 15.5   German Cybersecurity Laws and Regulations

Year	Law/Regulation	Description
1977	Federal Data Protection Act[38]	It protects personal privacy and prevents personal data from being infringed in the process of use.
1997	Information and Communication Services Act	It covers personal information protection, electronic signature, information crime, and minor protection.
2015	German Cybersecurity Act[39]	It improves IT security for companies and the federal government, and better protects citizens on the Internet.
2017	NIS Directive Implementation Act [12]	The NIS directive of transforming the EU is implemented in Germany.
2017	Data Protection Adaption Act[40]	It analyzes the relationship between EU regulations and Federal Data Protection Act.
2017	Act to Improve Enforcement of the Law in Social Networks (Network Enforcement Act)[41]	It is designed to enable users to share any content with other users and make them available to the public (Social Network).

[38] Federal Data Protection Act: J L. Riccardi, The German Federal Data Protection Act of 1977: Protecting the Right to Privacy?, 6B.C. Int'l & Comp. L. Rev. 243 (1983),https://lawdigitalcommons.bc.edu/iclr/vol6/iss1/8
[39] German Cybersecurity Act: https://www.bsi.bund.de/DE/Themen/KRITIS/IT-SiG/it_sig_node.html
[40] Data Protection Adaption Act: https://www.linkedin.com/pulse/adaptation-german-federal-data-protection-act-general-von-wilucki
[41] Network Enforcement Act: https://www.bmjv.de/SharedDocs/Gesetzgebungsverfahren/Dokumente/NetzDG_engl.pdf?__blob=publicationFile&v=2

The Information and Communication Services Act, also known as the *Multimedia Act,* is composed of three new laws (i.e., the personal data protection law of communication service, the communication service law, and the digital signature law), as well as six subsidiary provisions of the existing laws, such as the criminal law, the copyright law, and the administrative law, which apply to information networks. It is the first special network law in the world, which provides comprehensive special legal norms for the behavior of electronic cyberspace including network content. The law extends the concept of publication to "audio-visual media, data storage devices, pictures, and other forms of expression" and stipulates the content responsibility of network service providers, as well as the protection of minors. The *Multimedia Act* has become the basic law and unified law of network information security in Germany. Together with the special laws on information security successively promulgated in Germany in the future, it has formed such a legislative mode of combining unified law and separate law in the legislation of network security in Germany. Germany has also amended its criminal law to stipulate computer crimes and penalties such as data espionage, computer fraud, forgery of evidence, transaction fraud related to data processing, forgery of certificates, forgery of certification materials, destruction of documents, tampering with materials, computer destruction, forgery of official documents, etc.

The implementation law of the NIS directive issued in 2017 was the network and information system security directive transformed from Germany to the EU, and the data protection adaption law was formulated by Germany to transform the EU general data protection regulations. Because the German prior law is contrary to the EU's general data protection regulations, it is necessary to amend the existing laws to adapt to them.

■ France

As a major power in the world and a core member of the EU, France has strong scientific and technological strength and talent advantages, and it has established its information network at the early stage of the Internet. The French government has always attached great importance to Cyberspace Security and continuously formulated a series of policies and regulations. Historically, the governance of cyberspace in France has experienced three periods, from the initial "regulation" to "automatic regulation" and so far to "joint regulation".

In the 1970s, as the initial "regulation" period, the regulation of the Internet and the development of information technology were completely controlled by the government. In 1978, the French government established the "French information and Freedom Commission" to protect citizens' privacy. In the same year, *the Information Technology and Freedom Act* was promulgated to protect personal data. In 1980, the French government formulated the *Communication Circuit Plan*. In 1986, a large-scale *"Plan for Building Information Superhighway"* was drawn up and approved by the government in 1994. In 1986, the *Freedom of the Press Act* made special provisions on the filtering of Internet content.

With the expansion and development of the network and the rapid growth of network users, the French government gradually realized that it was impractical to manage and control the Internet from the perspective of the state. It should take a step-by-step approach and negotiate with network technology developers and service providers. It required network technology developers and service providers to pay attention to the management of the network and popularize network knowledge to users' "Automatic control". In this period, the government paid attention to the construction of network coordination organizations and did not issue relevant legal and policy documents.

Subsequently, the French government realized that the problems in cyberspace could not be solved only by individuals, institutions, or a certain country. Only with the participation of everyone and the joint efforts of various parties could the problems be solved, and the harm or loss could be minimized. Therefore, in early 1999, the French government put forward the management policy of "joint control". Under the guidance of this idea, the *Information Society Act* was drafted to clarify everyone's rights and responsibilities in law, to ensure the freedom of online communication and trade, and the safety and reliability of information dissemination. After that, a series of laws and regulations were issued. The representative laws are as follows:

In 2004, the *Trust Act of Digital Economy* clarified the potential threats of the Internet to social life, citizens' privacy, intellectual property rights, and national information security. Besides, it clarified the rights and responsibilities of Internet users.

In 2008, *White Paper on French National Defense and National Security* for the first time raised network security to the level of national security regarded network information attack as one of the biggest threats in the next 15 years and emphasized that France should have effective information defense capability, carry out reconnaissance, defense, counterattack against network attacks, and develop high-level network security products.

In 2011, the *French Information System Defense and Security Strategy* was the first national information security strategy report in French history, which formulated four strategic measures and seven measures for France's information security roadmap. The four strategic objectives were: (a) become a cybersecurity power; (b) protect sovereign information and ensure decision-making ability; (c) protect national infrastructure; (d) ensure cyberspace security.

In 2019, the *5G Network Security Act* established a new authorization system before French operators used 5G devices to ensure network information security and national science and technology sovereignty. In the same year, the *"Anti-Cyber Hatred Act"* was promulgated, stipulating that online social media with more than 2 million visits per month should strengthen control over online activities in France to curb hate speech.

In addition, the French government also paid attention to the protection of minors in cyberspace. In 1998, the *Act on the Protection and Elimination of Sexual Harm and the Protection of Minors* was promulgated to punish the use of the Internet to poison minors severely. In 2009, *Internet Copyright Protection Act* was promulgated, and a special organization was set up to supervise the network copyright and effectively crackdown on network infringement and privacy. In the same year, the HADOPI Act was also promulgated to crack down on the illegal downloading of network works, and the high office for the dissemination and protection of network works was established accordingly. In 2016, *Digital Republic Act* was promulgated, to emphasize the importance of personal data copyright.

■ Russia

The construction of network information security legal system in Russia began in the 1990s. Before that, Russia developed spontaneously in cyberspace without government supervision and the application of normative legal rules. After the completion of Russia's domestic political and economic changes, there was a good situation of political stability and economic recovery in China. Russia's pace of entering the information society was gradually accelerating, and the problem of network information security also appeared. In this context, to seek the security, stability, and development of cyberspace, Russia formulated a series of laws, regulations, and policies on network information security according to its national conditions. In the 21st century, Russia also formed a relatively perfect legal system of network information security, which completely reversed the regressive situation in the field of network security.

In 1994, the *Trade Secret Act of the Russian Federation* was promulgated. In 1995, the network information security bureau was incorporated into the scope of legal protection through the provisions of the *Russian Constitution* for the first time. In the same year, *Federal Information, Informatization, and Information Protection Act* were promulgated, which stipulated the protection subject of network information security. The law also proposed to add a computer crime charge in the new *Criminal Code*. According to this suggestion, in 1996, the *Criminal Code of the Russian Federation* specially set up a chapter on "crimes in the field of computer information", which stipulated network information security in the form of the *Criminal Code*. *Bill on the Conceptual Basis of the Formation of the Information Society in the Russian Federation* was promulgated in 1998; *Act on Information Security Doctrine of Russian Federation* was promulgated in 2000 and signed again in 2016. In terms of the protection of minors, the *Act on the Protection of Children from Interference with Information Harmful to their Health and Development* was adopted in 2009. In 2019, the *Network Sovereignty Act of the Russian Federation* was promulgated to further strengthen the autonomous interconnection and active protection capabilities of the Russian national network in the global cyberspace.

15.3.3 Asia

■ China

In the early stage, China focused on the regulation of physical architecture, including the construction of the backbone network in China and the implementation of government-led comprehensive supervision on the global

Internet and access nodes of the backbone network. However, the legal construction was relatively backward, making the planning of related problems more dependent on departmental regulations and other documents. After introducing Internet technology in the 1990s, more attention was paid to the impact of information globalization on political stability and social order. For the network public opinion propaganda, similar supervision to traditional media was adopted, which extended a series of applicable laws to the network space. Since Snowden disclosed the global electronic monitoring plan of the U.S. in 2013, Internet security has been raised to a strategic level by many countries, including China. After establishing the central network security and Informatization Leading Group in 2014, the *Act on Network Security of the People's Republic of China* became the top priority of legislation, and the whole network security legislation construction began to systematize. At present, China's cyberspace security legal system mainly governs Cyberspace Security through three levels, as shown in Table 15.6.

If we divided China's legislative documents into departmental rules, normative documents, and policy documents, China's cyberspace security legislation will be more comprehensive, as shown in Figure 15.1.

■ Japan

Japan has issued a series of laws on the prevention of cybercrime, such as the *"Act on the Prohibition of Illegal Access"* passed in 1999 to stop illegal access and prevent computer crime explicitly. In addition, the *Criminal Act* has been amended to extend the content of the criminal law to the field of network, add computer crime provisions, and stipulate computer crimes and penalties such as the crime of false use of electromagnetic records, the crime of damaging or deliberately obstructing the use of others, the crime of fraud in the use of electronic computers, and the crime of discarding electromagnetic records. After entering the 21st century, Japan has successively promulgated laws and regulations such as *Act on Standardizing the Responsibility of Internet Service Providers, Act on Combating the Use of Dating Websites to Lure Minors, Act on the Preparation of Safe Internet Environment for Young People*, and *Act on Standardizing E-mail*, which has effectively curbed crimes, as well as illegal and harmful information in cyberspace.[4]

Japan formed its network privacy protection system in a short period through relatively perfect laws and regulations to protect network privacy and personal information. In 1998, the *Act on the Protection of Personal Information Processed by Computers* held by administrative organs was issued to strengthen the protection of personal information processed by computers held by central government organs. In 2000, *Anti-hacker Act* was issued to protect the safe and free transmission of personal data. In 2003, the *Personal Information Protection Act* was issued to protect personal information and

---

[4] chinadaily.com.cn/hqzx/2011-04/22/content_12378354.htm. Accessed: 2021.1.14

Table 15.6   China's Cyberspace Legislation System[42]

Level	Bill	Year
Law	The decision of the Standing Committee of the National People's Congress on safeguarding Internet Security	2000
	The People's Republic of China on Electronic Signature Act	2004
	The decision of the Standing Committee of the National People's Congress on strengthening the protection of network information	2012
	The People's Republic of China on network security Act	2016
	E-commerce Act of the People's Republic of China	2018
	The cryptography of the People's Republic of China	2019
Administrative regulations	Regulations of the People's Republic of China on the Safety Protection of Computer Information Systems	1994
	Provision Rules of the People's Republic of China on the Management of International Networking of Computer Information Webs	1996
	Regulations of the People's Republic of China on Telecommunications	2000
	Measures for the administration of Internet information services	2000
	Regulations on the administration of foreign-invested telecommunication enterprises	2008
	Regulations on the protection of information network dissemination	2013
	Regulations on the protection of computer software	2013
	Notice of the State Council on authorizing the state Internet information office to be responsible for the management of Internet information content	2014
	Measures for the security protection and management of computer information network international networking	2014
	Regulations on the administration of Internet service business places	2016

(Continued)

Table 15.6 (*Continued*)   China's Cyberspace Legislation System

Level	Bill	Year
Judicial interpretation	Interpretation on the specific application of law in handling criminal cases of making, copying, publishing, selling, and disseminating obscene electronic information using the Internet, mobile communication terminals, and voice stations.	2004
	Interpretation on the specific application of law in handling criminal cases involving the production, reproduction, publication, trafficking, and dissemination of obscene electronic information through the Internet, mobile communication terminals, and voice stations	2010
	Interpretation of several issues concerning the application of law in handling criminal cases such as defamation through information network	2013
	Provision on several issues concerning the application of law in the trial of civil disputes over infringement of the right of information network dissemination	2014
	Provisions on the application of law in the trial of civil disputes involving infringement of personal rights and interests through information network	2014
	Legal interpretation on handling criminal cases such as illegal use of information network and assistance in criminal activities of information network	2019

[42] http://www.cac.gov.cn/index.htm

promote the effective use of personal information. In 2013, The Identification Number Act is formulated by the Japanese governement to improve administractive efficiency of user identitfication numbers in terms of social insurance and taxation. In 2014, *Basic Act on Cyber Security* was passed to strengthen the coordination and operation between the Japanese government and the private sector in the field of cybersecurity to better respond to cyberattacks.

■ Korea

Korea was the first country in the world to establish a special Internet censorship agency, and it was also the first country to enforce the network real-name system, which implemented a relatively strict mobile phone real-name system and a limited network real-name system. In 2001, the *Act on Promoting the Use of Information and Communication Networks* was passed to manage the content of cyberspace; in 2005, the privacy of many Korean

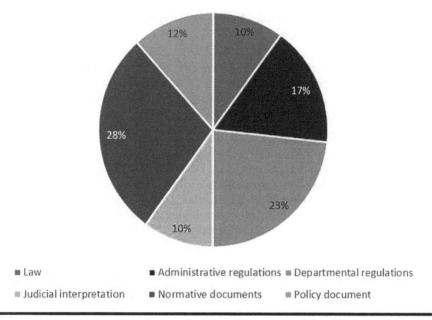

■ Law   ■ Administrative regulations ■ Departmental regulations

▨ Judicial interpretation ■ Normative documents ▨ Policy document

Figure 15.1 The proportion of Chinese legal norms from 1994 to 2020.[7]

[7] http://www.cac.gov.cn/index.htm

stars was exposed, and the government immediately promulgated the *Act on the Protection of Information and Communication* and *the Basic Act on Promoting Informatization* to protect personal privacy. In 2008, *Amendment to the Implementation Order of Information and Communication Network* was issued, which was the first legal norm specially formulated in the world to crack down on Internet rumors. It attracted worldwide attention. With the development of new technologies, South Korea continues to supplement and improve the legal system of network security. In 2015, it formulated the *Act on Development of Cloud Computing and User Protection*, which required cloud service providers to inform users in times of infringement accidents, user information leakage, any service interruption. In 2017, the South Korean government officially proposed the *National Cyber Security Act*, which aimed to prevent cyberattacks that threaten national security, quickly and actively respond to cyber crises, and contribute to the protection of national security and national interests.

■ Singapore

  Singapore's network security legislation mainly involves network content security, spam control, and personal information protection. *The Broadcasting Act* passed in 1996 and *the Broadcasting (Classified Permission) Notice and the Internet Code of Conduct* are the basic laws for the content management of cyberspace in Singapore. Other regulatory contents are scattered in the

Criminal Act, Domestic Security Act, Sedition Act, Act on Safeguarding Religious Integration, Bad Publications Act, and other laws and regulations.[5] In 2007, *Spam Control Act* was passed to control spam. To strengthen personal information protection, *Personal Information Protection Act* was passed in 2012. After that, Cyberspace Security was upgraded to the national strategic stage, and *Cyberspace Security Act* was passed in 2018.

15.4 Technology Developed by Cyberspace Law: Digital Forensic

National Institute of Justice (NIJ) defined electronic data as information stored or transmitted in binary form, which could be relied on in court and could be found in computer hard disk, mobile phone, personal digital assistants, and flashcards in digital cameras. Electronic data evidence could be used to prosecute all types of crimes, not just electronic crimes.[6] In 1991, the term of computer forensics was first put forward in the International Association of Computer Specialties held in the U.S. In 1993, the first international conference on computer evidence was held. In 1995, the international organization on computer evidence was established.

Many countries have formulated relevant laws to promote the development of electronic data forensics technology and formulated standards to regulate the process of electronic data forensics. The U.S. promulgated *Unified Electronic Transaction Act, Unified Evidence Rules of 1999, Unified Computer Information Act,* and *California Evidence Code*; Canada promulgated the *Unified Electronic Evidence Act of 1998*; the Philippines promulgated *the Electronic Evidence Rules*; in 2001, Russia promulgated the *Electronic Digital Signature Act*, which clearly stipulated the legal requirements of electronic digital signature, certification authority, application situation, in addition to stipulating key management mode and legal obligation of key holder; in 1999, China's *Contract Act* incorporated the data message contract into the written contract for the first time, admitting its legitimacy; in 2004, *Road Traffic Safety Act* stipulated the evidential status of data message and traffic technology monitoring records; in 2005, *Electronic Signature Act* was an important legal document that directly and clearly stipulated the electronic data in China; Article 4–8 of the electronic evidence specifically stipulated the concept, written form, original form, preservation requirements, admissibility, and probative force of electronic evidence. These provisions applied not only to electronic commerce and electronic transactions but also to judicial activities. From 2012 to 2014, the three procedural laws of civil, criminal, and administrative officially took electronic data as one of the independent litigation pieces of evidence.

---

[5] http://www.npc.gov.cn/npc/c16115/201211/a4fa87828d0444d7904a3372b1ad800e.shtml
[6] http://www.nij.gov/topics/forensics/evidence/digital/pages, Accessed on: 2021.1.15

15.5 Discussion for Cyberspace Legislation

Through the introduction of cyberspace legislation of the previously mentioned countries, various countries pay more and more attention to the safety, governance, and norms of cyberspace. Besides, other countries have raised this to national strategy. This section discusses cyberspace legislation as follows:

a. Cyberspace legislation is gradually increasing, and the legislative field is gradually subdivided

In the era of the digital economy, extortion software, terrorism, network hackers, leakage, and false information are rampant. Strengthening the legal governance of Cyberspace Security has gained international attention. In the future, under the premise of affirming the current legal framework, countries around the world will introduce some new laws to solve the new problems in the development of information networks. That includes strengthening the protection of cyberspace infrastructure, strengthening the specification and management of network service providers, and standardizing the digital certification authority, which are the three key issues to be solved in the Cyberspace Security Legislation of various countries.

b. Cyberspace legislation tends to be internationalized

Cyberspace is the common activity space of human beings, which needs the joint construction and governance of all countries in the world. The legislation of cyberspace should first adhere to multilateral participation. All countries, big or small, strong or weak, rich or poor, are equal members of the international community. They have the right to participate equally in the construction of international order and rules in cyberspace through the international cyberspace governance mechanism and platform, according to their basic national conditions, to jointly maintain the peace and security of cyberspace and promote the nationalization, systematization, institutionalization, and legalization of cyberspace.

c. Strengthen data security and protect citizens' privacy

Data security is the focus of cyberspace legislation in various countries. Emphasizing the security of data and information resources, including the economic information represented by trade secrets and the protected information of government departments, is one of the specific contents of relevant legislation. Another issue to pay attention to is the security protection of personal data, including the prohibition of interception and theft of personal data, and the security protection requirements of personal data storage and processing. At present, the U.S., France, Germany, and other countries have formulated laws to protect personal data information. In the future, more countries will focus on this field and establish a suitable legal framework to protect data security and citizen privacy.

References

1. Y. Xia, Jurisprudential analysis of network law, *Social Scientist*, Vol. 23; No. 10, pp. 81–83, 2008.[in Chinese]
2. D. R. Johnson and D. Post, Law and borders: The rise of law in cyberspace, *Standford Law Review*, Vol. 48; No. 5, pp. 1367–1402, 1996.
3. S. J. Ethan, H. S. Truman, *National Security Act of 1947*, VolvPress, United States, 1945.
4. B. J. George, *The Comprehensive Crime Control Act of 1984*, Aspen Pub, United States, 1984.
5. G. W. Milor, The computer security act of 1987, *Computers & Security*, Vol. 7; No. 3, pp. 251–253, 1988.
6. B. Wei and R. Zhou, American information security legislation and its enlightenment and analysis, *Cyberspace Security*, Vol. 5; No. 111, pp. 5–10, 2019.[in Chinese]
7. G. W. Bush, Executive order 13231--Critical infrastructure protection in the information age, Weekly Compilation of Presidential Documents, No. 42, pp. 1485, 2001.
8. R. J. Samuels, Homeland security act, *Encyclopedia Britannica*, 2020, https://www.britannica.com/topic/Homeland-Security-Act [Accessed: 23 January 2021].
9. J. R. Reagan, *Federal Information Security Management Act (FISMA): Policy Analysis and Examination of Agency Implementation*, ResearchGate, Berlin, 2010.
10. P. F. Kunzlik, Proposed EC council directive on the legal protection of databases, *Computer Law & Security Review*, Vol. 8; No. 3, pp. 116–120, 1992.
11. M. A. Min-Huand and C. Zhao. The review of European Union information security law frame, *Hebei Law Science*, Vol. 11; pp. 152–156, 2008.[in Chinese]
12. S. D. Park, The changes of German cybersecurity legal system by the NIS directive implementation act, *IT & Law Review*, Vol. 17; pp. 153–189, 2018.

Chapter 16

A Brief History of Cyber War

16.1 Introduction

With the birth and rise of the Internet, the field of military operations has expanded from the original water, land, air, and outer space to cyberspace, which has a profound impact on the form of military operations and endows a modern war with new features of intelligence, interconnectedness, and destructiveness [1]. During the operation in the fifth space, great changes have taken place in the operation form and winning mechanism. In the increasingly complex network war situation, it is the key to win the war to obtain the support of the military strategy, organization, personnel training, weapons, and equipment with more cyber wisdom. In addition, effective cyber war rehearsal and actual combat will accumulate more data and experience, and promote the further development of military confrontation in cyberspace. This chapter mainly describes the development process of cyber war under descriptions, strategies, education, and organizations. In addition, the major rehearsals and actual combats are listed in chronological order to give readers an intuitive understanding of cyber war.

16.2 Descriptions of Cyber War

The development of information technology leads to continuous changes in the form of cyber war, and the degree of intelligence in war is also constantly increasing. From the initial destruction of government computers to the transformation and upgrading of weapons and equipment to the advent of unmanned weapons and equipment, the operational form of cyber war is constantly changing, leading to the cognitive change of cyber war and related terms. Table 16.1 lists different

DOI: 10.1201/9781003257387-16   **189**

**Table 16.1   Description of Cyber War and its Related Terms
in Different Periods**

Date	Reference	Term	Description
1993	Cyberwar is coming! [2] (U.S.)	Cyberwar	Cyberwar is "a series of network attack and defense actions taken to interfere with and destroy the enemy's network information system and ensure the normal operation of its own network information system". It is "a Blitzkrieg in the 21st century".
2005	Dictionary of Military and Associated Terms (U.S.)	Cyberspace operations	Operations that use cyber capabilities in cyberspace or through cyberspace to achieve military purposes, including computer network operations that operate and protect the global information grid.
2006	National Military Strategy for Cyberspace Operations[50] (U.S.)	Cyberspace operations	Military, intelligence, and operational activities are carried out in or through cyberspace.
2008	Definition of cyberspace operations (U.S.)	Cyberspace operations	Cyberspace operation is the application of cyberspace capability, whose purpose is to achieve goals in or through cyberspace. Such operations include computer network operations and activities to operate and defend the global information grid.
2010	On Cyber War (U.S.)	Cyberspace operations	For political, economic, and territorial purposes, cyberspace operations are forms of conflicts among countries that use precise and reasonable forces to attack military and industrial targets.

(Continued)

Table 16.1 (*Continued*)   Description of Cyber War and its Related Terms in Different Periods

Date	Reference	Term	Description
2011	The People's Liberation Army military China (CN)	Cyber war	In information cyberspace, operations are carried out to destroy the enemy's network system and network information, weaken its use function, and protect its own network system and network information.
2012	Cyber War (U.S.)	Cyber war	Cyber war is the act of disrupting or destroying the computer or network of another country by one country.
2014	Cyberspace Operations (U.S.)	Cyberspace operations	It consists of military activities, intelligence activities, and daily business operations that use cyberspace.
2015	STRATEGIC PLAN 2015–2020 (U.S.)	Cyberspace operations	The purpose of using network capabilities is to achieve goals in or through cyberspace.
2021	Britannica[51] (U.K.)	Cyberwar	Cyberwar, also spelled cyber war, also called cyberwarfare or cyber warfare, war conducted in and from computers and the networks connecting them, waged by states or their proxies against other states.

[50] https://www.abbreviations.com/term/592806
[51] https://www.britannica.com/topic/cyberwar

descriptions of cyber war and related terms. These descriptions are caused by many factors, such as technological development and operational form.

16.3 Strategies in Cyber War

The transformation from weaponized war to information war and intelligent war will lead to the original military strategies without complete applicability. The pursuit of effective strategies and programs in line with the changes in the war situation has become an important research content of countries and regions. In addition, the joint research between the government and technology companies has begun to become closer, which will help the military rely on the latest information technology to deploy strategic guidelines that conform to the development of the local military.

16.3.1 The United States

For ground-based unmanned weapons, the U.S. military has issued a series of technical development plans, including *Unmanned Aircraft Systems Roadmap 2005–2030*[1] (in 2005), *Pentagon Unmanned Systems Integrated Roadmap 2017–2042*[2] (in 2018), etc. In 2008, International Business Machines Corporation (IBM) began to develop a pulsed neural network chip and then jointly developed a brain-heuristic supercomputer system with the U.S. Air Force. In 2009, U.S. president Bush signed presidential order No. 54 on national security and presidential order No. 23 on homeland security, requiring all security-related departments of the U.S. government (including the Department of Homeland Security, the National Security Agency, etc.) to participate in the implementation of "The Comprehensive National Cybersecurity Initiative".[3] The construction of the "National Cyber Range" was an important part of the project. In 2011, the U.S. Department of Defense (DoD) formulated the *Department of Defense Strategy for Operating in Cyberspace.*[4] In 2012, the Defense Advanced Research Projects Agency (DARPA) announced the PLAN X[5] project. The main goal of the project was to develop innovative technologies for understanding, planning, and management of cyber war in a complex network environment. In 2014, the U.S. military proposed the *Third Offset Strategy,*[6] with research focuses on machine learning and machine-assisted operations. In 2015, the U.S. DoD issued *THE DEPARTMENT OF DEFENSE CYBER STRATEGY,*[7] and the U.S. military continued to increase its investment in cyber training. In 2017, the U.S. DoD officially issued a memorandum called *Project Maven,*[8] which aimed

[1] https://rosap.ntl.bts.gov/view/dot/18248
[2] https://news.usni.org/2018/08/30/pentagon-unmanned-systems-integrated-roadmap-2017-2042
[3] https://obamawhitehouse.archives.gov/issues/foreign-policy/cybersecurity/national-initiative
[4] https://en.wikipedia.org/wiki/U.S._Department_of_Defense_Strategy_for_Operating_in_Cyberspace
[5] https://en.wikipedia.org/wiki/Plan_X
[6] https://en.wikipedia.org/wiki/Offset_strategy
[7] https://cyberdefensereview.army.mil/CDR-Content/Articles/Article-View/Article/1136144/the-new-2015-dod-cyber-strategy-general-alexander-was-right/
[8] https://www.defense.gov/Explore/News/Article/Article/1356172/project-maven/igphoto/2001897580/

to further develop the application of artificial intelligence (AI) and other technologies in war. In 2018, the U.S. Center for Strategic and Budgetary Assessments (CSBA) released the report named *Human-Machine Teaming for Future Ground Forces*,[9] which mainly described the driving factors, main forms, and main challenges of future ground forces man-machine formation. In February 2019, to promote the development of human-machine integration, DARPA released *Intelligent Neural Interfaces*[10] (INI) and *Science of Artificial Intelligence and Learning for Open-world Novelty*[11] (SAIL-ON) project announcement. In September of the same year, the U.S. Air Force released the *2019 Artificial Intelligence Strategy*,[12] which specifically emphasized the importance of AI in the current military development. In November 2019, the U.S. DoD received a report titled *Cyborg Soldier 2050: Human/Machine Fusion and the Implications for the Future of the DoD*.[13] The U.S. Army began the development of "Cyborg Warrior".

16.3.2 Russia

In 2014, the Russian Ministry of Defense formulated and approved a comprehensive goal plan, and named it *Creation of Prospective Military Robotics through 2025*.[14] In 2016, Russia held the *Robotization of the Armed Forces of the Russian Federation*. In 2017, Russia released *Russia's Military Modernization Plans: 2018–2027*,[15] aiming to narrow the gap in the fields of unmanned aerial vehicles (UAVs) and precision-guided munitions. According to a 2017 report from Harvard University, the Russian Military Industry Council had approved the plan to obtain 30% of combat power from the remote control and human–machine intelligent robot platforms in 2030.[16] At the Russian Federation Security Conference held in November 2019, Putin emphasized that the main tasks in the new era included the development of modern new high-precision weapons, aerospace defense equipment, and the integration of AI technology into military equipment.

---

[9] https://csbaonline.org/uploads/documents/Human_Machine_Teaming_-_25Apr2018.pdf

[10] https://www.darpa.mil/program/intelligent-neural-interfaces

[11] https://www.darpa.mil/program/science-of-artificial-intelligence-and-learning-for-open-world-novelty

[12] https://www.csis.org/analysis/fly-fight-ai-air-force-releases-new-ai-strategy

[13] https://community.apan.org/wg/tradoc-g2/mad-scientist/m/articles-of-interest/300458

[14] https://thestrategybridge.org/the-bridge/2017/12/12/red-robots-rising-behind-the-rapid-development-of-russian-unmanned-military-systems

[15] https://www.ponarseurasia.org/memo/russias-military-modernization-plans-2018-2027

[16] https://www.providencejournal.com/story/opinion/columns/2020/11/28/opinion-artificial-intelligence-and-future-warfare/6382288002/

16.3.3 China

In July 2017, the State Council of the People's Republic of China announced a detailed strategy for turning China into a "leading country in the field of AI and a global innovation center" by 2030.[17] The strategy included increasing investment in research and development using AI to consolidate national defense and defend national security while paying special attention to the use of this technology in the field of combat automation and prediction. In 2019, China published the white paper *China's National Defense in the New Era*,[18] which further elaborated on the tremendous changes in the form of war and combat methods driven by AI.

16.3.4 Other Countries/Regions

Japan issued the *Information Security Strategy* in May 2010, which required all departments to build a system that can respond to large-scale cyberattacks to ensure cyberspace security. In 2016, the United Kingdom (U.K.) government issued the *National Cyber Security Strategy 2016–2021*.[19] It believed that cyberattacks were the greatest threat to the U.K. economy and national security. In 2018, France released the *2018 Strategic Review of Cyber defense*, which outlined France's overall cyber defense strategy. In 2019, France announced a new *French Cyber Military Strategy*, which included the *Ministerial Policy for Defensive Cyber Warfare* and the *Public Elements for the Military Cyber Warfare Doctrine*.[20] The military strategies related to cyberspace have been being constantly adjusted to best adapt to the development of national/regional military intelligence. Table 16.2 lists the military policies, reports, and strategies related to cyberspace of some countries in recent years.

16.3.5 Multilateral Cooperation

In November 2009, during the nuclear disarmament negotiations between the U.S. and Russia, the U.S. agreed for the first time to conduct cyber arms control negotiations with Russia. In December 2009, the U.S. and Russia held consultations on cyber arms control during the nuclear disarmament negotiations in Geneva.[21] In 2013, Japan and the U.S. held the first "cyber dialogue" and issued a joint statement on strengthening cooperation in cyber defense. In the same year, at the "2+2" Security Agreement Committee Meeting, Japan and the U.S. confirmed that the two countries cooperated to deal with cyberattacks.[22] In the 2015 new edition of *THE GUIDELINES FOR JAPAN-U.S. DEFENSE COOPERATION*,[23] the two countries also joined the content of network security cooperation.

---

[17] http://www.gov.cn/zhengce/content/2017-07/20/content_5211996.htm
[18] http://www.mod.gov.cn/regulatory/2019-07/24/content_4846424.htm
[19] https://www.gov.uk/government/publications/national-cyber-security-strategy-2016-to-2021
[20] https://warontherocks.com/2019/04/a-close-look-at-frances-new-military-cyber-strategy/
[21] http://cpc.people.com.cn/n/2015/0417/c83083-26860167.html?ol4f
[22] http://www.xinhuanet.com//mil/2015-04/17/c_127700063_2.htm
[23] https://www.mofa.go.jp/region/n-america/us/security/guideline2.html

Table 16.2   Military Policies/Reports/Strategies Related to Cyberspace in Recent Years

Country	Date	*Military Policies/Reports/Strategies Covering Cyberspace Related Content*
U.S.	2014	Cyberspace Operations
	2015	The Department of Defense Cyber Strategy
	2015	Third Offset Strategy
	2018	Summary of the 2018 National Defense Strategy of The United States of America
	2018	The Joint Enterprise Defense Infrastructure (JEDI) contract
	2018	DoD Cloud Strategy
	2019	Summary of the 2018 Department of Defense Artificial Intelligence Strategy: Harnessing AI to Advance Our Security and Prosperity
	2019	DoD Digital Modernization Strategy 2019
	2019	AI Principles: Recommendations on the Ethical Use of Artificial Intelligence by the Department of Defense
	2019	National Defense Authorization Act for Fiscal Year 2020
	2020	The U.S. National Defense Authorization Act for Fiscal Year 2021
Russia	2014	Information Security Doctrine of the Russian Federation (draft)
	2017	Law on Security of Critical Information Infrastructure
	2019	National Strategy for the Development of Artificial Intelligence
Singapore	2016	Cybersecurity strategy
	2018	Factsheet on National Cyber Security Masterplan
U.K.	2016	National Cyber Security Strategy 2016–2021
	2017	Civil Nuclear Cyber Security Strategy
China	2017	New Generation Artificial Intelligence Development Plan
	2019	China's National Defense in the New Era
France	2018	2018 Strategic Review of Cyber defense
	2019	French Cyber Military Strategy

16.4 Education in Cyber War

To build an excellent cyber army or organization, it is necessary to cultivate professional talents as a prerequisite to complete high-quality preparatory work. To this end, many countries and regions have set up research institutes and explained relevant cyber military knowledge in university courses to cultivate military professionals in information technology. For example, In 1999, the U.S. National Security Agency began to implement the "National Information Security Education and Training Program". This plan had set up "Information Security Education and Academic Exchange Center" in 23 domestic colleges and universities, offering a series of courses from vocational training, bachelor's degree, master's degree to doctor's degree.[24] In 2014, West Point Military Academy established the Cyber Warfare Research Institute, which was responsible for training cyber military talents.[25]

16.5 Institutions in Cyber War

Professional cyber military organizations and armies can be used to maintain the security of the country/region in cyberspace. In order to achieve this goal, various countries and regions carefully prepare highly professional cyber armies, use these organizations to monitor cyberspace, timely respond to potential cyber military threats, and even launch cyber wars against other countries and organizations.

As early as the 1990s, the Information Security Committee was established in Russia. Currently, this agency was conducting cyber war under the leadership of the Federal Security Agency. In 1998, the U.S. established the Joint Task Force-Computer Network Defense (JTF-CND) to protect network security.[26]

In 2002, the Indian army established a Tri-Service Joint Computer Emergency Unit and a "Hacker" unit. The main task of these two units was to deal with any network insecure behavior in a timely manner. In 2005, the U.S. military established a Joint Functional Component Command–Network Warfare (JFCC-NW).[27] The main responsibility of the command was to be responsible for cyberattacks. In the same year, the Indian army established a

---

[24] http://www.81.cn/wjsm/2015-01/05/content_6294600_2.htm

[25] https://www.workboat.com/viewpoints/cybersecurity-training-revs-up-at-military-academies

[26] https://military.wikia.org/wiki/Joint_Task_Force-Global_Network_Operations

[27] https://itlaw.wikia.org/wiki/Joint_Functional_Component_Command_for_Network_Warfare

cyber security department in the army headquarters, dedicated to cyber war and maintaining the Indian army's cyber security.

In 2006, the U.S. 67th Information Operations Wing was reorganized into the 67th Network Warfare Wing, becoming the only professional cyber war force of the U.S. military.[28] In the same year, the U.S. DoD established the Cyber Media Warfare Force. In addition, Korea announced the establishment of a Cyber Command this year. In May 2007, the first Cyber Warfare Command established by the U.S. Air Force had formed combat effectiveness. In 2009, the U.K. government established two departments related to cyber security.[29] The first was the Office of Cyber Security, which was used to ensure cybersecurity between government departments. The second was the Cyber Security Operations Centre, which was used to ensure cybersecurity between the government and civilian agencies. In the same year, the U.S. military established the "Network Joint Functional Command", which was committed to the integrated construction of network attack and defense, and striding forward to the direction of actual combat.

In January 2013, the Japanese government established a "Cyber Security Strategy Headquarters" composed of cabinet members. In March 2013, the U.S. Cyber War Command announced that it would add 40 new cyber forces.[30] Among them, 13 cyber forces were attack forces used to counterattack when the country is attacked by major cyberattacks. Another 27 cyber forces were used to provide relevant support to other commands. In the same year, the U.S. DoD clearly put forward the goal of building 133 cyber task forces in the *Four-year Defense Evaluation Report*. In 2015, Russia established the National Center for the Development of Technology and Basic Elements of Robotics.[31] This center fully supported high-tech innovation in national defense and national security.

In February 2017, the U.K. National Cyber Security Center (NCSC) became operational.[32] The center was part of the Government Communications Headquarters of the U.K. Intelligence Agency and was used to strengthen the security of national networks. In 2017, when the U.S. president Trump came to power, he set up a network review group. This group, composed of the military, law enforcement agencies, and the private sector, comprehensively assessed the current situation of U.S. cyber defense. In August 2017, Trump announced that the U.S. Cyber Command would be upgraded to the 10th U.S. Joint Operations Command to strengthen the U.S. capabilities in cyberspace. In the same year, the U.S. DoD established the "Algorithmic Warfare Cross-Functional Team" to promote the application of

---

[28] https://military.wikia.org/wiki/67th_Cyberspace_Wing
[29] https://www.sciencedirect.com/topics/computer-science/cyber-security-strategy
[30] https://www.strategypage.com/htmw/htiw/articles/20130320.aspx
[31] https://futureoflife.org/2019/05/09/state-of-ai
[32] https://www.ncsc.gov.uk/

technologies such as AI, machine learning, and big data. In December 2018, the U.S. Air Force established the Air Force Artificial Intelligence Cross-Functional Group. One of the group's first tasks was to ensure that the latest AI technologies were introduced into the Air Force. According to the plan, the entire U.S. military's cyber war unit would be established around 2030 and fully assume the network offensive and defensive tasks to ensure that the U.S. military has a comprehensive information advantage.

It can be seen from the above history that various countries/regions are actively carrying out military informatization, digitization, and intelligence construction, to achieve a higher technological level of information attack and defense as much as possible. So far, various countries/regions are still implementing new informatization military or digital transformation of the original military to meet the needs of military organizations in cyber war.

16.6 Typical Cyber War Rehearsals

More and more countries, regions, and organizations have begun to actively rehearse cyber war to guard against all kinds of network threats and unsafe behaviors. These rehearsal activities can enhance the vigilance of the army, strengthen the network supervision and emergency response by simulating various possible network attack activities, and avoid huge losses in actual combat.

16.6.1 Unilateral Rehearsal

Take the U.S. as an example. This country has organized several cyber war rehearsals to test the attack and defense capabilities of its military in the cyber environment.

In 2007, the U.S. Central Intelligence Agency held a three-day "Silent Horizon" cyber antiterrorism exercise in Virginia.[33] The exercise simulated a network attack similar to the scale of the "9.11" incident to test the actual defense capabilities of network security.

In 2008, the U.S. DoD Advanced Research Projects Agency planned to develop the "National Cyber Range" project and clearly stated that the project was part of the National Cyber Security Plan.[34] "National Cyber Range" refers to the construction of a virtual environment to simulate real cyber offensive and defensive operations to achieve effective simulation of cyber war.

---

[33] https://www.coursehero.com/file/p6mm9pdh/The-CIAs-annual-cyber-war-exercise-Silent-Horizon-has-been-happening-since-2007
[34] https://www.wired.com/2008/05/the-pentagons-w/

The *JOINT TRAINING MANUAL FOR THE ARMED FORCES OF THE UNITED STATES*[35] issued in 2015 believed that the DoD should incorporate real cyberspace conditions into all exercises. Thus, the U.S. military has made flexible adjustments to the actual combat content and its own conditions when building the cyber war simulation environment.

The 2015 version of the *Department of Defense Cyber Strategy* stipulated that all large-scale cyber exercises organized by the U.S. military must include a cyber "red team" to test the U.S. military's cyber defense capabilities. So far, the U.S. military had established a professional "red team" and adopted the form of red-blue confrontation in the exercise.

16.6.2 Multilateral Rehearsal

In addition to conducting military cyber-enabled rehearsals in their own countries, some countries and organizations have also joined forces to conduct military rehearsals of cyber war to enhance cooperation in cyberspace.

The 2006 "Cyber Storm I" exercise was jointly conducted by the U.S., U.K., Canada, Australia, and New Zealand.[36] This exercise was dedicated to improving the ability to respond to cyberattacks between countries.

In the 2008 "Cyber Storm II" exercise, these five countries were still involved.[37] This exercise also included the private sectors, the federals, and the states in the U.S.

In the 2010 "Cyber Storm III" exercise, participating countries expanded to 13 countries, including Australia, Canada, France, Germany, Hungary, Italy, Japan, the Netherlands, New Zealand, Sweden, Switzerland, and the U.K.[38]

In 2010, the North Atlantic Treaty Organization Cooperative Cyber Defense Centre of Excellence (NATO CCD COE) first launched the "Locked Shields" cyber exercise, aiming to promote international cooperation in cybersecurity among different countries.[39]

In 2013, "Cyber Storm IV" exercise was held with the participation of 11 countries.[40] In addition, "Cyber Storm V" exercise[41] and "Cyber Storm VI" exercise[42] were launched in 2016 and 2018, respectively. "Cyber Storm 2020[43]" has also held smoothly in 2020.

---

[35] https://www.jcs.mil/Portals/36/Documents/Library/Manuals/m350003.pdf?ver=2016-02-05-175706-067
[36] https://www.cisa.gov/cyber-storm-i
[37] https://www.cisa.gov/cyber-storm-ii
[38] https://www.cisa.gov/cyber-storm-iii
[39] https://ccdcoe.org/exercises/locked-shields/
[40] https://www.cisa.gov/cyber-storm-iv
[41] https://www.cisa.gov/cyber-storm-v-national-cyber-exercise
[42] https://www.cisa.gov/cyber-storm-vi
[43] https://www.cisa.gov/cyber-storm-2020

16.7 Typical Cyber War

16.7.1 Cyber War Based on Information Attack and Defense

Early cyber wars mainly invaded the important electronic equipment of other countries. After completing the invasion, the attacker may monitor intelligence, steal secrets, deliberately tamper with normal procedures, and implant Trojan virus.

In 2008, the conflict between Russia and Georgia broke out [3]. The Russian army launched a "swarm" network deterrence attack on Georgia, which paralyzed the enemy's important systems in finance, transportation, and other fields. In addition, the attack caused the breakdown of communications, logistics, and other important networks. Besides, military supplies could not be delivered to the designated locations in time, which had a serious impact on Georgia's military command and dispatch. Beginning this year, "Lei Jin" had been used to attack the computer networks of government departments and other important organizations including Russia, Afghanistan, Pakistan, and many other countries to obtain important data. This was a piece of malicious software used by the U.S. and the U.K. intelligence agencies to conduct cyberattacks on European Union (EU) computer systems for many years. In 2010, a worm called "Stuxnet" spread arbitrarily around the world, and Iran suffered the most serious attacks, including nuclear power plants and other important institutions.[44]

Until recently, the suppression of the enemy's confidential information systems remained an important form of cyber war.

In 2011, the U.S. launched the "Cyber Dawn" program in the "Odyssey Dawn" military operation in Libya, which directly destroyed the Libyan oil production system and became a typical hard-destructive cyberattack. In May 2012, the "Flame" virus spread in Middle Eastern countries such as Iran, Israel, and Palestine.[45] The virus had a variety of data theft functions. It was a new type of "electronic spy" that stole confidential information from other countries and represented the latest development trend of cyberspace intelligence activities. At the end of 2012, the first batch of the U.S. military's Cyber Mission Units had just passed the acceptance check and began to support the U.S. military operations in Syria and Iraq, and focused on accumulating actual combat data. In December 2015, a major targeted cyberattack occurred in Ukraine, which caused continuous power outages in nearly one-third of the country.[46]

16.7.2 Cyber War Based on Intelligent Weapons

With the development of information technology, more and more old weapons begin to undergo intelligent transformation, and weapons and equipment are also given the important characteristics of digitization. In addition, with the emergence of new technologies such as AI and computer vision, unmanned armored vehicles,

---

[44] https://en.wikipedia.org/wiki/Stuxnet

[45] https://cn.reuters.com/article/net-us-cyberwar-flame-idINBRE84R0E420120528

[46] https://en.wikipedia.org/wiki/December_2015_Ukraine_power_grid_cyberattack

unmanned aerial vehicles, and unmanned submarines have begun to appear and occupy an important position in military equipment.

In 2003, during the Second Gulf War, the U.S. military applied radio frequency identification (RFID) technology to the logistics support system, which greatly shortened the supply time. In addition, the U.S. military also sewed RFID tags into the cuffs of soldiers' clothes to track the location of wounded soldiers and improve the efficiency of the rescue of wounded soldiers.

In 2008, the first unmanned vehicle "Guardium" was equipped with Israeli armored forces. The "Guardium" is the world's first controllable autonomous unmanned vehicle, which exhibits a high degree of self-control ability after parameter setting. The "Guardium" unmanned vehicle is equipped with day/night situational awareness cameras, allowing remote operators to monitor events that occur around the vehicle.[47]

In 2016, Russia used six platform-M tracked unmanned combat vehicles and four secret languages wheeled unmanned reconnaissance vehicles for the first time in Syrian military operations. This practice used ground unmanned equipment from auxiliary combat to main combat. In the same year, the Israeli military began to use autonomous vehicles for border patrols.[48]

In December 2020, Russian peacekeepers used the "Uran-6" minesweeper robot for the first time to conduct minesweeping operations on the territory of Nagorno-Karabakh, with good results.[49] The operator of "Uran-6" can remotely control it within a distance of no more than 800 meters. At the same time, "Uran-6" has four high-definition cameras, which can provide a full range of vision.

16.8 Conclusion

The development of cyberspace provides a new platform for military operations. With the continuous development of information technology, countries and regions worldwide have paid attention to this new combat form. They have continuously strengthened the military application and development of these technologies. The evolution and development of cyber war is the result of the joint action of many aspects. These aspects include the cognition of cyber war, cyber military strategy and education, cyber military construction, cyber war rehearsal, and actual combat. Therefore, starting from the above aspects, this chapter lists major international events in chronological order. There are reasons to believe that the future combat form will further advance in the direction of informatization and digitization and present new characteristics such as intelligence and concealment.

---

[47] https://en.wikipedia.org/wiki/Guardium
[48] https://www.foxnews.com/tech/robot-patrol-israeli-army-to-deploy-autonomous-vehicles-on-gaza-border
[49] https://armenpress.am/eng/news/1037491.html

References

1. Z. Zhang, F. Shi, Y. Wan, Y. Xu, F. Zhang, and H. Ning, Application progress of artificial intelligence in military confrontation, *Chinese Journal of Engineering*, Vol. 42; No. 9, pp. 1106–1118, 2020.
2. A. John and R. David, Cyberwar is coming! *Comparative Strategy*, Vol. 12; No. 2, pp. 141–165, 1997.
3. S. Lesley, The era of cyber warfare: Applying international humanitarian law to the 2008 Russian-Georgian cyber conflict, *Loy. L.A. Int'l & Comp. L. Rev.*, Vol. 32; pp. 303, 2010.

Index

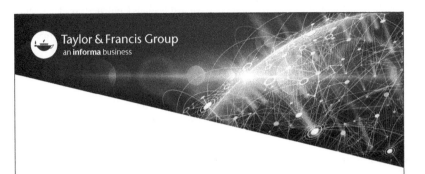